PEARSON

ALWAYS LEARNING

Patrick Frank

Prebles' Artforms

Second Custom Edition for Northeastern Illinois University

Taken From:
Prebles' Artforms, Tenth Edition
by Patrick Frank

Cover Art: Front cover art courtesy of Artiss
          Back cover art courtesy of Todd A. Irwin

Taken from:

Prebles' Artforms, Tenth Edition
by Patrick Frank
Copyright © 2011, 2009, 2006, 2004, 2002 by Pearson Education, Inc.
Published by Prentice Hall
Upper Saddle River, New Jersey 07458

This special edition published in cooperation with Pearson Learning Solutions.

All trademarks, service marks, registered trademarks, and registered service marks are the property of their respective owners and are used herein for identification purposes only.

Pearson Learning Solutions, 501 Boylston Street, Suite 900, Boston, MA 02116
A Pearson Education Company
www.pearsoned.com

Printed in the United States of America

1 2 3 4 5 6 7 8 9 10 XXXX 16 15 14 13 12 11

000200010270744691

SD

ISBN 10: 1-256-10585-6
ISBN 13: 978-1-256-10585-5

BRIEF CONTENTS

CONTENTS

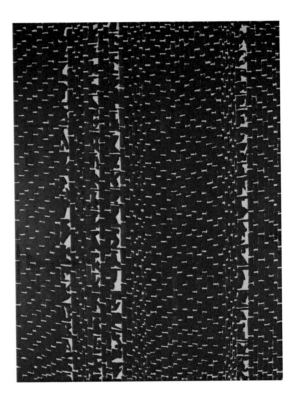

ABOUT THE AUTHOR

Patrick Frank has taught in several higher education environments, from rural community colleges to private research universities. His recent scholarly work has focused on Latin American graphic arts. He is author of *Posada's Broadsheets: Mexican Popular Imagery 1890–1910* and *Los Artistas del Pueblo: Prints and Workers' Culture in Buenos Aires* (University of New Mexico Press). He has curated five exhibitions of Latin American prints. He has also edited a volume of artists' writings, *Readings in Latin American Modern Art* (Yale University Press). He served as collaborating author for the modern section of Marilyn Stokstad's *Art History* (third edition). He earned M.A. and Ph.D. degrees at George Washington University in Washington, D.C. He is currently an adjunct faculty member in the Art Department of Pitzer College, and lives in Venice, California.

ABOUT THE COVER

David Hockney (b. 1937) embodies the variety and mobility that are possible in the work and life of a contemporary artist. In a career spanning five decades, Hockney has lived and traveled globally, creating art that reflects multiple influences and an exploration of many media. Not only has he produced a lifetime of paintings, but also photo collages, set designs, book illustrations, opera staging, and, most recently, hundreds of images using iPhone and iPad apps. His classic 1967 acrylic painting *A Bigger Splash* is a reference to his move from England to Los Angeles and his adoption of a new life in the United States. Hockney utilizes the versatility of acrylics in this artwork as he contrasts the flat brushwork of the geometric shapes that dominate the scene with the quick, unblended application of paint that creates the electric splash of an unseen swimmer. Bright and exciting, this book's cover also represents the invitation *Prebles' Artforms* extends to its readers: to dive into the world of art.

ACKNOWLEDGMENTS

I greatly appreciate the help and encouragement of the many people who have been directly involved in this tenth edition. A few people deserve special mention for their contributions: Image researcher Francelle Carapetyan was her usual tireless self, securing rights to pictures of artworks from across the world. Production Project Manager Barbara Cappuccio kept us all on track while also keeping a welcome sense of humanity. Production Editor Doug Bell's laser-like focus prevented several catastrophes that are best left untold here. Developmental Editor Margaret Manos cleaned up my prose and helped bring it to the (I hope!) clear and jargon-free state that you are reading here. Cory Skidds was my guardian spirit at the Imaging Center, warding off evil influences that can adversely affect pictures of artworks in books.

This book also benefitted from assistance in specialized content areas from Elizabeth East, Charles James, Philip James, Rebecca Fraser, and Anthony Lee. Many artists opened their studios and homes to me as I was researching this book; I greatly appreciate their generosity, just as I hope that I have communicated the vigor and inspiration of their creativity.

I also express my appreciation to the following reviewers, who offered many helpful suggestions during the revision of the text:

Ingrid Cartwright, *Western Kentucky University*
Andrea Donovan, *Minot State University*
Cindy Grant, *Mississippi Delta Community College*
Bobette Guillory, *Carl Albert State College*
Claire Hampton, *Volunteer State Community College*
Jean Janssen, *Kankakee Community College*
Anne Perry, *University of Texas at El Paso*
Karen Stabley, *York College of Pennsylvania*
Paige Wideman, *Northern Kentucky University*
Sandra Williams, *Palm Beach Community College*

Leo Tolstoy wrote that art can be a "means of union" for people, "joining them together in the same feelings." I hope that this book facilitates such unions, because if we study and enjoy the cultural productions of the world's diverse peoples, we will build bridges of human understanding.

PATRICK FRANK

PREFACE

Prebles' Artforms **continues to lead the field with its steadfast focus on contemporary art, global artists, and cutting-edge technology for the art-appreciation classroom.**

WE FORM ART. ART FORMS US.

The title of this book has a dual meaning. Besides the expected discussion of the various forms of art, the title also reflects the fact that art does, indeed, help to form us as people. As we create forms, we are in turn formed by what we have created. Several years ago, the title was changed to *Prebles' Artforms*, acknowledging the pioneering contribution of the original authors, Duane and Sarah Preble, to the study of art. Their vision and spirit have touched hundreds of thousands of students who have studied this book.

Artforms grew out of a desire to introduce art through an engaging visual experience, and to expose students to a culturally diverse body of creative work. It is written and designed to help readers build an informed foundation for individual understanding and enjoyment of art. By introducing art theory, practice, and history in a single volume, this book aims to draw students into a new or expanded awareness of the visual arts.

Beyond fostering appreciation of major works of art, this book's primary concern is to open students' eyes and minds to the richness of the visual arts as unique forms of human communication and to convey the idea that the arts enrich life best when we experience, understand, and enjoy them as integral parts of the process of living.

WHY USE THE NEW EDITION?

This new edition stems from my belief that students deserve to be exposed to cutting-edge, contemporary art. Experiencing visual creativity on a global scale will broaden their minds and open up their own creative faculties. Moreover, they will benefit from reading discussions and contemporary thought on both. For this tenth edition I've added two new features throughout the book to enrich these aspects of the learning experience for students:

At the Edge of Art: This new set of boxes helps to expand our definition of art by focusing on works at its boundaries. Highlighted are artworks that are unexpected, unintended, or perhaps not ordinarily deemed "art," that push students to reconsider and perhaps broaden their definition of art. These boxes show digital expressions of creativity online (page 147) or sculpture built from equations using mathematical logic (page 180). Not all of the featured works are contemporary; one is an ancient decorated stone from the earliest historic fringe of human creativity (page 215); another is a mask used in healing ceremonies that its creator never regarded as art (page 312). *At the Edge of Art* leads students to reconsider fundamental questions such as, "What is art?" and "Why is art important?"

MyArtsLab: This dynamic website provides a wealth of resources geared to meet the diverse teaching and learning needs of today's instructors and students. Throughout the text, icons will indicate where topics are enhanced and can be experienced online in different ways.

The **'LEARN MORE'** icon directs students to MyArtsLab to view **Closer Look** tours, which let them experience and interact with works of art.

The **'HEAR MORE'** and **'SEE MORE'** icons let students know where they can hear accompanying chapter audio or watch the **podcasts** that I created specifically for *Artforms*.

The **'EXPLORE MORE'** icon lead students online to expand their visual interaction with art by allowing them to view 360-degree architectural panoramas and simulations, or watch videos of artists at work.

Designed to amplify a traditional course in numerous ways or to administer a course online, **MyArtsLab** combines pedagogy and assessment with an array of multimedia activities. See the book's complete resources pages (pages xii–xiv) for more information.

ADDITIONAL UPDATES TO THE NEW EDITION INCLUDE:

- **Contemporary Art.** I continue to expand our coverage of the most recent creativity as I keep this book at the top of its field in coverage of contemporary art. In this edition are fifty-seven new images of work by living artists, 45 percent of them women and 30 percent of them global.

- **Inclusiveness.** Readers from diverse backgrounds want to know how earlier people who share their origins have contributed to human creativity. *Artforms* has always honored this quest, and this edition deepens that commitment. This edition includes work by six new African-American artists, and twenty new works by artists from around the globe. Latino and Latin American artists included for the first time here include Teddy Cruz, Lucio Fontana, Joaquín Torres-García, Nicola López, Jesús Rafael Soto, Vik Muniz, and the performance group Asco, in addition to two colonial Latin American paintings.

- **Photography.** Photography has been an important locus of new creativity for the entire postmodern period, and we recognize that fact by giving it its own chapter here, with significant expansion. The following chapter, now focusing on film and digital arts, has also been rewritten to include more films by artists, and some new digital art.

- **Interactive Design.** This cutting-edge area of graphic arts gets a titled section in Chapter 9, with a look at creators who design for interactive environments.

Pedagogy. Each chapter begins with questions that set out key learning outcomes, stimulate critical thinking, and focus the discussion that follows. The terms in the glossary are now also in boldface at their initial introduction in the text.

I have always welcomed feedback and input from readers, students, and teachers. Here is a direct way to communicate with me: Send any thoughts, concerns, questions, and comments to patrickfrank@ artformstext.com.

Patrick Frank
Venice, California

FACULTY AND STUDENT RESOURCES

my arts lab Designed to save instructors time and to improve students' results, MyArtsLab, is keyed specifically to the chapters of *Prebles' Artforms*, Tenth Edition. In addition, MyArtsLab's many features will encourage students to experience and interact with works of art. Here are some of those key features:

- A complete **Pearson eText** of the book, enriched with multimedia, including: a unique human-scale figure adjoining all works of fine art, an audio version of the text read by the author, primary source documents, video demonstrations, and much more. Students can highlight, make notes and bookmark pages.

- **Closer Look Tours** These interactive walk-throughs offer an in-depth look at key works of art, enabling the student to zoom in to see detail they could not otherwise see on the printed page or even in person. Enhanced with expert audio, they help students understand the meaning and message behind the work of art.

- Robust **Quizzing** and **Grading Functionality** is included in MyArtsLab. Students receive immediate feedback from the assessment questions that populate the instructor's gradebook. The gradebook reports gives an in-depth look at the progress of individual students or the class as a whole.

- MyArtsLab is your one stop for instructor material. Instructors can access the Instructor's Manual, Test Item File, PowerPoint images, and the Pearson MyTest assessment generation program from the MyArtsLab's instructor's tab.

MyArtsLab with eText is available for no additional cost when packaged with *Prebles' Artforms*. MyArtsLab with eText may also be used as a stand-alone item, which costs less than a used text. To order this text with MyArtsLab, please use: ISBN: 978-0-205-02696-8 www.myartslab.com.

 Instructors who adopt *Prebles' Artforms* will receive access to **MyClassPrep,** an online site designed to make lecture preparation simpler and less time consuming. The site includes the images from the text in both high resolution jpegs, as well as ready made PowerPoints® for your lectures. **MyClassPrep** can be accessed through your **MyArtsLab** instructor account.

CourseSmart online textbooks are an exciting new choice for students looking to save money. As an alterative to purchasing the print textbook, students can subscribe to the same content online and save up to 60 percent off the suggested list price of the print text.

With a **CourseSmart eText,** students can search the text, make notes online, print out reading assignments that incorporate lecture notes, and bookmark important passages for later review. For more information, or to subscribe to **CourseSmart,** visit www.coursesmart.com

Books a la carte

Give your students flexibility and savings with the new Books a la carte edition of *Prebles' Artforms*. This edition features exactly the same content as the traditional textbook in a convenient three-hole-punched, loose-leaf version— allowing students to take only what they need to class. The Books a la carte edition costs less than a used text—which helps students save about 35 percent over the cost of a used book.
ISBN: 978-0-205-01148-3
ISBN with MyArtsLab: 978-0-205-01149-0

Classroom Response System (CRS) In-Class Questions

Get instant, class-wide responses to beautifully illustrated chapter-specific questions during a lecture to gauge students' comprehension—and keep them engaged. Available for download under the instructor's tab in your MyArtsLab course. www.myartslab.com.

Instructor's Manual and Test Item File

This is an invaluable professional resource and reference for new and experienced faculty. Each chapter contains the following sections: Chapter Overview, Chapter Objectives, Key Terms, Lecture and Discussion Topics, Resources, and Writing Assignments and Projects. The test bank includes multiple choice, true/false, short answer, and essay questions. Available for download under the instructor's tab in your MyArtsLab course. www.myartslab.com.

MyTest

This flexible, online test-generating software includes all questions found in the printed Test Item File. Instructors can quickly and easily create customized tests with MyTest. http://www.pearsonmytest.com

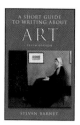

A Short Guide to Writing About Art, Tenth Edition
-Sylvan Barnet
This best-selling text has guided tens of thousands of art students through the writing process. To order *Prebles' Artforms* and the Barnet text together at a discounted price, please use this ISBN: 978-0-205-06342-0

Writing About Art, Sixth Edition
-Henry Sayre
This efficient supplement features a step-by-step approach to writing—from choosing a work to write about, to essay organization, to research techniques, to footnote form, to preparing the final essay. To order Prebles' Artforms and the Sayre text together at a discounted price, please use this ISBN: 978-0-205-05871-6

Custom Publishing Opportunities
Prebles' Artforms is available in a custom version specifically tailored to meet your needs. You may select the content that you would like to include or add your own original material. See you local publisher's representative for further information.

THE NATURE OF ART AND CREATIVITY

When Janet Echelman's huge artwork *Her Secret Is Patience* was hoisted into the air above Phoenix in mid-2009, even most of the doubters became admirers. This is because the work is simply stunning: It defies gravity as it dances and waves slowly in the breeze. Suspended from three leaning poles between 40 and 100 feet above the ground, its colored circles of netting seem both permanent and ever changing, both solid and spacious.

The artist chose the cactus flower shape to symbolize the Arizona desert city of Phoenix. She was inspired by the patience of the saguaro cactus, she said, "a spiny cactus putting down roots in search of water in the desert, saving up every ounce of energy until, one night, in the middle of the cool darkness, it unfurls one succulent bloom." The work also refers to the character of nature itself. Echelman drew her title from the words of American poet and philosopher Ralph Waldo Emerson, who wrote, "Adopt the pace of nature; her secret is patience." Thus, the sculpture both resembles and reflects the surrounding nature; it catches and moves with every breeze as if choreographed by the wind.

The citizens who advocated the piece over the extended waiting time between conception and completion were patient as well. Doubters objected to the price tag ($2.4 million), the shape (one said it resembled a giant jellyfish), and the artist's origins (she is not from Arizona). Those misgivings and a few technical issues kept *Her Secret Is Patience* on the drawing boards for a year and a half. But today most Arizonians look on the work with pride: this unique

1.1 Janet Echelman.
Her Secret Is Patience. 2009.
Polyester fiber twine and rope. Height 100′.
Width at top 100′.
Civic Space Park, Phoenix, AZ. Courtesy Janet Echelman, Inc.
Photo: Peter Vanderwarker.

HEAR MORE: Listen to an audio file of your chapter at
www.myartslab.com

1

visual delight will forever mark the city of Phoenix just as the Eiffel Tower marks Paris. The *Arizona Republic* editorialized: "This is just what Phoenix needs: a distinctive feature that helps create a real sense of place."[1]

The creation and reception of *Her Secret Is Patience* embody a central theme of this book: artistic creation is a two-way street. That is, humans form artworks, and then the art forms us. Hence, the title of this book: *Artforms*. In this chapter, we will look at some of the ways in which art can affect or influence us.

Not all of us regularly create works of art, but we are all creative in some way. We create a home life. We create relationships. We create events, goals, projects, and accomplishments. Even the common acts of arranging furniture in a room or pictures on the wall can be creative. Visual art is one type of human creativity, and art viewers, when contemplating a work, create their own responses to it. When we respond to a work of art, we activate our own creativity; the artist's work evokes the artist within us. In this chapter, we will also discuss the meaning of creativity and look at a few examples.

WHAT IS ART?

First, some definitions: Within this book a **work of art** is the visual expression of an idea or experience, formed with skill, through the use of a medium. A **medium** is a particular material, along with its accompanying technique. (The plural is *media*.) Artists select media to suit the ideas and feelings they wish to present. When a medium is used in such a way that the object or performance contributes to our understanding or enjoyment of life, we experience the final product as art.

For *Her Secret Is Patience*, the artist sought to create a work that would say something about the Phoenix area, in a way that harmonized with the forces of nature. Thus, she chose flexible netting for the medium because it responds gracefully to the wind. Echelman similarly chose the size, scale, shape, and color of the work that would best support and express her message.

Media in use for many centuries include clay, fiber, stone, wood, and paint. By the mid-twentieth century, modern technology had added more new media, including video and computers, to the nineteenth-century contributions of photography and motion pictures. Many artists today combine media in a single work. Whatever the medium, art grows from our common need to give expressive substance to feelings, ideas, insights, and experiences. In this book, the focus is the visual arts, including drawing, painting, sculpture, film, architecture, and design.

Much of our communication is verbal, yet any single medium of expression has its limitations. Some ideas and feelings can be communicated only through visual forms, while other insights can be expressed best through music. American painter Georgia O'Keeffe said: "I found that I could say things with colors and shapes that I couldn't say in any other way—things I had no words for."[2] The arts communicate meanings that go far beyond ordinary verbal exchange, and artists use the entire range of thought, feeling, and observation as the subjects of their art.

PURPOSES AND FUNCTIONS OF ART

Art forms us in many ways: by telling us things, embellishing our lives, elevating our spirits, showing us who we are, waking us up to injustice, or just flooring us with beauty. A given work of art may serve several functions all at once. To understand their purposes and functions, let us examine some works as examples.

Art for Communicating Information

Because art makes a statement that can be understood by many people, it has often been used to impart information and ideas. During the Middle Ages in Europe, stained-glass windows and stone sculpture of the cathedrals taught Bible stories to an illiterate population. Many artworks provide evidence about the historical period in which they were created. Today, many artists use photographs and movies to make works that inform us.

In 2009, photographer Lauren Greenfield went to the Mideastern emirate of Dubai to document the impact of the global economic downturn on that formerly high-flying city. She returned with many

1.2 Lauren Greenfield.
The View North, toward Burj Dubai. 2009.
Photograph.
© Lauren Greenfield/Institute for Artist Management.

remarkable images, among them *The View North, toward Burj Dubai*. No verbal essay could do as well at showing us both the glamorous aspirations and the current desolate state of the region. Here we see frozen cranes, hollow buildings, and nearly empty streets that meander between dead construction sites. The sidewalks have almost no people; the pool at the lower right is empty. The view from above contributes to the haunted feeling of this now-ghostly city. Through careful composition and skillful execution, she made information more accessible and memorable than it would be through words alone.

Art for Day-to-Day Living

Objects of all kinds, from ancient, carefully crafted flint knives to today's personal music players, have been conceived to delight the eye as well as to serve more obviously useful functions. Well-designed objects and spaces—from spoons to cities—bring pleasure and efficiency into our daily lives. A recent example of good design that can also help us get from Point A to Point B is the *Mission One*

motorcycle. Notice that the lines all seem to lean forward, suggesting speed. (And that is not merely a suggestion, as the *Mission One* can top 150 m.p.h.) The black body shields the engine, which is powered by rechargeable lithium-ion batteries rather than gasoline. It leans forward in both design and technology. It is fast, quiet, green, and also beautiful.

1.3 *Mission One.* Electric-powered motorcycle. 2009.
Mission Motors, San Francisco.
Designer: Yves Behar.
Courtesy Mission Motors.

Most societies value the artistic embellishment of everyday things. This *Dish* from ancient Persia is simply decorated in a few colors. The circular patterns in the central motif echo the shape of the plate itself. Dancing around its border is a line of stylized Arabic writing from Muslim scripture, which underlines the plate's function in hospitality: "Generosity is one of the qualities of the people of Paradise."

Nearly all the objects and spaces we use in our private and public lives were designed by artists and designers. The best of our buildings, towns, and cities have been designed with the quality of their visual form—as well as their functions—in mind. Each of us is involved with art and design whenever we make decisions about how to style our hair, what clothes to wear, or how to furnish and arrange our living spaces. As we make such choices, we are engaged in universal art-related processes, making visual statements about who we are and the kind of world we like to see around us.

Art for Worship and Ritual

In many societies, the arts have a spiritual component. People throughout history have used their best skills to fashion beautiful objects to aid in prayer, contemplation, worship, magic, and ceremony.

A great deal of traditional African art has a spiritual emphasis, as worshippers use objects in rituals to attract the attention of the gods. The *Dance Wand in Honor of Eshu* is draped with strands of the shells that were once used as currency, alluding to Eshu's lordship of the marketplace. A worshipper uses the statue by hanging it over a shoulder and literally dancing with it to the appropriate chants and songs. The bulbs protruding from Eshu's bladelike hairdo signify the medicines that Eshu uses.

1.5 *Dance Wand in Honor of Eshu.*
Elegba Cult. Yoruba, Nigeria. Wood, leather, cowrie shells, brass, bone. Height 19¾″.
© 2010, Indiana University Art Museum: Raymond and Laura Wielgus Collection 87.24.2.
Photographers: Michael Cavanagh and Kevin Montague.

1.4 *Dish.*
10th Century. East Iran. Lead-glazed earthenware with colored slips. Diameter 8¼″.
Courtesy of the Freer Gallery of Art, Smithsonian Institution, Washington, D.C. F1965.27

Many objects created for ritual use look precious, befitting their use in divine ceremonies. The *Chalice* by American potter Beatrice Wood seems to radiate warm light. Muslim potters centuries ago developed the technique that produces this glowing, metallic surface. The profile of the piece shows its origins in the natural forms of the earth, as it lacks straight lines and square edges. Its resemblance to a human form may echo the Christian belief that Christ is present in the communion ritual, for which this chalice is designed. The *Chalice* has many symmetrical handles that seem to invite eager grasping. These handles suggest that the most natural approach to it is to stand before it and hold it up, which is in fact what priests do in the Roman Catholic Mass. The *Chalice* could hold consecrated wine for Christian ritual, but its earthy, rounded shape and glowing body make it a compelling decorative piece as well.

A likely location for using the *Chalice* might be *St. Anselm's Altar*, a recently consecrated piece at

1.6 Beatrice Wood (1893–1998).
Chalice. 1986.
Pottery. 7⅝″ × ⅞″.
Collection of The Newark Museum. Inv.: 86.4. © The Newark Museum, Newark, New Jersey, U.S.A.

1.7 Stephen Cox.
St. Anselm's Altar. 2006.
Aosta marble. Height 35″.
Chapel of St. Anselm, Canterbury Cathedral, England.
Stephen Cox.

Canterbury Cathedral in England. Artist Stephen Cox fashioned beautiful green marble from Italy into a shape that brings a modern look to that ancient church. The marble has striking white veins that the artist included in the design. The symmetrical front suggests the upper part of a cross, with the arms of Christ extended.

Art continues to fulfill personal, spiritual needs for many people, and most of the world's major religions have used art to inspire and instruct the faithful.

Art for Personal Expression

We all share the basic human need to know and be known by others. Many artists help meet this need by expressing their personalities or feelings or worldviews in art; the artwork then becomes a meeting site between artist and viewer. Certain artists reveal themselves so clearly that we feel we know them. Seventeenth-century Dutch artist Rembrandt van Rijn expressed his attitude toward life in well over one thousand paintings, drawings, and prints.

From the age of twenty until his death at sixty-three, Rembrandt created dozens of self-portraits. He was fascinated by the expressive possibilities of the human body and found himself to be the most readily available model. Like a good actor, he used his own face as a resource for studying life.

In most of his self-portraits, Rembrandt viewed himself straightforwardly and with disarming honesty. His *Self-Portrait* of 1658 is brought to life by the eyes, which suggest a person of penetrating insight. By examining himself objectively, Rembrandt went beyond himself; he created a statement about how it feels to be alive, to be human.

Korean-American artist Yong Soon Min projects an altogether contemporary sense of the self in her mixed-media piece *Dwelling*. Born in a small village in Korea just before the end of the Korean War, she and her mother joined her

1.8 Rembrandt van Rijn.
Self-Portrait. 1658.
Oil on canvas. 52⅝" × 40⅞".
Copyright The Frick Collection, New York.

father in California when she was seven. Thus, while she was raised mainly in the United States, it is not her native land; yet on trips back to Korea she feels distant from her country of origin as well.

If Rembrandt's *Self-Portrait* shows a powerful presence, *Dwelling* expresses alienation and absence. The artist inserted personal mementoes into a traditional Korean-style dress and hung it over a pile of books, maps, and photographs. Inside the dress, barely visible, is a script from a Korean poet, which gives voice to the loss of identity. The hauntingly empty dress seems to await a Korean occupant who will never put it back on.

SEE MORE See a video interview with Yong Soon Min about *Dwelling* by going to **www.myartslab.com**

1.9 Yong Soon Min.
Dwelling. 1994.
Mixed media. 72″ × 42″ × 28″.
Photo by Erik Landsberg.
Courtesy of the artist.

1.10 Romare Bearden.
Rocket to the Moon. 1971.
Collage on board. 13″ × 9¼″.
© Romare Bearden Foundation/Licensed by VAGA, New York, NY.

This sense of divided nationality is increasingly common among Americans, many of whom were born elsewhere.

Twentieth-century American artist Romare Bearden was fascinated by the pageant of daily life he witnessed in the rural South and in Harlem, New York. In *Rocket to the Moon*, collage fragments build a scene of quiet despair and stoic perseverance. A barely visible rocket at the very top heads for the moon, while urban life below remains punctuated by a red stop-light. The artist makes an ironic visual statement, placing America's accomplishments in space alongside the stalled social and economic progress of many urban areas.

Not all art is meant to express the personality of the maker; the designs of a coin or a telephone offer much less information about the personal concerns of the artist than do the designs of a painting or a piece of sculpture. Yet an element of self-expression exists in most art, even when the art is produced cooperatively by many individuals, as in filmmaking and architecture.

ROMARE BEARDEN

Jazz, Memory, and Metaphor

1.11 Romare Bearden.
Bernard Brown & Associates.

ROMARE BEARDEN PAID tribute to the richness of his African-American experience through his art. He sought:

to paint the life of my people as I know it ... because much of that life is gone and it had beauty.[3]

The child of educated, middle-class parents, Bearden spent his early childhood in rural North Carolina, then moved north with his family to Harlem, in New York City. His first paid job as an artist was cartooning. During the Depression he attended the Art Students League in New York, where he was encouraged to say more in his drawings than he said in his cartoons. He held his first exhibition in a private studio in 1940—about the same time that he became a social worker in New York, a job he held on and off until 1966.

LEARN MORE: Read an interview with Romare Bearden at **www.myartslab.com**

After serving in the army during World War II, Bearden used his G.I. Bill education grant to study at the Sorbonne in Paris. There he came to know a number of intellectuals and writers of African descent, including poet Leopold Senghor and novelist James Baldwin. Bearden was inspired to make his ethnic heritage a cornerstone of his art. He said of his experience at the Sorbonne, "The biggest thing I learned was reaching into your consciousness of black experience and relating it to universals."[4]

He believed that, just as African Americans had created their own musical forms such as jazz and blues, they should invent their own visual art. He urged his fellow African-American artists to create art out of their own life experiences, as had jazz greats Duke Ellington, Count Basie, Fats Waller, and Earl "Fatha" Hines, who were among Bearden's friends. Bearden himself was a musician and songwriter who said he painted in the tradition of the blues.

He combined his stylistic search with institutional activism. In 1963, he founded the Spiral Group, an informal group of African-American artists

who met in his studio. A year later, he became art director of the Harlem Cultural Council, a group devoted to recognizing and promoting the arts of Harlem residents.

His work shows that Bearden admired and carefully studied Cubist paintings and African sculpture. Also important to his creative development was the rapid-cut style of contemporary documentary filmmakers. Bearden worked in a variety of styles prior to the 1960s, when he arrived at the combined collage and painting style for which he is best known.

Bearden observed, distilled, and then reconstructed the life he saw around him to create memorable images of humanity. In *Prevalence of Ritual: Tidings,* an angel

seems to console an introspective young woman. Borrowed picture fragments, with a few muted colors, make up an otherwise gray world. There is a mood of melancholy and longing. Does the train suggest departure from this world, or escape to the lure of a better life in the North?

Despite his emphasis on his own experiences, Bearden's work has meaning far beyond the African-American community. He said, "What I try to do with art is amplify. If I were just creating a picture of a farm woman from back home, it would have meaning to her and people there. But art amplifies itself to something universal"[5].

1.12 Romare Bearden.
Prevalence of Ritual: Tidings. 1967.
Photomontage. 36" × 48".
© Romare Bearden Foundation/Licensed by VAGA, New York, NY.

Art for Social Causes

What we see influences how we think. Artists in many societies have used their work to criticize or influence public opinion. Often the criticism is clear and direct, as with Francisco Goya's expression of outrage at the Napoleonic Wars in his country. *The Disasters of War* is a series of works that vividly documents atrocities committed by Napoleon's troops as they invaded Spain in 1808. Some of the abuses that Goya depicted are still committed today, a grim fact that gives *The Disasters of War* continuing relevance. This series is a landmark of social criticism in art, and still influences artists today.

Cuban-American artist Félix González-Torres works in a similar vein. In 1990, he printed large sheets showing photographs of all the victims of gunfire in the United States in a randomly selected week. *Untitled (Death by Gun)* is exhibited in what the artist called "endless copies": Placed in a large stack on the floor, they are free for the taking by viewers. González-Torres said of these pieces,

1.13   Francisco Goya.
The Disasters of War, No. 18: Bury Them and Say Nothing. 1818.
Etching and aquatint. 5⅞″ × 8⅜″.
S.P. Avery Collection, Miriam and Ira D. Wallach Division of Art, Prints and Photographs.
The New York Public Library, Astor, Lenox, and Tilden Foundations.

1.14   Félix González-Torres.
Untitled (Death by Gun). 1990.
Nine inch stack of photolithographs, offset printed in black. 44½″ × 32½″.
a.   Installation view.
b.   Single sheet.
The Museum of Modern Art, New York/Licensed by Scala-Art Resource, New York. Purchased in part with funds from Arthur Fleisher, Jr., and Linda Barth Goldstein.
Photograph: © 2002 The Museum of Modern Art, New York.

"I need the public to complete the work. I ask the public to help me, to take responsibility, to become a part of my work, to join in."[6]

Architecture, painting, and sculpture have often been used to project and glorify images of deities, political leaders, and now corporations. In seventeenth-century France, King Louis XIV built an enormous palace and formal garden at Versailles. His purpose was to symbolize the strength of his monarchy—to impress and intimidate the nobility with the Sun King's power (see Chapter 16).

Advertising designers often use the persuasive powers of art to present a version of the truth. We see their messages every day on television and in the media. Not all persuasive art is commercial, however. Art can be an effective instrument for educating, directing popular values, molding public opinion, and gaining and holding political power.

Some artists have been calling attention to the problem of global warming for years. In 1997, Zimbabwean graphic designer Chaz Maviyane-Davies made the poster *Global Warning* for a United Nations conference in Kyoto, Japan. Here we see the Earth literally roasting under the impact of the hot breath of the man at the lower left. The poster leaves no doubt about the global nature of the problem, and also the idea that

1.15 Chaz Maviyane-Davies.
Global Warning. 1997.
Poster for 3rd United Nations Convention on Climate Change, Kyoto.
Courtesy of Chaz Maviyane-Davies.

humans are causing it. Maviyane-Davies remains active with various issues and frequently distributes his work for free over the Internet.

The art of our culture reflects who we are, as well as our relationships to our surroundings and to one another. Art can be pleasing and beautiful, but it can also shout us awake and inspire us to action.

Art for Visual Delight

Many of us probably think of visual delight as the first function of art. Indeed, art can provide pleasure, enjoyment, amusement, diversion, and embellishment in our world. Art that is visually attractive and well crafted can "lift us above the stream of life," as one aesthetician put it. Absorbed in contemplating such works, we forget where we are for a moment.

Islamic art often abounds with lavish decorations of this sort. For example, the fourteenth-century

Decorative Panel from the Alhambra is made of colored mosaic tile laid in dazzling patterns. Our eyes follow pathways that enclose geometric figures of many different shapes, sizes, and colors. These small polygons are elements in a larger rhythm of black starbursts between rows of geometric interlace. The piece shown here is only a small fragment of the lower portion of a wall enclosing a room in the Alhambra, a palace that reached its full glory under the Nasrid rulers of Granada in the fourteenth century.

Some contemporary artists have achieved impressive decorative effects with very different materials. Miriam Schapiro's *Heartland* depends partly on sheer size for its impact, since it measures nearly seven by eight feet. Here, a rich texture of mixed media calls to mind traditional art forms of quilting and flower arranging, once considered the province of women. Schapiro coined the term "femmages" to describe her pieces, which combine paint, fabric, and glitter in a collage format.

1.16 *Decorative Panel from the Alhambra.*
Granada, Spain. Nasrid Period, 14th Century.
Glazed mosaic tile. 60″ × 50⅝″.
Museo de la Alhambra.

1.17 Miriam Schapiro.
Heartland. 1985.
Acrylic, fabric, and glitter on canvas. 85″ × 94″.
Collection of Orlando Museum of Art, Orlando, Florida. Gift of the Women for Special Acquisition and the Council of 101, 87.1.

The lush colors, bold patterns, and symbolic meanings of the shape of the work combine to create a garden of delight that encompasses our entire field of vision.

WHAT IS CREATIVITY?

The source of all art, science, and technology—in fact, all of civilization—is human imagination, or creative thinking. As scientist Albert Einstein declared, "Imagination is more important than knowledge."[7]

What do we mean by this talent that we call creativity? It is the ability to bring forth something new that has value. Mere novelty is not enough; the new thing must have some use, or unlock some new way of thinking. Creativity also has the potential to influence future thought or action. Wherever it happens, creativity is an asset to society.

Some believe that a divine power inspires creative people; others believe that creativity is a function of imagination. In any case, creativity is unpredictable. If we could predict the next innovation, it would not be new.

Psychological studies have described the traits that most creative people share. They include the abilities to:

- wonder and be curious
- be open to new experience
- see the familiar from an unfamiliar point of view
- take advantage of accidental events
- make one thing out of another by shifting its function
- generalize from particulars in order to see broad applications
- synthesize, integrate, find order in disorder
- be in touch with one's unconscious, yet be intensely conscious
- be able to analyze and evaluate

- know oneself, have the courage to be oneself in the face of opposition
- be willing to take risks
- be persistent: to work for long periods—perhaps years—in pursuit of a goal

He Got Game is a good example of visual creativity by simple means. Robin Rhode drew a basketball hoop on the asphalt surface of a street, and then photographed himself lying down in twelve positions as if he were flipping through the air performing an impossible slam dunk. The South African artist here imitates the slow-motion and stop-motion photography often seen in sports television to create a piece with transcendent dramatic flair. The work cleverly uses low-tech chalk drawing and a slangy title to celebrate the cheeky boastfulness of street culture.

As this example shows, creativity is an attitude. Creativity is as fundamental to experiencing a work of art as it is to making one. Insightful seeing is itself a creative act; it requires open receptivity, putting aside habitual modes of thought. When we come upon a work of art that baffles or infuriates us, it challenges our creativity as viewers.

Skill, training, and intelligence are helpful in creativity, but they are not always necessary. Children can be quite creative; so can people who have not graduated from art schools. In fact, the urge to create is universal; it has little to do with art training. We will conclude this chapter by discussing art by untrained artists and children.

UNTRAINED ARTISTS

People with little or no formal art education who make art are usually described as **outsider artists** or **folk artists**.

Untrained artists are largely unaware of art history or the art trends of their time. Unlike folk art,

1.18 Robin Rhode.
He Got Game. 2000.
Twelve color photographs.
Perry Rubenstein Gallery, New York. © Robin Rhode.

which is made by people working within a tradition, art by outsider artists is personal expression created apart from any conventional practice or style.

Many outsider artists seem to develop their art spontaneously, without regard to art of the past or present. Anna Zemankova was a Czech housewife with no art training who at age

1.19 Anna Zemankova.
Untitled (M). c. 1970s.
Pastel on paper. 24¼″ × 17¾″ (61.6 × 45.1 cm).
Courtesy of the artist and Cavin-Morris Gallery, NY.

1.20 Sabatino "Simon" Rodia.
Nuestro Pueblo.
Watts, Calif., 1921–1954. Mixed Media. Height 100′.
a. Distant View.
b. Detail of enclosing wall with construction tool
   impressions.
Photographs: Duane Preble.

fifty-two suddenly began making drawings. She would awaken each morning at about four o'clock and draw with pastel until seven. Seated at a special easel that her son designed, she seemed to work transfixed by an inner vision. All of her works are *Untitled*, including the work illustrated here, but they seem to depict plant life. Her imagery resembles in some ways the local decorative arts of her region, such as embroideries and ceramic glazes, but the combination is completely her own. In later years she began to embroider on the drawings. She said that in her art she grew plants that did not grow elsewhere, and indeed they resemble no known species.

One of the best-known (and largest) pieces of outsider art in the United States is *Nuestro Pueblo (Our People)* more commonly known as the Watts Towers. Creator Simon Rodia exemplifies the artist who visualizes new possibilities for ordinary materials. He worked on his cathedral-like towers for thirty-three years, making the fantastic structures from cast-off materials such as metal pipes and bed frames held together with steel reinforcing rods, mesh, and mortar. Incredibly, he built the towers without power tools, rivets, welds, or bolts.

As the towers rose in his triangular backyard, he methodically covered their surfaces with bits and pieces of broken dishes, tile, melted bottle glass, shells, and other colorful junk from the vacant lots of his neighborhood. Rodia's towers and the ideas they represent are testimony to the artist's creativity and perseverance.

The *Throne of the Third Heaven of the Nations' Millennium General Assembly* is another striking work by an untrained artist. James Hampton, a night janitor in Washington, D.C., for years brought home pieces of furniture and other objects he found on his rounds, laboriously covered them with gold and silver foil, and arranged them symmetrically in his garage. Hampton, a Baptist minister, believed that Jesus was coming again soon and would need a throne to sit on. So he built one. No one knew of this project until its creator died, when relatives going through his possessions discovered it. It now occupies an entire gallery in the Smithsonian Institution.

In contrast to outsider artists, folk artists are part of established traditions of style, theme, and craftsmanship. Most folk artists are untrained in traditional art skills and create more from enthusiasm than from professional commitment. Folk art can take many forms, including quilts, hand-stitched samplers, decorated weather vanes, or customized cars. In earlier times, particularly in rural areas, influences from beyond one's immediate community were limited, and thus many folk art traditions remained relatively unchanged for long periods.

1.21 James Hampton.
Throne of the Third Heaven of the Nations' Millennium General Assembly. c. 1950–1964.
Gold and silver aluminum foil, colored Kraft paper, plastic sheets over wood, paperboard, and glass.
180 pieces. 10′6″ × 27′ × 14′6″.
Copyright National Museum of American Art, Smithsonian, Washington, D.C./Art Resource, NY.

I'd like to study the drawings of kids. That's where the truth is, without a doubt.
ANDRÉ DERAIN[8]

THE ARTS COME from inborn human needs to create and to communicate. They come from the desire to explore, confirm, and share special observations and insights—a fact readily apparent in nine-year-old Kojyu's *Searching for Bugs in the Park* The arts are one of the most constructive ways to say "I did it. I made it. This is what I see and feel. I count. My art is me." Unfortunately, the great value of this discover-and-share, art-making process is only rarely affirmed in today's busy homes and schools.

We include art by children as the best way—other than actual hands-on art-making processes—to help you reexamine your relationship to your own creative powers and perhaps even to guide you as you prepare to become a parent, a teacher, or a caregiver for children.

Children use a universal visual language. All over the world, drawings by children ages two to six show similar stages of mental growth, from exploring with mark making to inventing shapes to symbolizing things seen and imagined. Until they are about six years old, children usually depict the world in symbolic rather than realistic ways. Their images are more mental constructions than records of visual observations.

During the second year of life, children enjoy making

marks, leaving traces of their movements. Sensitive exploration is visible in *First Lines,* by a one-and-a-half-year-old child. After marking and scribbling, making circles and other shapes fascinates young children. The *House* shape is by a two-year-old. *Hand with Line and Spots* is by a three-year-old, as is the smiling portrait of *Grandma* in which self-assured lines symbolize a happy face, shoulders, arms, body, belly button, and legs.

Being the son of a salt-water fish collector, and watching an octopus, gave almost four-year-old Jason the idea for his drawing of a smiling *Mother Octopus with Babies.* The excitement of joyful play with friends on unicycles inspired eight-year-old Yuki's *I Can Ride, I Can Ride My Unicycle.* Notice how she emphasized her own image by greatly exaggerating her size

1.22 Kojyu, age 9. *Searching for Bugs in the Park.*

1.23 Anonymous Child, age 18 months. *First Lines.*

1.24 Alana, age 2. *House.*

1.25 Jeff, age 3. *Hand with Line and Spots.*

1.26 Alana, age 3. *Grandma.*
Photographs: Duane Preble.

relative to others and how she included important information, such as her right leg seen through the spokes of the wheel.

Young children often demonstrate an intuitive

OCTOPUS

1.27 Jason, almost 4.
Mother Octopus with Babies.

1.28 Yuki, age 8.
I Can Ride, I Can Ride My Unicycle.
Photographs: Duane Preble.

sense of composition. Unfortunately, we lose much of this intuitive sense of balanced design as we begin to look at the world from a conceptual, self-conscious point of view. Most children who have been given coloring books, workbooks, and predrawn printed single sheets become overly dependent on such impersonal, stereotyped props. In this way, children often lose the urge to invent unique images based on their own experiences. A child's two drawings of *Birds* show this process: The child first interprets the bird in a personal, fresh way, but later adopts the trite forms of a conventional workbook. Without ongoing opportunities for personal expression, children lose self-confidence in their original creative impulses.

Children begin life as eager learners. If they are loved and cared for, they soon express enthusiasm for perceiving and exploring the world around them. Research shows that parents' ability to show interest in and empathy for their child's discoveries and feelings is crucial to the child's brain development. Before the age of one, and well before they talk, babies point tiny fingers at wonderful things they see. Bodies move in rhythm to music. Ask a group of four-year-olds "Can you dance?" "Can you sing?" "Can you draw?" and they all say, "Yes! Yes!" Ask twelve-year-olds the same questions, and they will too often say "No, we can't." Such an unnecessary loss

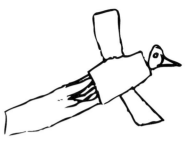

1.29 Anonymous Child.
Birds.
a. This picture shows one child's drawing of a bird before exposure to coloring books.

b. Then the child colored a workbook illustration.

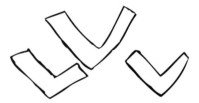

c. After coloring the workbook birds, the child lost creative sensitivity and self-reliance.
(a,b, and c) From *Creative Mental Growth* by Lowenfeld, ©1975, p. 23. Reproduced by permission of Pearson Education Inc, Upper Saddle River, NJ.

has ominous implications for the spiritual, economic, social, and political health of society.

Most abilities observed in creative people are also characteristic of children during interactions with the world around them. What becomes of this extraordinary capacity? According to John Holt, author of *How Children Fail,*

We destroy this capacity above all by making them afraid—afraid of not doing what other people want, of not pleasing, or of making mistakes, of failing, of being wrong. Thus we make them afraid to gamble, afraid to experiment, afraid to try the difficult and unknown.[9]

When the Southwest was a Spanish colony, a folk tradition of religious imagery evolved in Roman Catholic churches and family chapels. The saints, or *santos*, were the most common subjects, and the artists who made them were known as *santeros*. Many santeros are anonymous, such as the Arroyo Hondo Carver. *Our Lady of the Immaculate Conception* shows his typical method of carving, with its elongated figures and distant, other-worldly facial expressions. Compared with related folk arts of the same region, this piece also displays the carver's brighter color scheme. Our Lady of the Immaculate Conception is usually represented without a Christ Child, but some folk artists ignore those customs, as the carver has done here.

Visual creativity takes a great many forms. A film director places actors and cameras on a stage in order to emphasize a certain aspect of the script. A Hopi potter takes clay from the ground near her home and shapes it into a water jar. A graphic designer seated at a computer screen arranges a composition of typefaces, images, and colors in order to help get his message across. A carver in Japan fashions wood into a Buddha that will aid in meditation at a monastery. Most of us have at some time composed a picture for a camera. All of these actions involve artistic creativity, the use of visual imagery to communicate beyond what mere words can say.

Like beauty, truth, and life itself, art is larger than any single definition. One dictionary defines art in this way:

art, n. 1. the expression or application of creative skill and imagination, especially through a visual medium such as painting or sculpture.[10]

As we have seen from the works illustrated in just this chapter, it is difficult to arrive at a definition that includes all the possible forms of art. Hence, we will spend the rest of the book exploring them.

PRACTICE MORE: Get flashcards for images and terms and review chapter material with quizzes at **www.myartslab.com**

1.30 Arroyo Hondo Carver.
Our Lady of the Immaculate Conception.
1830–1850.
Carved and painted wood. 29″ high.
Taylor Museum, Colorado Springs Fine Arts Center, Museum Purchase. TM3858.

VISUAL COMMUNICATION

IS IT POSSIBLE TO EXPRESS FEELING USING LINES ONLY?

DO ARTISTS WHO WORK IN TWO DIMENSIONS MANIPULATE SPACE?

HOW CAN YOU TELL WHETHER COLORS WILL CLASH OR CO-ORDINATE?

WHAT ARE SOME WAYS THAT ARTISTS MANIPULATE TIME?

The language of vision determines, perhaps even more subtly and thoroughly than verbal language, the structure of our consciousness.

S. I. HAYAKAWA[1]

The most direct path to the mind is through the eyes. As philosopher and educator S. I. Hayakawa pointed out, our visual experience of the world is so profoundly influential that it constitutes a nonverbal language all its own. This is the language that artists use to communicate. In this chapter we will first discuss the art of looking and then consider various visual tools that artists use.

LOOKING AND SEEING

The verbs "look" and "see" indicate varying degrees of awareness. Looking implies taking in what is before us in a purely mechanical way; seeing is a more active extension of looking. If we care only about function, we simply need to look quickly at a doorknob in order to grasp and turn it. But when we get excited about the shape and finish of a doorknob, or the bright, clear quality of a winter day,

we go beyond simple functional looking to a higher level of perception called "seeing."

The twentieth-century French artist Henri Matisse wrote about the effort it takes to move beyond stereotypes and to see intently:

To see is itself a creative operation, requiring an effort. Everything that we see in our daily life is more or less distorted by acquired habits, and this is perhaps more evident in an age like ours when cinema, posters, and magazines present us every day with a flood of ready-made images which are to the eye what prejudices are to the mind. The effort needed to see things without distortion takes something very like courage.[2]

But, since words and visual images are two different "languages," talking about visual arts with words is always an act of translation one step removed from actually experiencing art. In fact, our eyes have their own connections to our minds and emotions. By cultivating these connections, we can take better advantage of what art has to offer.

HEAR MORE: Listen to an audio file of your chapter at **www.myartslab.com**

Ordinary things become extraordinary when we see them deeply. Is Edward Weston's photograph of a pepper meaningful to us because we like peppers so much? Probably not. To help us truly see, Weston created a memorable image on a flat surface with the help of a common pepper. A time exposure of over two hours gave *Pepper #30* quality of glowing light—a living presence that resembles an embrace. Through his sensitivity to form, Weston revealed how this pepper appeared to him. Notes from his *Daybook* communicate his enthusiasm about this photograph:

August 8, 1930

I could wait no longer to print them—my new peppers, so I put aside several orders, and yesterday afternoon had an exciting time with seven new negatives.

First I printed my favorite, the one made last Saturday, August 2, just as the light was failing—

quickly made, but with a week's previous effort back of my immediate, unhesitating decision. A week?—Yes, on this certain pepper,—but twenty-eight years of effort, starting with a youth on a farm in Michigan, armed with a No. 2 Bull's Eye [Kodak] 3½ × 3½, have gone into the making of this pepper, which I consider a peak of achievement.

It is a classic, completely satisfying—a pepper—but more than a pepper: abstract, in that it is completely outside subject matter . . . this new pepper takes one beyond the world we know in the conscious mind.[3]

Weston's photograph of a seemingly common object is a good example of the creative process at work. The artist was uniquely aware of something in his surroundings. He worked for a long time (perhaps 28 years!) to achieve the image he wanted. The photograph that resulted not only represents the object but also communicates a deep sense of wonder about the natural world.

THE VISUAL TOOLBOX

Remember that a picture—before being a war horse, a nude woman, or some anecdote—is essentially a plane surface covered with colors assembled in a certain order.
Maurice Denis[4]

Painter Maurice Denis might have gone on to say that the surface can also be covered with lines, shapes, colors, and other aspects of visual form. Sculpture consists of these same elements organized and presented in three-dimensional space. Because of their overlapping qualities, it is impossible to draw rigid boundaries between the elements of visual form.

A glance at Swiss artist Paul Klee's *Landscape with Yellow Birds* shows his fluent use of several visual tools. Fluid, curving **lines** define abstract **shapes**. Klee simplified and flattened the solid

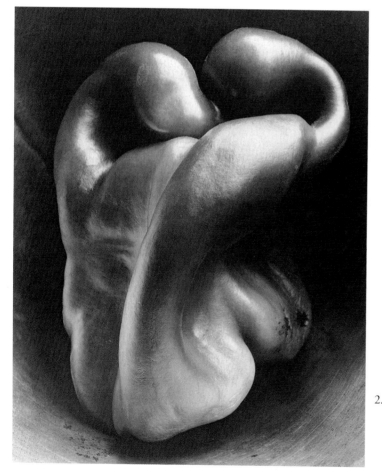

2.1 Edward Weston.
Pepper #30. 1930.
Photograph.
Photograph by Edward Weston.
Collection Center for Creative Photography, The University of Arizona.
©1981 Arizona Board of Regents.

2.2 Paul Klee.
Landscape with Yellow Birds. 1923.
Watercolor, newspaper, black base. 14″×17⅜″.
Photograph: Hans Hinz/Artothek.
© 2010 Artists Rights Society (ARS), New York/VG Bild-Kunst, Bonn.

masses of natural plant and bird forms so that they read as flat shapes against a dark background **space**. Such **abstraction** emphasizes the fantastic, dreamlike quality of the subject. The whimsical positioning of the upside-down bird suggests a moment in **time** without **motion**. **Light** illuminates and enhances the yellow **color** of the birds and the unusual colors of the leaves.

This chapter introduces the visual tools identified in *Landscape with Yellow Birds:* line, shape, mass, space, time, motion, light, and color, and abstraction. Not all these elements are important, or even present, in every work of art; many works emphasize only a few elements. To understand their expressive possibilities, it is useful for us to examine, one at a time, some of the expressive qualities of each of these aspects of visual form.

LINE

We write, draw, plan, and play with lines. Our individualities and feelings are expressed as we write our one-of-a-kind signatures or make other unmechanical lines. Line is our basic means for recording and symbolizing ideas, observations, and feelings; it is a primary means of visual communication.

A line is an extension of a point. Our habit of making all kinds of lines obscures the fact that pure geometric line—line with only one dimension, length—is a mental concept. Such geometric lines, with no height or depth, do not exist in the three-dimensional physical world. Lines are actually linear forms in which length dominates over width. Wherever we see an edge, we can perceive the edge as a line—the place where one object or plane appears to end and another object or space begins. In a sense, we often "draw" with our eyes, converting edges to lines.

In art and in nature, we can consider lines as paths of action—records of the energy left by moving points. Many intersecting and contrasting linear paths form the composition in Lee Friedlander's photograph *Bismarck, North Dakota.* Wires, poles, railings, building edges, and the shadows they cast all present themselves as lines in this work.

2.3 Lee Friedlander.
Bismarck, North Dakota. 2002.
Photograph.
© Lee Friedlander, courtesy Fraenkel Gallery, San Francisco.

2.4 *Line Variations.*

a. Actual line

b. Implied line

c. Actual straight lines and implied curved line

d. Line created by an edge

e. Vertical line (attitude of alert attention); horizontal line (attitude of rest).

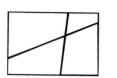
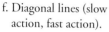
f. Diagonal lines (slow action, fast action).

g. Sharp, jagged line.

h. Dance of curving lines.

i. Hard line, soft line.

j. Ragged, irregular line.

Characteristics of Line

Lines can be active or static, aggressive or passive, sensual or mechanical. Lines can indicate directions, define boundaries of shapes and spaces, imply volumes or solid masses, and suggest motion or emotion. Lines can also be grouped to depict light and shadow and to form patterns and textures. Note the line qualities in these *Line Variations.*

Consider the range of uses artists found for lines in the works pictured on these two pages. In Anselm Reyle's *Untitled* neon work, colored lights describe lines in three-dimensional space. But artists have put lines to many other uses.

Bridget Riley created a powerful energy field of parallel, wavy lines in her painting *Current.* We cannot focus steadily on one spot in this work, and as our eyes move, the work seems to vibrate even though nothing in it moves. Jackson Pollock made his *Drawing* by pouring and dripping ink from a stick without touching the paper. The swirling

2.5 Anselm Reyle.
Untitled. 2006.
119 neon tubes, chains, cable, and 13 transformers.
16'4" × 32'8" × 26'4".

2.6 Bridget Riley.
Current. 1964.
Synthetic polymer paint on composition board.
58⅜"×58⅞" (148.1 × 149.3 cm).

2.7 Jackson Pollock.
Drawing. 1950. Duco on paper. 28.2 × 152.2 cm.
Staatsgalerie Stuttgart/Graphische Sammlung. © 2010 The Pollock-Krasner
Foundation/Artists Rights Society (ARS), New York.

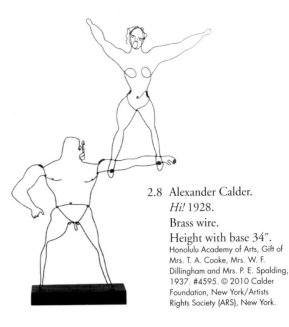

2.8 Alexander Calder.
Hi! 1928.
Brass wire.
Height with base 34″.
Honolulu Academy of Arts, Gift of
Mrs. T. A. Cooke, Mrs. W. F.
Dillingham and Mrs. P. E. Spalding,
1937. #4595. © 2010 Calder
Foundation, New York/Artists
Rights Society (ARS), New York.

lines tracked his expressive hand motions, varying the thickness with the speed of his wrist. The two acrobats in *Hi!* by Alexander Calder are drawn in space using wire that the artist flexed into shape with pliers; his whimsical lines captured their exuberant maneuvers. Many Japanese prints take as subject matter popular entertainers such as dancers and actors. The two prints pictured here use black contour lines in contrasting ways: *Woman Dancer* is curvy and sensuous, suggesting rhythmic motion, whereas Torii Kiyotada's *Actor* uses angular lines to express violent and swift action.

Many types of prints are made up almost entirely of lines, with little shading or color. Kiki Smith etched lines in a metal plate to create *Ginzer*, a depiction of her cat. She painstakingly drew one line for each of *Ginzer*'s hairs, it seems. The eyes and foot pads are slightly shaded, but all else was done with line. She successfully captured the cat's flexible limbs and back as *Ginzer* reclined, but she also showed a hint of the cat's wild side in the mouth and alert eyes.

2.9 Attributed to Torii
Kiyonobu I
(1664–1729).
*Woman Dancer with
Fan and Wand* (or possibly *Tsugawa Handayu*).
c. 1708.
Woodblock print.
21¾″×11½″.
The Metropolitan Museum of Art,
Harris Brisbane Dick Fund and
Rogers Fund, 1949 (JP 3098).
Photograph © 1979 The
Metropolitan Museum of Art.
Art Resource, NY.

2.10 Torii Kiyotada
(Japanese, worked c.
1710–1740).
*An Actor of the
Ichikawa Clan in a
Dance Movement of
Violent Motion.*
c. 1715.
Hand-colored
woodcut. 11¼″×6″.
The Metropolitan Museum of Art,
Harris Brisbane Dick Fund and
Rogers Fund, 1949. (JP 3075).
Photograph © 1979 The
Metropolitan Museum of Art.
Art Resource, NY.

2.11 Kiki Smith.
Ginzer. 2000.
Etching, aquatint, and drypoint on
mold-made paper.
22½″×31″.
Published by Harlan & Weaver, New York.

Implied Line

Implied lines suggest visual connections. Implied lines that form geometric shapes can serve as an underlying organizational structure. In *I and the Village*, Marc Chagall used implied lines to create a large circle at the lower center that brings together scenes of Russian Jewish village life. Notice that he also drew in the implied sightline between man and animal with a fine line.

2.12 Marc Chagall.
I and the Village. 1911.
Oil on canvas. 6′3⅝″ × 59⅝″ (192.1 × 151.4 cm).
The Museum of Modern Art/Licensed by Scala-Art Resource, NY.
Mrs. Simon Guggenheim Fund.
Photograph © 2002 The Museum of Modern Art, New York.
© 2010 Artists Rights Society (ARS), New York/ADAGP, Paris.

SHAPE

The words *shape*, *mass*, and *form* are sometimes used interchangeably, but they mean different things in the visual arts. Here *shape* is used to refer to the expanse within the outline of a two-dimensional area or within the outer boundaries of a three-dimensional object. When we see a three-dimensional object in natural light, we see that it has mass, or volume. If the same object is silhouetted against a sunset, we may see it only as a flat shape. Enclosing lines or changing color sets a shape apart from its surroundings so that we recognize it.

We can group the infinite variety of shapes into two general categories: geometric and organic. **Geometric shapes**—such as circles, triangles, and squares—tend to be precise and regular. **Organic shapes** are irregular, often curving or rounded, and seem relaxed and more informal than geometric shapes. The most common shapes in the human-made world are geometric. Although some geometric shapes exist in nature—in such forms as crystals, honeycombs, and snowflakes—most shapes in nature are organic. A related term with a similar meaning is **biomorphic**, which also suggests shapes based on natural forms.

In *I and the Village,* Chagall used a geometric structure of circles and triangles to organize the organic shapes of people, animals, and plants. He softened the severity of geometric shapes to achieve a natural flow between the various parts of the painting. Conversely, he abstracted natural subjects toward geometric simplicity in order to strengthen visual impact and symbolic content.

When a shape appears on a **picture plane** (the flat picture surface), it simultaneously creates a second shape out of the background area. The dominant shapes are referred to as **figures** or **positive shapes**; background areas are **ground** or **negative shapes**. The figure–ground relationship is a fundamental aspect of perception; it allows us to sort out and interpret what we see. Because we are conditioned to see only objects, and not the spaces between and around them, it takes a shift in awareness to see the white

2.13 *A Shape of Space.*
Implied shape.

negative shapes in *A Shape of Space.* Most artists consider both positive and negative shapes simultaneously and treat them as equally important to the total effectiveness of a composition.

Interactions between figure shapes and ground shapes are heightened in some images. *Night Life* can be seen as white shapes against black or as black shapes against white. Or, to say it another way, the figure–ground relationship can shift back and forth. In both this and M. C. Escher's woodcut *Sky and Water*, shifting of figure and ground contributes to a similar content: the interrelatedness of all things.

In the upper half of Escher's print, we see dark geese on a white ground. As our eyes move down the page, the light upper background becomes fish against a black background. In the middle, however, fish and geese interlock so perfectly that we are not sure what is figure and what is ground. As our awareness shifts, fish shapes and bird shapes trade places, a phenomenon called **figure–ground reversal**.

MASS

A two-dimensional area is called a shape, but a three-dimensional area is called a mass—the physical bulk of a solid body of material. When mass encloses space, the space is called **volume**.

Mass in Three Dimensions

Mass is often a major element in sculpture and architecture. For example, immense or bulky mass was an important characteristic of ancient Egyptian architecture and sculpture. Egyptians sought this quality and perfected it because it expressed their desire to make art for eternity.

2.14 Duane Preble.
Night Life.
Figure–ground reversal.
Duane Preble.

2.15 M. C. Escher.
Sky and Water I. 1938.
Woodcut. 17⅛″×17¼″.
© 2006 The M. C. Escher Company–Holland.
All rights reserved. www.mcescher.com.

Sennefer, Steward of the Palace was carved from hard black granite and retains the cubic, blocklike appearance of the quarried stone. None of the limbs project outward into the surrounding space. The figure sits with knees drawn up and arms folded, the neck obscured by a ceremonial headdress. The body is abstracted and implied with minimal suggestion. This piece is a good example of **closed form**—form that does not openly interact with the space around it. Here, compact mass symbolizes permanence. Egyptian portrait sculpture acted as a symbolic container for the soul of an important person to ensure eternal afterlife.

In contrast to the compact mass of the Egyptian portrait, modern sculptor Alberto Giacometti's *Man Pointing* conveys a sense of fleeting presence rather than permanence. The tall, thin figure appears eroded by time and barely existing. Because Giacometti used little solid material to construct the figure, we are more aware of a linear form in space than of mass. The figure reaches out; its **open form** interacts with the surrounding space, which seems to overwhelm it, suggesting the fragile, impermanent nature of human existence.

Giacometti's art reveals an obsession with mortality that began when he was twenty, following the death of an older companion. Later, expressing the fleeting essence of human life became a major concern of his work. For Giacometti, both life and art

2.16 *Sennefer, Steward of the Palace.*
c. 1450 B.C.E.
Black granite. Height 2′9″.
The British Museum, Department of Egyptian Antiquities.
© The British Museum/Art Resource, NY.

2.17 Alberto Giacometti (1901–1966).
Man Pointing. 1947.
Bronze. 70½″×40¾″×16⅜″, at base, 12″×13¼″.
Gift of Mrs. John D. Rockefeller 3rd. (678.1954) The Museum of Modern Art, New York, NY, U.S.A. Digital Image The Museum of Modern Art/Licensed by SCALA/Art Resource, NY. © 2010 Succession Giacometti/Artists Rights Society (ARS), New York/ADAGP, Paris.

making were continuous evolutions. He never felt that he succeeded in capturing the changing nature of what he saw, and therefore he considered all of his works unfinished.

Mass in Two Dimensions

With two-dimensional media such as painting and drawing, mass must be implied. In *Bread*, Elizabeth Catlett drew lines that seem to wrap around and define a girl in space, implying a solid mass. The work gives the appearance of mass because the lines both follow the curvature of the head and build up dark areas to suggest mass revealed by light. Her use of lines convinces us that we are seeing a fully rounded person.

SPACE

Space is the indefinable, general receptacle of all things—the seemingly empty space around us. How artists organize space in the works they create is one of their most important creative considerations.

Space in Three Dimensions

Of all the visual elements, space is the most difficult to convey in words and pictures. To experience three-dimensional space, we must be in it. We experience space beginning with our own positions in relation to other people, objects, surfaces, and voids at various distances from ourselves. Each of us has a sense of personal space—the area surrounding our bodies—that we like to protect, and the extent of this invisible boundary varies from person to person and from culture to culture.

Architects are especially concerned with the qualities of space. Imagine how you would feel in a small room with a very low ceiling. What if you raised the ceiling to fifteen feet? What if you added skylights? What if you replaced the walls with glass? In each case you would have changed the character of the space and, by doing so, would have radically changed your experience.

We experience the outside of a building as mass, but we experience the inside as volume, and as a sequence of enclosed spaces. Cesar Pelli's design for the *North Terminal* at Ronald Reagan Washington

2.18 Elizabeth Catlett.
Bread. 1962.
Linocut on paper. 15⅝″ × 11⅝″.
Courtesy of the Library of Congress.
© Elizabeth Catlett/Licensed by VAGA, New York, NY.

2.19 Cesar Pelli and Associates.
North Terminal, Ronald Reagan Washington National Airport. 1997.
Photographer: Jeff Goldberg/Esto Photographics, Inc.

National Airport takes the passenger's experience of space into account. Large windows offer views of the runways and also of the Potomac River and the nearby Washington Monument. The architect divided the huge interior space into smaller modules to give the concourse a more domestic feel: "The module has an important psychological value in that each one is like a very large living room in size," the architect said.[5] "It's a space that we experience in our daily life. . . . The domes make spaces designed on the scale of people, not on the scale of big machines."

Space in Two Dimensions

With three-dimensional objects and spaces, such as sculpture and architecture, we must move around to get the full experience. With two-dimensional works, such as drawing and painting, we see the space of the surface all at once. In drawings, prints, photographs, and paintings, the actual space of each picture's surface (picture plane) is defined by its edges—usually the two dimensions of height and width. Yet within these boundaries, a great variety of possible pictorial spaces can be implied or suggested, creating depth in the picture plane.

2.20 *Pool in the Garden.*
    Wall painting from the tomb of Nebamun.
    Egypt. c. 1400 B.C.E.
    Paint on dry plaster.
    Photograph © The British Museum, London.

Paintings from ancient Egypt, for example, show little or no depth. Early Egyptian painters made their images clear by portraying objects from their most easily identifiable angles and by avoiding the visual confusion caused by overlap and the appearance of diminishing size. *Pool in the Garden* demonstrates this technique. The pool is shown from above while the trees, fish, and birds are all pictured from the side.

Implied Depth

Almost any mark on a picture plane begins to give the illusion of a third dimension: depth. Clues to seeing spatial depth are learned in early childhood. A few of the major ways of indicating space on a picture plane are shown in the diagrams of *Clues to Spatial Depth.*

When shapes overlap, we immediately assume from experience that one is in front of the other (diagram a). Overlapping is the most basic way to achieve the effect of depth on a flat surface. (Note that *Pool in the Garden* uses very little overlapping.) The effect of overlap is strengthened by diminishing size, which gives a sense of increasing distance between each of the shapes (diagram b). Our perception of distance depends on the observation that distant objects appear smaller than near objects. A third method of achieving the illusion of depth is vertical placement: objects placed low on the picture plane (diagram c) appear to be closer to the viewer than objects placed high on the plane. This is the way we see most things in actual space. Creating illusions of depth on a flat surface usually involves one or more such devices (diagram d).

When we look at a picture, we may be conscious of both its actual flat surface and the illusion of depth that the picture contains. Artists can emphasize either the reality or the illusion, or strike a balance between these extremes. For centuries, Asian painters have paid careful attention to the relationship between the reality of the flat pic-

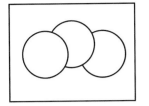

a. Overlap.

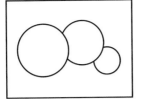

b. Overlap and
diminishing size.

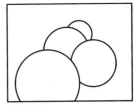

c. Vertical placement.

d. Overlap, vertical placement,
and diminishing size.

ture plane as well as the illusion of depth they wish to imply. Mu Qi's ink painting *Six Persimmons* has only a subtle suggestion of depth in the overlap of two of the persimmons. By placing the smallest persimmon lowest on the picture plane, Mu Qi further minimized the illusion of depth; because we interpret the lower part of the picture as being closer to us, we might expect the persimmon there to be larger.

The persimmons appear against a pale background that works as both flat surface and infinite space. The shapes of the fruit punctuate the open space of the ground. Imagine what would happen to this painting if some of the space at the top were cut off. Space is far more than just leftovers; it is an integral part of the total visual design.

Linear Perspective. In general usage, the word **perspective** refers to point of view. In the visual arts, perspective refers to any means of representing three-dimensional objects in space on a two-dimensional surface. In this sense it is correct to speak of the perspective of Persian miniatures, Japanese prints, Chinese Song Dynasty paintings, or Egyptian murals—although none of these styles are similar to the **linear perspective** system, which was developed during the Italian Renaissance. Different traditions, rather than mere skill, give us various ways of depicting depth.

In the West, we have become accustomed to linear perspective (also called simply, perspective) to depict the way objects in space appear to the eye. This system was developed by Italian architects and painters in the fifteenth century, at the beginning of the Renaissance.

Linear perspective is based on the way we see. We have already noted that objects appear smaller when seen at a distance than when viewed close up.

Because the spaces between objects also appear smaller when seen at a distance, parallel lines appear to converge as they recede into the distance, as shown in the first of the *Linear Perspective* diagrams on the following page. Intellectually, we know that the edge lines of the road must be parallel, yet they seem to converge, meeting at last at what is called a **vanishing point** on the horizon—the place where land and sky appear to meet. On a picture surface,

2.22 Mu Qi (Japanese, d. after 1279).
Six Persimmons (Six Kakis). c. 1269.
Pen and ink on paper, width 36.2 cm.
Daitoku–ji Monastery, Kyoto, Japan.
The Bridgeman Art Library International Ltd.

the horizon (or **horizon line**) also represents your eye level as you look at a scene.

Eye level is an imaginary plane, the height of the artist's eyes, parallel with the ground plane and extending to the horizon, where the eye level and ground plane appear to converge. In a finished picture, the artist's eye level becomes the eye level of anyone looking at the picture. Although the horizon is frequently blocked from view, it is

2.23 *Linear Perspective.*

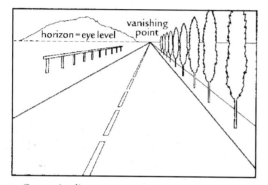

a. One-point linear perspective.

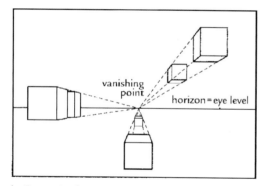

b. One-point linear perspective. Cubes above eye level, at eye level, and below eye level.

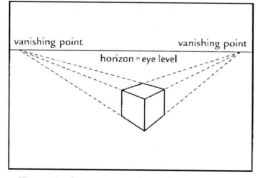

c. Two-point linear perspective.

necessary for an artist to establish a combined eye-level/horizon line to construct images using linear perspective.

With the linear perspective system, an entire picture can be constructed from a single, fixed position called a **vantage point**, or viewpoint. Diagram a shows **one-point perspective**, in which the parallel sides of the road appear to converge and trees in a row appear smaller as their distances from the vantage point increase. A single vanishing point is used for all shapes.

Diagram b shows cubes drawn in one-point linear perspective. The cubes at the left are at eye level; we can see neither their top nor their bottom surfaces. We might imagine them as buildings.

The cubes in the center are below eye level: we can look down on their tops. These cubes are drawn from a high vantage point: a viewing position above the subject. The horizon line is above these cubes, and their perspective lines go up to it. We may imagine these as boxes on the floor.

The cubes at the right are above our eye level; we can look up at their bottom sides. These cubes are drawn from a low vantage point. The horizon line is below these cubes. and their perspective lines go down to it. Imagine that these boxes are sitting on a glass shelf high above our heads.

In one-point perspective, all the major receding "lines" of the subject are actually parallel, yet visually they appear to converge at a single vanishing point on the horizon line. In two-point perspective, two sets of parallel lines appear to converge at two points on the horizon line, as in diagram c.

When a cube or any other rectilinear object is positioned so that a corner, instead of a side, is closest to us, we need two vanishing points to draw it. The parallel lines of the right side converge to the right; the parallel lines of the left side converge to the left. There can be as many vanishing points as there are sets and directions of parallel lines. Horizontal parallel lines moving away from the viewer above eye level appear to go down to the horizon line; those below eye level appear to go up to the horizon line.

2.24a Raphael.
The School of Athens. 1508. Fresco. Approximately 18′ × 26′. Stanza della Segnatura, Vatican Palace, Vatican State.
Copyright Erich Lessing/Art Resource, NY.

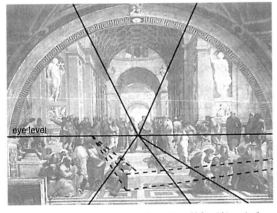

Perspective lines showing eye level, main vanishing point, and left vanishing point for the stone block in the foreground.

2.24b Raphael.
The School of Athens. 1508.
Stanza della Segnatura, Vatican Palace, Vatican State.
Copyright Erich Lessing/Art Resource, NY.

2.25 *Study of The School of Athens*
Stanza della Segnatura, Vatican Palace, Vatican State.
Copyright Erich Lessing/Art Resource, NY.

In *The School of Athens*, Raphael invented a grand architectural setting in the Renaissance style to provide an appropriate space for his depiction of the Greek philosophers Plato and Aristotle and other important thinkers. The size of each figure is drawn to scale according to its distance from the viewer; thus, the entire group seems natural. Lines superimposed over the painting reveal the basic one-point perspective system Raphael used. However, the cube in the foreground is not parallel to the picture plane or to the painted architecture and is in two-point perspective.

Raphael used perspective for emphasis. We infer that Plato and Aristotle are the most important figures in this painting because of their placement at the center of receding archways in the zone of greatest implied depth.

If the figures are removed, as shown in the *Study of the School of Athens*, our attention is pulled right through the painted setting into implied infinite space. Conversely, without their architectural background defined by perspective, Plato and Aristotle lose importance; picking them out from the crowd becomes difficult.

Atmospheric Perspective. Atmospheric or **aerial perspective** is a nonlinear means for giving an illusion of depth. In atmospheric perspective, the illusion of depth is created by changing color, value, and detail. In visual experience of the real world, as the distance increases between the viewer and faraway objects such as mountains, the increased quantity of air, moisture, and dust causes the distant objects to appear increasingly bluer and less distinct. Color intensity is diminished, and contrast between light and dark is reduced.

Asher Brown Durand used atmospheric perspective in his painting *Kindred Spirits* to provide a sense of the vast distances in the North American wilderness. The illusion of infinite space is balanced by dramatically illuminated foreground details, by the figures of the men, and by Durand's lively portrayal of trees, rocks, and waterfalls. We identify with the figures of painter Thomas Cole and poet William Cullen Bryant as they enjoy the spectacular landscape. As in *The School of Athens*, the implied deep space appears as an extension of the space we occupy.

Traditional Chinese landscape painters have another way of creating atmospheric perspective. In Shen Zhou's painting *Poet on a Mountain Top*, near and distant mountains are suggested by washes of ink and color on white paper. The light gray of the farthest mountain at the upper right implies space and atmosphere. Traditional Chinese landscape paintings present

2.26 Asher Brown Durand.
Kindred Spirits. 1849.
Oil on canvas. 44″ × 36″.
Courtesy Crystal Bridges Museum of American Art, Bentonville, Arkansas.

白雲如帶東山腰石
磴飛空細路遙攀倚
杖藜舒眺望欲因鳴
澗谷吹簫洗聞
蘭

2.27 Shen Zhou (Chinese, 1427–1509).
Poet on a Mountain Top. Ming Dynasty (1368–1644).
From series: *Landscape Album: Five Leaves*
Album leaf mounted as a handscroll. Ink and
watercolor on paper. Silk mount.
15¼" × 23¾" (38.73 × 60.32 cm) overall.
The Nelson-Atkins Museum of Art, Kansas City, Missouri.
(Purchase: Nelson Trust) 46-51/2.

poetic symbols of landforms rather than realistic representations. Whereas *Kindred Spirits* draws the viewer's eye into and through the suggested deep space, *Poet on a Mountain Top* leads the eye across (rather than into) space.

TIME AND MOTION

Time is the non-spatial continuum, the fourth dimension, in which events occur in succession.

Because we live in an environment combining space and time, our experience of time often depends on our movement in space and vice versa. Although time itself is invisible, it can be made perceptible in art. Time and motion become major elements in visual media such as film and video.

Many traditional non-Western cultures teach that time is cyclic. The Aztecs of ancient Mexico, for example, held that the Earth was subject to

2.28 *Aztec Calendar Stone.* 1479.
Dagli Orti\Picture Desk, Inc./Kobal Collection.

center. He first comes into view as he approaches the wilderness in the upper left; we next see him encountering the centaur at upper right; finally, he emerges into the clearing in the foreground, where he meets Saint Paul. The road on which he travels implies continuous forward movement in time.

Comics also generally express a linear conception of time, as we read the frames from left to right and top to bottom. Gary Panter's six-panel comic *Back to Nature* shows the progression of his thoughts as he comes to grips with the attacks of September 11, 2001. Although he thinks of the past and hopes for the future, the sequence of frames implies succession in time.

2.29 Sassetta and Workshop of Sassetta.
The Meeting of Saint Anthony and Saint Paul. c. 1440.
Tempera on panel, .475 × .345 cm (18¾″ × 13⅝″)
framed: .616 × 1.254 × .076 cm (24¼″ × 49⅜″ × 3″).
Samuel H. Kress Collection. Photograph © 2001 Board of Trustees,
National Gallery of Art, Washington. 1939.1.293.(404)/PA.

periodic cycles of destruction and recreation, and their calendar stone embodies this idea. At the center of the *Aztec Calendar Stone* is a face of the sun god representing the present world, surrounded by four rectangular compartments that each represent one previous incarnation of the world. The whole stone is round, symbolizing the circular nature of time.

The Judeo-Christian tradition of Western culture teaches that time is linear—continually moving forward. The early Renaissance painter Sassetta implied the passage of linear time in his painted narration of *The Meeting of St. Anthony and St. Paul.* The painting depicts key moments during Saint Anthony's progression through time and space, including the start of his journey in the city, which is barely visible behind the trees at the top

LEARN MORE: For a Closer Look at the *Aztec Calendar Stone,* go to **www.myartslab.com**

2.30 Gary Panter.
Back to Nature. 2001.
Self-published comic. 5″ × 3¼″.
Gary Panter.

Manipulated Time

Most movies compress time to varying degrees. Doug Aitken's 2007 video work *Sleepwalkers* manipulated time by presenting five parallel narratives of actors awakening at sunset and going about urban rounds in the city at night. The five actors played various roles, from bike messenger to corporate executive. Their stories were edited down to 13 minutes each and projected in random sequence onto eight exterior walls of the Museum of Modern Art in New York. The piece interacted with viewers' urban errands as well, since the work was on view from 5 to 10 P.M. each night for a month. The artist said of the work, "I wanted to create something that transformed architecture into a moving, flowing space." As viewers moved about the city block that the museum occupies, they saw five workers in parallel narratives also moving about the city.

2.31 Doug Aitken (b. 1968).
Doug Aitken: Sleepwalkers.
2007.
Installation view of the exhibition.
January 16, 2007 through February 12, 2007. (IN1991.25) Location: The Museum of Modern Art, New York, NY, U.S.A. Courtesy 303 Gallery, New York.

Implied Motion

To give lifelike feeling, artists often search for ways to create a sense of movement. Sometimes movement itself is the subject or a central quality of the subject. An appealing depiction of movement, *Dancing Krishna* portrays the Indian Hindu god as a playful child who just stole his mother's butter supply and now dances with glee. The cast bronze medium provides the necessary strength to hold the dynamic pose as the energy-radiating figure stands on one foot, counterbalancing arms, legs, and torso.

Artists of the Futurist movement in the early twentieth century found innovative ways to depict motion and speed, which they regarded as the most important new subjects for art. Gino Severini lived near railroad tracks outside Paris and he made the churning, chugging trains a subject of several works. *Suburban Train Arriving in Paris* needs very little explanation, as the train shatters the landscape into jagged, slanting forms. The overlapping planes and diagonal lines suggest powerful left-to-right motion. The inscription at the top (Kneipp) refers to a billboard advertisement for a drink.

Contemporary artist Jenny Holzer made a clever use of implied motion in an *Untitled* work, in which she installed light boards on the inner edge of the spiral ramp in the Guggenheim Museum in New York. These boards are commonly used for advertising, but she populated this extended helix with sayings of her own invention. The sayings seem to progress down the ramp in a continuous flow, but in reality the lights go on and off only at carefully programmed intervals. In this welter of constantly shifting slogans, she hoped to show how the mass media bombard us with input.

2.32 *Dancing Krishna.*
Tanjor, Tamil Nadu. South India. Chola dynasty.
c. 1300. Bronze, 23⅜″.
Honolulu Academy of Arts. Partial gift of
Mr. and Mrs. Christian H. Aall; partial purchase,
The Jhamandas Watumull Family Fund, 1997. (8640.1)
Photo by Shuzo Uemoto.

2.33 Gino Severini (1883–1966).
Suburban Train Arriving in Paris. 1915.
Oil on canvas. 35″ × 45½″.
Tate Modern, London © 2010 ARS, NY.
Photo Credit: Tate, London/Art Resource, NY.

2.34 Jenny Holzer.
Untitled.
(Selections from Truisms, Inflammatory Essays,
The Living Series, The Survival Series, Under a
Rock, Laments, and Child Text), 1989. Extended
helical tricolor L.E.D. electronic display signboard.
Site-specific dimensions: 41.9 cm × 49 m × 37.8 cm
× 15.2 cm (16½″ × 162′ × 6″).
Solomon R. Guggenheim Museum, New York. Partial gift of the artist,
1989. 89.3626. Photograph by David Heald © The Solomon R.
Guggenheim Foundation, New York. © 2010 Jenny Holzer, member
Artists Rights Society (ARS), New York.

Actual Motion

Before the advent of electric motors, artists created moving sculpture by harnessing the forces of wind and water. Fountains, kites, banners, and flags have been popular since ancient times.

Alexander Calder's mobiles, such as his *Untitled* work in the National Gallery, rely on air movement to perform their subtle dances. As viewers enter and leave the galleries of the East Building, the sculpture slowly moves in space. Calder, a leading inventor of **kinetic art**, was one of the first twentieth-century artists who made actual motion a major feature of their art.

LIGHT

Our eyes are light-sensing instruments. Everything we see is made visible by the radiant energy we call light. Sunlight, or natural light, although perceived as white, actually contains all the colors of light that make up the visible part of the electromagnetic spectrum. Light can be directed, reflected, refracted, diffracted, or diffused. The source, color, intensity,

2.35 Alexander Calder.
Untitled. 1976.
Aluminum and steel. 9.103 × 23.155 cm (358½″ × 912″).
Gift of the Collectors Committee. Photograph © 2001 Board of Trustees, National Gallery of Art, Washington. 1977.76.1.(A-1799)/SC.
© 2010 Calder Foundation, New York/Artists Rights Society (ARS), New York.

and direction of light greatly affect the way things appear; as light changes, surfaces illuminated by it also appear to change.

Seeing Light

A simple shift in the direction of light dramatically changes the way we perceive the sculpture of *Abraham Lincoln* by Daniel Chester French. When the monumental figure was first installed in the Lincoln Memorial in Washington, D.C., the sculptor was disturbed by the lighting: Sunlight reflected off the floor seemed to radically change Lincoln's character, making it seem that the president had seen a ghost! The problem was corrected by placing spotlights in the ceiling above the statue. This made Lincoln resemble the inspiring leader that the sculptor intended to portray. Because the spotlights are stronger than the natural light reflected from the white marble floor, they illuminate the figure with overhead light that creates an entirely different expression.

Most of us know this from trying to take pictures outdoors: Light coming from a source directly in front of or behind objects seems to flatten three-dimensional form and emphasize shape. Light from above or from the side, and slightly in front, most clearly reveals the form of objects in space.

In the terminology of art, **value** (sometimes called *tone*) refers to the relative lightness and darkness of surfaces. Value ranges from white through various grays to black. Value can be considered a property of color or an element independent of color. Subtle relationships between light and dark areas determine how things look. To suggest the way light reveals form, artists use changes in value.

2.36 Daniel Chester French (1850–1931).
Abraham Lincoln (1911–1922). Detail, seated statue, Lincoln Memorial.
a. As originally lit by daylight.
b. With the addition of artificial light.
Historical professional composite photograph (1922) of full-sized plaster model of head (1917–1918). 50½" tall.
Chapin Library, Williams College; gift of the National Trust for Historic Preservation Chesterwood Archive.
Photographer: De Witt Ward.

A gradual shift from lighter to darker tones can give the illusion of a curving surface, while an abrupt value change usually indicates an abrupt change in surface direction.

Light in Art

The diagram *Dark/Light Relationships* shows that we perceive relationships rather than isolated forms: the gray bar has the same gray value over its entire length, yet it appears to change from one end to the other as the value of the background changes.

2.37 *Dark/Light Relationships.*
Value scale compared to uniform middle gray.

2.38 Annibale Carracci
(1560–1609).
Head of a Youth.
Charcoal and white chalk
on green/gray paper.
27.1 × 24 cm.
Hermitage, St. Petersburg, Russia.
The Bridgeman Art Library
International Ltd.

Using charcoal and white chalk on middle-value paper, Annibale Carracci used **chiaroscuro** (shading from light to dark) to create the illusion of roundness in his drawing *Head of a Youth.* The face on its brighter side is close to the shade of the paper. At times the distinction between subject and background is difficult to see, as in the clothing. On the areas where light strikes the subject most directly, the artist used white chalk, as on the forehead and nose, making these areas brighter than the background. Areas around the mouth and chin are delicately shaded, showing that the artist is sensitive to the subtlest curves of the face. The shadowy areas stand in contrast both to the white highlights and to the color of the paper; the darkest area, at the left, forms a silhouette against the background.

The choice of colored paper is in some ways advantageous because we tend to perceive white areas as flooded with light. Middle-value paper tends to heighten the contrasts of light and dark within the subject itself.

The preoccupation with mass or solid form as revealed by light is a Western tradition that began in the Renaissance. When the Japanese first saw Western portraits, they wanted to know why one side of the face was dirty!

Color, direction, quantity, and intensity of light strongly affect our moods, mental abilities, and general well-being. California architect Vincent Palmer has experimented with the color and intensity of interior light, and he has found that he can modify the behavior of his guests by changing the color of the light around them. Light quality affects people's emotions and physical comfort, thereby changing the volume and intensity of their conversations and even the lengths of their visits.

Light as a Medium

Some contemporary artists use artificial light as their medium. They enjoy using light because it gives pure, intense colors that radiate into the viewer's space. Others who use light are drawn to the idea of making electric power into art. Keith Sonnier placed an array of neon tubes in the outdoor lobby of a new government building in Los Angeles and called it *Motordom*, to express the reality of car culture that Southern Californians live with. The tubes slowly flicker in a pattern that repeats every five minutes, as if taillights are passing along the sides of the walls and around the lobby. The agency that commissioned the building operates the state's roads and bridges, making *Motordom* particularly appropriate for that space.

Paul Chan uses light from a digital projector to display his haunting creations. For his series of seven works called *The 7 Lights*, he installed the projector at various angles so that it sent an irregular window of light onto the floor or wall of the gallery space. Over each work's 14-minute duration, a bewildering variety of objects seem to tumble or glide or fall

2.39 Keith Sonnier.
Motordom. 2004. Light Installation at Caltrans District 7 Headquarters, Los Angeles.
Photo Roland Halbe. © 2010 Keith Sonnier/Artists Rights Society (ARS), New York.

HEAR MORE: For a podcast interview with Keith Sonnier about *Motordom*, go to **www.myartslab.com**

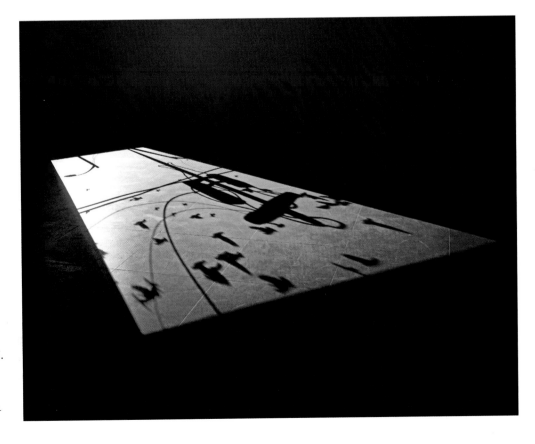

2.40 Paul Chan.
The 7 Lights. 2005–2007. Still from video projection.
Image Courtesy of the Artist and Greene Naftali Gallery, New York. Photo Credit: Jean Vong.

through the projected field of light. We see shadows of all kinds of things, from pets to people, luggage to locomotives. These shadows are "light that has been struck out," said the artist, and thus the word ~~Lights~~ of the title has been struck through. It is as if we are witnessing some silent catastrophe, as the laws of gravity are suspended and everything has come loose from its moorings.

COLOR

Color, a component of light, affects us directly by modifying our thoughts, moods, actions, and even our health. Psychologists, as well as designers of schools, offices, hospitals, and prisons, understand that colors can affect work habits and mental conditions. People surrounded by expanses of solid orange or red for long periods often experience nervousness and raised blood pressure. In contrast, some blues have a calming effect, causing blood pressure, pulse, and activity rates to drop to below normal levels.

Dressing according to our color preferences is one way we express ourselves. Designers of everything from clothing and cars to housewares and interiors recognize the importance of individual color preferences, and they spend considerable time and expense determining the colors of their products.

Most cultures use color symbolically, according to established customs. Leonardo da Vinci was influenced by earlier European traditions when he wrote, "We shall set down for white the representative of light, without which no color can be seen; yellow for earth; green for water; blue for air; red for fire; and black for total darkness."[6] In traditional painting in North India, flat areas of color are used to suggest certain moods, such as red for anger and blue for sexual passion. A modern artist may paint the sky or the ground with a bright shade that relates not to the appearance of the area, but to the feeling appropriate to the work. In Austrian slang, yellow describes a state of envy or jealousy, while blue means intoxicated.

Between the fifteenth and nineteenth centuries, color was used in limited, traditional ways in Western art. In the 1860s and 1870s, influenced by the new discoveries in optics, the French Impressionist painters revolutionized the way artists used color.

The Physics of Color

What we call "color" is the effect on our eyes of light waves of differing wavelengths or frequencies. When combined, these light waves make white light, the visible part of the spectrum. Individual colors are components of white light.

The phenomenon of color is a paradox: color exists only in light, but light itself seems colorless to the human eye. Objects that appear to have color are merely reflecting the colors that are present in the light that illuminates them. In 1666, British scientist Isaac Newton discovered that white light is composed of all the colors of the spectrum. He found that when the white light of the sun passes through a glass prism, it is separated into the bands of color that make up the visible spectrum, as shown in the diagram *White Light Refracted by a Prism.*

Because each color has a different wavelength, each travels through the glass of the prism at a different speed. Red, which has the longest wavelength, travels more rapidly through the glass than blue, which has a shorter wavelength. A rainbow results when sunlight is refracted and dispersed by the spherical forms of raindrops, producing a combined effect like that of the glass prism. In both cases, the sequence of spectral colors is: red, orange, yellow, green, blue, and violet.

Pigments and Light

Our common experience with color is provided by light reflected from pigmented surfaces. Therefore,

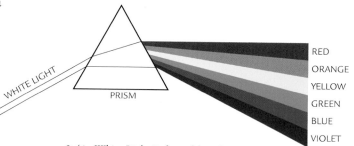

2.41 *White Light Refracted by a Prism.*

the emphasis in the following discussion is on pigment color rather than on color coming from light alone.

When light illuminates an object, some of the light is absorbed by the surface of the object and some is reflected. The color that appears to our eyes as that of the object (called **local color**) is determined by the wavelengths of light being reflected. Thus, a red surface illuminated by white light (full-spectrum light) appears red because it reflects mostly red light and absorbs the rest of the spectrum. A green surface absorbs most of the spectrum except green, which it reflects, and so on with all the hues.

When all the wavelengths of light are absorbed by a surface, the object appears black; when all the wavelengths are reflected, the surface appears white. Black and white are not true colors: white, black, and their combination, gray, are **achromatic** (without the property of hue) and are often referred to as **neutrals**.

Each of the millions of colors human beings can distinguish is identifiable in terms of just three variables: hue, value, and intensity.

- **Hue** refers to a particular wavelength of spectral color to which we give a name. Colors of the spectrum—such as yellow and green—are called hues.
- **Value** refers to relative lightness or darkness from white through grays to black. Pure hues vary in value. On the color chart shown in *The Three Dimensions of Color*, hues in their purest state are at their usual values. Pure yellow is the lightest of hues; violet is the darkest. Red and green are middle-value hues. Black and white pigments can be important ingredients in changing color values. Adding black to a hue produces a **shade** of that hue. For example, when black is added to orange, the result is a brown; when black is mixed with red, the result is maroon. White added to a hue produces a **tint**. Lavender is a tint of violet; pink is a tint of red.
- **Intensity**, also called **saturation**, refers to the purity of a hue or color. A pure hue is the most intense form of a given color; it is the hue at its

highest saturation, in its brightest form. With pigment, if white, black, gray, or another hue is added to a pure hue, its intensity diminishes and the color is thereby dulled.

2.42 *The Three Dimensions of Color.*

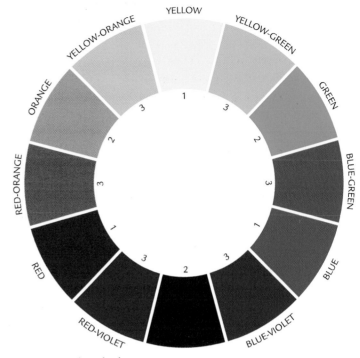

a. Hue—the color wheel.

b. Value—from light to dark. Value scale from white to black.

+ WHITE   PURE HUE   + BLACK

c. Value variation in red.

PURE HUE   DULLED   PURE HUE

d. Intensity—from bright to dull.

2.43 *Pigment Primaries: Subtractive Color Mixture.*

Most people are familiar with the three *Pigment Primaries*: red, yellow, and blue. Mixtures of these are what we usually experience as local color when we look at a leaf, a wall, or a painting. When the pigments of different hues are mixed together, the mixture appears duller and darker because pigments absorb more and more light as their absorptive qualities combine. For this reason, pigment mixtures are called **subtractive color mixtures**. Mixing red, blue, and yellow will produce a dark gray, almost black, depending on the proportions and the type of pigment used.

A lesser-known triad is the three *Light Primaries*: red-orange, green, and blue-violet. These are actual electric light colors that produce white light when combined; they are the colors that our televisions and computer screens use. Such mixtures are called *additive color mixtures*. Combinations of the light primaries produce lighter colors: red and green light, when mixed, produce yellow light.

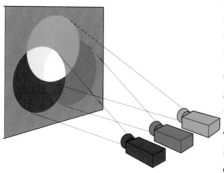

2.44 *Light Primaries: Additive Color Mixture.*

Color Wheel

The color wheel is a twentieth-century version of a concept first developed in the seventeenth century by Isaac Newton. After Newton discovered the spectrum, he found that both ends could be combined into the hue red-violet, making the color wheel concept possible. Numerous color systems have followed since that time, each with its own basic hues. The color wheel shown here is based on twelve pure hues and can be divided into the following groups:

- **Primary hues** (see 1 on the color wheel): red, yellow, and blue. These pigment hues cannot be produced by an intermixing of other hues. They are also referred to as primary colors.

- **Secondary hues** (see 2 on the color wheel): orange, green, and violet. The mixture of two primaries produces a secondary hue. Secondaries are placed on the color wheel between the two primaries of which they are composed.

- **Intermediate hues** (see 3 on the color wheel): red-orange, yellow-orange, yellow-green, blue-green, blue-violet, and red-violet. Each intermediate is located between the primary and the secondary of which it is composed.

The blue-green side of the wheel seems **cool** in psychological temperature, and the red-orange side is **warm**. Yellow-green and red-violet are the poles dividing the color wheel into warm and cool hues. The difference between warm and cool colors may come chiefly from association. Relative warm and cool differences can be seen in any combination of hues. Color affects our feelings about size and distance as well as temperature. Cool colors appear to contract and recede; warm colors appear to expand and advance, as in the *Warm/Cool Colors* diagram.

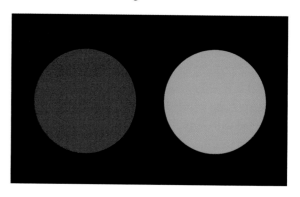

2.45 *Warm/Cool Colors.*

The most vibrant color sensations come not from blending colors, but from placing tiny dots of purer hues next to each other so that they blend in the eye and the mind. This is what happens in modern four-color printing, in which tiny dots of ink in the printer's three primary colors—magenta, yellow, and cyan—are printed together in various amounts with black ink on white paper to achieve the effect of full color. See the *Color Printing* separations and the enlarged detail of the reproduction of Botticelli's *Birth of Venus*; the eye perceives subtle blends as it optically mixes tiny dots of intense color.

2.46 *Color Printing.*

a. Yellow.

b. Magenta.

c. Yellow and magenta.

d. Cyan.

e. Yellow, magenta, and cyan.

f. Black.

g. Yellow, magenta, cyan, and black.

h. Color printing detail of Sandro Botticelli's *Birth of Venus*, 1486. Detail.
Tempera on canvas, 69″ × 52¾″.
Erich Lessing/Pearson Education/PH College.

Color Schemes

Color groupings that provide distinct color harmonies are called color schemes.

Monochromatic color schemes are based on variations in the value and intensity of a single hue. In a monochromatic scheme, a pure hue is used alone with black and/or white, or mixed with black and/or white. Artists may choose a monochromatic color scheme because they feel that a certain color represents a mood. Pablo Picasso, for example, made many blue paintings in the early years of the twentieth century, at a time in his life when he was poor. Other artists adopt the monochromatic color scheme as a kind of personal discipline, in order to experiment with the various shades and gradations of a relatively narrow band of the spectrum. James Abbott McNeill Whistler did just that in the 1870s when he embarked on a series of works called *Nocturnes.* The series began when he noticed that after sunset the world becomes in effect more monochromatic as the brightest hues disappear. We see his exploration in *Nocturne: Blue and Gold—Old Battersea Bridge,* where he created a visually rich surface with limited tonal means. The gold flecks are the only counterfoil to the monochromatic blue-green scheme.

Analogous color schemes are based on colors adjacent to one another on the color wheel, each containing the same pure hue, such as a color scheme of yellow-green, green, and blue-green. Tints and shades of each analogous hue may be used to add variations to such color schemes.

Jennifer Bartlett's three-dimensional installation *Volvo Commission* uses the analogous colors

2.47 James Abbott McNeill Whistler.
Nocturne: Blue and Gold—Old Battersea Bridge.
1872–1875.
Tate Gallery, London, Great Britain. Copyright Erich Lessing/
Art Resource, NY.

2.48 Jennifer Bartlett.
Volvo Commission. 1984.
Relaxation room, detail: table, painted wood,
29″ × 35″ × 35″; chair, painted wood,
35″ × 18″ × 18″; portfolio of twenty-four drawings,
pen, brush, and ink on paper, 20″ × 16″; house
cigarette box, painted wood, 5″ × 5″; boat
ashtray, silver, 5″ × 2″; screen, enamel on six
wood panels, 6″ × 10′3″.
Volvo Corporate Headquarters, Sweden. Courtesy of the artist.

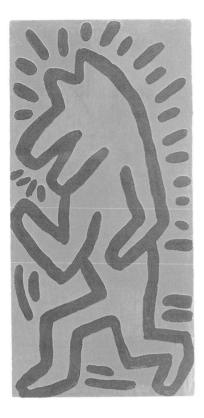

2.49 Keith Haring.
Untitled. 1982.
Dayglo paint on wood. 8½″ × 4½″.
© The Keith Haring Foundation.

together they vibrate. This "loud" color scheme supports the simple execution and brash subject matter of the painting in providing an almost comically crude effect. The artist used Dayglo paints, which are known for their gaudy brightness.

These examples provide only a basic foundation in color theory. In fact, most artists work intuitively with color harmonies more complex than the schemes described above.

ART AND REALITY

The way artists approach reality is part of their visual toolbox: Artists may depict much of what they see in the physical world, they may alter appearances, or they may invent forms that no one has seen. The terms **representational**, abstract, and **nonrepresentational** (or **nonobjective**) are used to describe a work's relationship to the physical world.

Representational Art

Representational art depicts the appearance of things. (When the human form is the primary subject, it is called **figurative art.**) It represents—or presents again—objects we recognize from the everyday world. Objects that representational art depicts are called **subjects.**

There are many ways to create representational art. The most "real"-looking paintings are in a style called **trompe l'oeil** (pronounced "tromp loy")—French for "fool the eye." Paintings in this illusionistic style impress us because they look so "real." In Harnett's painting *A Smoke Backstage* (on the following page), the assembled objects are close to life-size, which contributes to the illusion. We almost believe that we could touch the pipe and match.

Belgian painter René Magritte shows a different relationship between art and reality. The subject of the painting appears to be a pipe, but written in

yellow-orange, yellow, and yellow-green, which are adjacent to one another in the spectrum and on the color wheel. The analogous color scheme supports the mood of quiet relaxation appropriate to the pleasant rural subject.

Complementary color schemes emphasize two hues directly opposite each other on the color wheel, such as red and green. When actually mixed together as pigments in almost equal amounts, complementary hues form neutral grays, but when placed side by side as pure hues, they contrast strongly and intensify each other. Complementary hues red-orange and blue-green tend to "vibrate" more when placed next to each other than do other complements because they are close in value and produce a strong warm/cool contrast. The complements yellow and violet provide the strongest value contrast possible with pure hues. The complement of a primary is the opposite secondary, which is obtained by mixing the other two primaries. For example, the complement of yellow is violet.

Keith Haring's *Untitled* shows the effect of complementary colors. The bright red and green are near-opposites on the color wheel. When seen

2.50 William Harnett.
A Smoke Backstage. 1877.
Oil on canvas. 7″ × 8½″.
Honolulu Academy of Arts, Gift of John Wyatt Gregg Allerton, 1964.
(3211.1).

Ceci n'est pas une pipe.

2.51 René Magritte (1898–1967).
La Trahison des Images (Ceci N'est Pas une Pipe). 1929.
Oil on canvas. 60 × 81 cm.
Los Angeles County Museum of Art, Los Angeles, CA, California, U.S.A.
Art Resource, NY. Banque d'Images ADAGP. © 2010 Artist Rights
Society (ARS), NY.

French on the painting are the words, "This is not a pipe." The viewer wonders, "If this is not a pipe, what is it?" The answer, of course, is that it is a painting! Magritte's title, *The Treason of Images (La Trahison des Images),* suggests the visual game that the artist had in mind.

Modern artist Henri Matisse told of an incident that illustrated a similar view on the difference between art and nature. A woman visiting his studio pointed to one of his paintings and said, "But surely, the arm of this woman is much too long." Matisse replied, "Madame, you are mistaken. This is not a woman, this is a picture."[7]

California artist Ray Beldner further complicated the relationship between art and reality. He created a reproduction of Magritte's painting out of sewn dollar bills, and called it *This Is Definitely Not a Pipe.* Modern artists are so famous these days, and their works sell for such high prices, that they may as well be "made of money." Beldner's point is that even representational art has a complex relationship to reality; artists almost never merely depict what they see. Rather, they select, arrange, and compose reality to fit their personal vision. The process can take them several steps away from the fact of a pipe on a tabletop.

SEE MORE: To see a video interview with Ray Beldner, go to **www.myartslab.com**

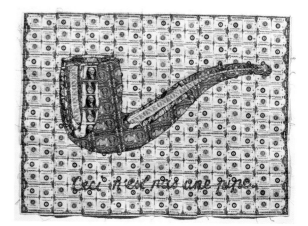

2.52 Ray Beldner.
This Is Definitely Not a Pipe. 2000.
Sewn. 24″ × 33″.
Courtesy of the artist and Catharine Clark Gallery,
San Francisco, CA.

Abstract Art

The verb "to abstract" means "to take from"; it means to extract the essence of an object or idea. In art, the word *abstract* can mean either (1) works of art that have no reference at all to natural objects, or (2) works that depict natural objects in simplified, distorted, or exaggerated ways. In this book, we use abstract in the second sense.

In abstract art the artist changes the object's natural appearance in order to emphasize or reveal certain qualities. Just as there are many approaches to representational art, there are many approaches to abstraction. We may be able to recognize the subject matter of an abstract work quite easily, or we may need the help of a clue (such as a title). The interaction between how the subject actually looks and how an artist presents it is part of the pleasure and challenge of abstract art. In a basic sense, all art is abstraction because it is not possible for an artist to reproduce exactly what is seen.

2.53 *Chilkat Blanket.*
Tlingit. Before 1928.
Mountain goat wool and shredded cedar bark. 4'7" × 5'4".
Neg./Transparency no. 3804. Photo by Steve Myers. Courtesy Department of Library Services, American Museum of Natural History.

Abstraction in one form or another is common in the art of many cultures. Native peoples of the Northwest Coast decorate many objects with forms abstracted from the animals that populate their mythology. For example, the *Chilkat Blanket* woven by Tlingit women contains in its center a face of such a composite figure. Below the face, along the bottom edge, claw feet point outward. Elsewhere in the design, shapes that symbolize eyes, fins, and wings of other animals fill the surface in a symmetrical arrangement. This blanket, once the prized possession of a high tribal official, was woven in a regional style. The weaver employed abstraction in the decorative use of meaningful symbols.

We see stages of abstraction in Theo van Doesburg's series of drawings and paintings,

Abstraction of a Cow. The artist apparently wanted to see how far he could abstract the cow through simplification and still have his image symbolize the essence of the animal. Van Doesburg used the subject as a point of departure for a composition made up of colored rectangles. If we viewed only the final painting, and none of the earlier ones, we would probably see it as a nonrepresentational painting.

Nonrepresentational Art

A great deal of the world's art was not meant to be representational at all. Amish quilts, many Navajo textiles, and most Islamic wood carvings consist primarily of flat patterns that give pleasure through mere variety of line, shape, and color. Nonrepresentational art (sometimes called nonobjective or nonfigurative art) presents visual forms

2.54 Theo van Doesburg (C. E. M. Kupper).
Abstraction of a Cow (1916).

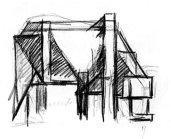

Studies for Composition *(The Cow)*. Pencil on paper. Each 4⅝″ × 6¼″ (11.7 × 15.9 cm).
The Museum of Modern Art/Licensed by Scala-Art Resource, NY. Purchase. Photograph © 2002 The Museum of Modern Art, New York. © 2010 Artists Rights Society (ARS), New York/Beeldrecht, Amsterdam.

Theo van Doesburg (C. E. M. Kupper)
Composition (The Cow). c. 1917 (dated 1916).
Tempera, oil and charcoal on paper. 15⅝″ × 22¾″
(39.7 × 57.8 cm).
The Museum of Modern Art/Licensed by Scala-Art Resource, NY.
Purchase. Photograph © 2002 The Museum of Modern Art, New York.
© 2002 Artists Rights Society (ARS), New York/Beeldrecht, Amsterdam.

Theo van Doesburg (C. E. M. Kupper).
Composition (The Cow). c. 1917
Oil on canvas. 14¾″ × 25″ (37.5 × 63.5 cm).
The Museum of Modern Art/Licensed by Scala-Art Resource, NY.
Purchase. Photograph © 2002 The Museum of Modern Art, New York.
© 2002 Artists Rights Society (ARS), New York/Beeldrecht, Amsterdam.

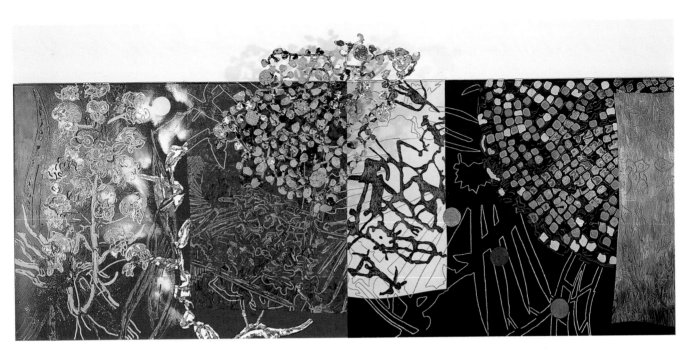

2.55 Nancy Graves.
Footscray, from the *Australian Series.* 1985.
Oil, acrylic, and glitter on canvas with painted aluminum sculpture.
6'4½" × 14'5" × 12½" (diptych).
© Nancy Graves Foundation/Licensed by VAGA, New York, NY.

with no specific references to anything outside themselves. Just as we can respond to the pure sound forms of music, so can we respond to the pure visual forms of nonrepresentational art.

While nonrepresentational art may at first seem more difficult to grasp than representational or abstract art, it can offer fresh ways of seeing. Absence of subject matter actually clarifies the way all visual forms affect us. Once we learn how to "read" the language of vision, we can respond to art and the world with greater understanding and enjoyment.

Here are two very different types of nonrepresentational art. In *Footscray* by Nancy Graves, oil paint on canvas combines with brightly colored aluminum elements that hover above the surface of the work. She used a great variety of colors and shapes, so that the total composition suggests organic, exuberant motion.

In contrast, Alma Woodsey Thomas's *Gray Night Phenomenon* uses only two colors, and brushstrokes that are more or less regular. She created a pattern across the picture plane that is neither gray nor nightlike. The subject of this work is not from the visible world; rather, it depicts a mood that might strike the artist in the middle of a gray night.

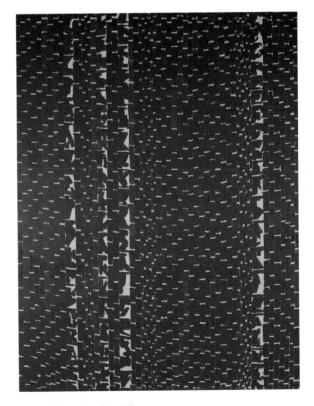

2.56 Alma Woodsey Thomas.
Gray Night Phenomenon. 1972.
Acrylic on canvas. 68⅛" × 53⅛" (175 × 134.8 cm).
Gift of Vincent Melzac. Smithsonian American Art Museum, Washington, DC/Art Resource NY.

2.57 Auguste Rodin.
The Kiss. 1886.
Marble. Height 5′11¼″
Musée Rodin, Paris, France. Photograph: Bruno Jarret.
© 2010 Artists Rights Society (ARS), New York/ADAGP, Paris.

embrace. Our emotions are engaged as we overlook the hardness of the marble from which he carved it. The natural softness of flesh is heightened by the rough texture of the unfinished marble supporting the figures.

In contrast to Rodin's sensuous approach, Brancusi used the solid quality of a block of stone to express lasting love. Through minimal cutting of the block, Brancusi symbolized—rather than illustrated—the concept of two becoming one. He chose geometric abstraction rather than representational naturalism to express love. We might say that Rodin's work expresses the feelings of love while Brancusi's expresses the idea of love.

FORM AND CONTENT

Form is what we see; **content** is the meaning we get from what we see. In this book, form refers to the total effect of the combined visual qualities within a work, including such components as materials, color, shape, line, and design. Content refers to the message or meaning of the work of art—what the artist expresses or communicates to the viewer. Content determines form, but form expresses content; thus, the two are inseparable. As form changes, content changes, and vice versa.

One way to understand how art communicates experience is to compare works that have the same subject but differ greatly in form and content. *The Kiss* by Auguste Rodin and *The Kiss* by Constantin Brancusi show how two sculptors interpret an embrace. In Rodin's work, the life-size human figures represent Western ideals of the masculine and feminine: Rodin captured the sensual delight of that highly charged moment when lovers

2.58 Constantin Brancusi.
The Kiss. c. 1916.
Limestone.
23″ × 13″ × 10″.
Photo by Graydon Wood, 1994. 1950-135-4.
Art Resource/Philadelphia Museum of Art.
© 2010 Artists Rights Society (ARS),
New York/ADAGP, Paris.

Seeing and Responding to Form

Obviously, artists expend effort to produce a work of art; less obvious is the fact that responding to a work of art also requires effort. The artist is the source or sender; the work is the medium carrying the message. We viewers must receive and experience the work to make the communication complete. In this way, we become active participants in the creative process.

Whether we realize it or not, learning to respond to form is part of learning to live in the world. We guide our actions by "reading" the forms of people, things, and events that make up our environment. Even as infants, we have an amazing ability to remember visual forms such as faces, and all through life we interpret events based on our previous experiences with these forms. Every form can evoke some kind of response from each of us.

Subject matter can interfere with our perception of form. One way to learn to see form without subject is to look at pictures upside down. Inverting recognizable images frees the mind from the process of identifying and naming things. Familiar objects become unfamiliar.

When confronted with something unfamiliar, we often see it freshly only because we have no idea what we are looking at. When we see the twisting, curving green and rust-red shapes in Georgia O'Keeffe's painting, we may not at first realize that the work depicts a *Jack-in-the-Pulpit* flower. The artist greatly enlarged it—the work is four feet high—and she focused closely on the flower, omitting nearly all else. We may wonder for a moment if we are looking at abstract or representational art.

O'Keeffe hoped that her way of seeing would cause us to sense the natural rhythms present in a flower. She said of this painting:

Everyone has many associations with a flower—the idea of flowers. Still—in a way—nobody sees a flower— really—it is so small—we haven't the time—and to see takes time, like to have a friend takes time. If I could paint the flower exactly as I see it no one would see what I see because I would paint it small like the flower is small.

So I said to myself—I'll paint what I see—what the flower is to me but I'll paint it big and they will be surprised into taking time to look at it.[8,9]

Those who have seen O'Keeffe's paintings of flowers and of the American Southwest often go on to see actual flowers and desert landscapes in new ways.

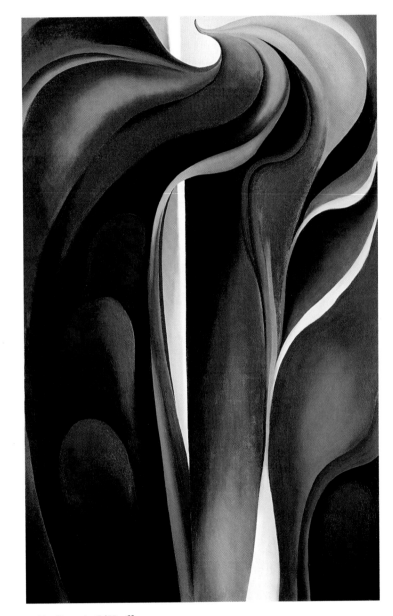

2.59 Georgia O'Keeffe.
Jack-in-the-Pulpit No. V. 1930. Oil on canvas. 48″ × 30″. Framed. 1.256 × .799 × .043 cm (49⁷⁄₁₆″ × 31⁷⁄₁₆″ × 1¹¹⁄₁₆″).
Alfred Stieglitz Collection, Bequest of Georgia O'Keeffe. Photograph © 2001 Board of Trustees, National Gallery of Art, Washington, D.C. 1987.58.4./PA. Photograph: Malcolm Varon/ © 2010 Georgia O'Keeffe Museum/Artists Rights Society (ARS), New York.

GEORGIA O'KEEFFE

A Personal Vision

DURING HER LONG, productive life, Georgia O'Keeffe became nearly as well known as her distinctive paintings. She represented, to many people, the popular concept of the isolated, eccentric "artist." She lived a spare, often solitary life, and approached both her life and her art in her own unique way.

O'Keeffe was born in Sun Prairie, Wisconsin, and spent her childhood on her family's farm. While in high school, she had a memorable experience that gave her a new perspective on the art-making process.

As she passed the door to the art room, O'Keeffe stopped to watch as a teacher held up a jack-in-the-pulpit plant so that the students could appreciate its unusual shapes and subtle colors. Although O'Keeffe had enjoyed flowers in the marshes and meadows of Wisconsin, she had done all of her drawing and painting from plaster casts or had copied them from photographs or reproductions. This was the first time she realized that one could draw and paint from real life. Twenty-five years later, she produced a powerful series of paintings based on flowers.

2.61 Georgia O'Keeffe.
Oriental Poppies. 1927.
Oil on canvas. 30″ × 40⅛″.
Collection Frederick R. Weisman Art Museum, University of Minnesota, Minneapolis, Museum Purchase. 1937.1. © 2010 Georgia O'Keeffe Museum/Artists Rights Society (ARS), New York.

2.60 Yousuf Karsh.
Georgia O'Keeffe. 1956.
Photograph.
Photograph: Yousuf Karsh, Woodfin Camp & Associates, Inc.

She studied at the Art Institute of Chicago, the Art Students League in New York, and Columbia University Teachers College. From 1912 to 1918, she spent four winters teaching school in the Texas Panhandle. The Southwestern landscape left a strong impression on her and influenced her later decision to move to New Mexico—where the desert became her favorite subject.

O'Keeffe's first mature works, produced in 1915, consisted of vivid watercolor landscapes and abstract charcoal drawings suggesting natural forms. Although she exhibited with other American modern artists, O'Keeffe developed her own style, which is both sensuous and austere. Her paintings of the 1920s include geometrically structured views of New York City, landscapes, and greatly enlarged flowers. An example is *Oriental Poppies*, a more representational treatment than the *Jack-in-the-Pulpit* series.

From 1929 to 1949, O'Keeffe spent summers in Taos, New Mexico, surrounded by the desert she loved. Then she settled permanently on an isolated ranch near the village of Abiquiu, where she remained until her death in 1986 at age ninety-eight. In most people's minds, she lives on as a model of creative individuality and strength.

Iconography

As we have noted, form conveys content even when no nameable subject matter is represented. But when subject matter is present, meaning is often based on traditional interpretations.

Iconography is the symbolic meaning of signs, subjects, and images. Not all works of art contain iconography. In those that do, it is often the symbolism (rather than the obvious subject matter) that carries the deepest levels of meaning. The identification and specific significance of subjects, motifs, forms, colors, and positions are the central concern of iconographic interpretation.

Artists' use of iconography can reveal a wealth of cultural information. For example, the Peruvian painting *The Virgin of Carmel Saving Souls from Purgatory* contains many iconographic details that add to its meaning. Some of these are obvious: The two winged figures standing in the foreground are angels; at the top is God the Father holding the orb of the world; below him is a dove that represents the Holy Spirit; Mary wears a crown to show that she is the Queen of Heaven. People emerge from a flaming pit that is purgatory. One angel holds a cross that symbolizes the sacrifice of Christ. The meaning of these details is established by convention and long use; we probably know these meanings and apply them unconsciously when we look at a work such as this.

Other details are less familiar but equally meaningful: The angel at the lower right holds a balance, symbolizing the weighing of souls that takes place in purgatory. The Virgin of Carmel is an appearance of Mary that took place in the thirteenth century; at that time she promised that anyone who wore a special garment called a scapular

2.62 Circle of Diego Quispe Tito.
The Virgin of Carmel Saving Souls in Purgatory.
Late 17th century.
Oil on canvas. 41″ × 29″.
The Bridgeman Art Library International.

2.63 *Descent of the Ganges.* Detail.
Mamallapuram, India. 7th Century. Granite.
Height approximately 30′.
Photograph: Duane Preble.

would not suffer the fires of hell. Both Mary and the child Jesus carry purselike objects that represent the scapulars that people wore or carried for protection. In this painting, Mary makes a special effort to save souls from purgatory who may not have owned the protecting scapular. Thus, the work was a sign of hope.

An excellent example of Hindu iconography called *Descent of the Ganges* was carved in a huge granite outcropping in the town of Mamallapuram, in southern India. Included in the large composition are more than a hundred human figures, deities, flying pairs of angels without wings, life-size elephants, and a variety of other animals, all converging at the Ganges River in an elaborate depiction of intertwining Hindu legends. The composition is filled with symbolic subject matter.

The central gorge in the carving symbolizes the descent of the sacred Ganges from heaven to earth, making the land fertile. The cobra-like figures in the gorge are the King and Queen of the Nagas,

serpent deities that portray the great river. While these figures occupy the center of the relief, other legends are illustrated around them.

In front of the largest elephant is a comical depiction of a cat and mice. According to an old folktale, a cat pretending to be an ascetic stood beside the Ganges with upraised paws and gazed at the sun. The cat convinced the mice that it was holy and thus worthy of worship. As the mice closed their eyes in reverence, the cat snatched them for dinner.

The whole sculpture relates to the annual miracle of the return of the life-giving waters of the river. Appropriately, the many figures appear to be emerging from the stone as if from flowing water.

Now that we have considered some of the tools that artists use, we will next consider how they place them in art works.

PRACTICE MORE: Get flashcards for images and terms and review chapter material with quizzes at **www.myartslab.com**

HAVE YOU EVER THOUGHT THAT A PHOTO OR AN ARTWORK IS TOO CHAOTIC TO READ CLEARLY?

HOW DO ARTISTS LET YOU KNOW WHERE TO LOOK IN AN ARTWORK?

HOW DOES VISUAL RHYTHM COMPARE WITH RHYTHM IN MUSIC?

HAVE YOU EVER LAUGHED AT SOMETHING THAT IS OUT OF PROPORTION OR NOT TO SCALE?

3.1 Charles Demuth (1883–1935).
The Figure 5 in Gold. 1928.
Oil on cardboard. 35½″ × 30″ (90.2 × 76.2 cm).
Alfred Stieglitz Collection, 1949 (49.59.1). The Metropolitan Museum of Art, New York, NY, U.S.A. Image copyright © The Metropolitan Museum of Art/Art Resource, NY.

In 1928, American artist Charles Demuth set out to make a portrait of his friend, the poet William Carlos Williams. Demuth visualized a line from a poem that Williams wrote when he saw a fire engine racing through the streets on a rainy night: "I saw the figure 5 in gold." To Demuth, that vivid line of poetry seemed to symbolize the poet, and it provided a compelling subject for an artwork. He named the painting after the line: *The Figure 5 in Gold*.

Artists design their works in order to communicate a message or a vision. The process of creation involves choosing between and among methods of arrangement in order to arrive at a final design that will best say what the artist had in mind.

In creating *The Figure 5 in Gold*, Demuth used the large numeral 5 to **unify** the composition. Though the work is not symmetrical, it seems **balanced**. The other inscriptions on the work, such as "Bill" at the top for William Carlos Williams, are **subordinated** to the central figure 5. The diagonals in the work suggest slanting raindrops, establishing a strong **directional force**. The red color (presumably of the fire engine) **contrasts** with the gray background of the rainy city night. The numeral is **repeated** in a way that suggests the approach and

HEAR MORE: Listen to an audio file of your chapter at **www.myartslab.com**

passing of the truck. We see the numeral in various **scales** of size.

In the preceding chapter, we considered the basic elements of the visual vocabulary that artists use; now we need to examine how they use those building blocks to create artworks. In two-dimensional arts, such as painting and photography, this organization is usually called **composition**, but a broader term that applies to the entire range of visual arts is **design**. The word "design" indicates both the process of organizing visual elements and the product of that process.

As he created *The Figure 5 in Gold,* Demuth used seven key principles of design that we will consider in this chapter:

unity and variety
balance
emphasis and subordination
directional forces
contrast
repetition and rhythm
scale and proportion

These terms provide an understanding not only of how artists work, but also of how design affects us. The process at its best is a lively give-and-take between the creator and the viewer. The organization of the work is perhaps the most important task for an artist; it can be done well or poorly, effectively or ineffectively. The Pop artist Roy Lichtenstein recognized this when he said, "Organized perception is what art is all about."[1]

3.2 Tony Smith (1912–1980).
Die. 1962.
Steel. Overall: 72⅜″ × 72⅜″ × 72⅜″.
Whitney Museum of American Art, New York;
Purchase, with funds from the Louis and Bessie
Adler Foundation, Inc., James Block, The Sondra
and Charles Gilman, Jr. Foundation Inc., Penny
and Mike Winton, and the Painting and
Sculpture Committee 89.6 © Estate of Tony
Smith/Artists Rights Society (ARS), New York.

UNITY AND VARIETY

Unity and **variety** are complementary concerns. Unity is the appearance or condition of oneness. In design, unity describes the feeling that all the elements in a work belong together and make up a coherent and harmonious whole. When a work of art has unity, we feel that any change would diminish its quality.

Yet very few artworks are absolutely unified into one homogeneous thing; most such works were created as experiments. For example, the French artist Yves Klein made several paintings in the 1960s that were solid blue in color, with no variation. An example from sculpture is *Die* by Tony Smith. This block is a six-foot cube, resembling one of a huge pair of unmarked black dice. The title may also refer to the finality of death. Few works have ever been as unified as this.

3.3 Jacob Lawrence.
Going Home. 1946.
Gouache.
21½" × 29½".

Variety, on the other hand, provides diversity. Variety acts to counter unity. The sameness of too much unity can be boring, and the diversity of uncontrolled variety may be chaotic; most artists strive for a balance between unity and variety that can yield interesting compositions.

In his painting *Going Home*, Jacob Lawrence balanced unity and variety. He established visual themes with the lines, shapes, and colors of the train seats, figures, and luggage, and then he repeated and varied those themes. Notice the varied repetition in the green chair seats and window shades. As a unifying element, the same red is used in a variety of shapes. The many figures and objects in the complex composition form a unified design through the artist's skillful use of abstraction, theme, and variation.

Lawrence was known for the lively harmony of his distinctive compositions. Although he worked in a manner that may seem unsophisticated, he was always resolving his designs through adjustments of unity and diversity. Lawrence studied other artists' work, and he was influenced by painters who were design problem solvers. He said, "I like to study the design to see how the artist solves his problems and brings his subjects to the public."[2]

The flat quality of *Going Home* contrasts with the illusion of depth in *Interior of a Dutch House* by Pieter de Hooch. Each artist depicted daily life in a style relevant to his times. In both, the painter's depiction of space provides the unity in the composition. De Hooch used the unity of the room to unify pictorial space and provide a cohesive setting for the interaction of figures.

Pattern refers to a repetitive ordering of design elements. In de Hooch's painting, the patterns of floor tiles and windows play off against the larger rectangles of map, painting, fireplace, and ceiling. These rectangular shapes provide a unifying structure. The nearly square picture plane itself forms the largest rectangle. He then created a whole family of related rectangles, as indicated in the accompanying diagram. In addition, the shapes and colors in the figures around the table relate to the shapes and colors of the figures in the painting above the fireplace—another use of theme and variation.

3.4 Pieter de Hooch.
Interior of a Dutch House. 1658.
Oil on canvas. 29″ × 35″.
National Gallery, London.

Just as few works strive for perfect unity, even fewer display absolute chaos. Robert Rauschenberg sought to duplicate the randomness of modern life in his works, such as *Gift for Apollo*. He began with a sawed-off door, turned it upside down, and casually applied paint strokes in various colors. He then attached a green necktie, some old postcards, a cloth pocket from a shirt, and part of a sign. He then placed the whole assemblage on small, spoked wheels, and "finished" the work by chaining a bucket to it. Yet even this level of disorder still has some sense of harmony: As in *Interior of a Dutch House*, we see repeated rectangles; the chain extends at a right angle to the axles and seems to anchor the work. Glue and gravity still hold it all in place. Rauschenberg made this work over 50 years ago, so the passage of time probably makes it seem less random than it was at first. Complete disorder in art is very difficult to achieve, though some works such as this one attempt it.

Alberto Giacometti's sculpture *Chariot* also combines diverse elements—a standing female figure and two wheels. Unity is achieved through the thin lines and rough texture in the figure, wheels, and axle, as well as through the use of bronze for the entire piece. The unity of handling leads us to see the sculpture as a single mysterious entity. Our interest is held by the varied components and by the precariousness of the figure poised atop a two-legged table on two wheels. And these bring us to the principle called balance.

BALANCE

For sculptors such as Giacometti, balance is both a visual issue and a structural necessity. The interplay between the opposing forces of unity and variety is a common condition of life. The dynamic process of seeking balance is equally basic in art, though many artists seek lack of balance in their work for one expressive reason or another.

3.5 Robert Rauschenberg.
Gift for Apollo. 1959.
Combine: oil, pant fragments, necktie, wood, fabric, newspaper, printed reproductions on wood with metal bucket, metal chain, door knob, L brackets, metal washer, nail and rubber wheels with metal spokes. 43¾″ × 29½″ × 41″ (111.1 × 74.9 × 104.1 cm).
The Museum of Contemporary Art, Los Angeles. The Panza Collection.
Art © Estate of Robert Rauschenberg/Licensed by VAGA, New York, NY.

3.6 Alberto Giacometti.
Chariot. 1950.
Bronze. 57″ × 26″ × 26⅛″
(114.8 × 65.8 × 66.2 cm).
The Museum of Modern Art/Licensed by Scala-Art Resource, NY. Purchase. Photograph © 2002 The Museum of Modern Art, New York. © 2010 Succession Giacometti/Artists Rights Society (ARS), New York/ADAGP, Paris.

3.7 James Hoban.
A Design for the President's House. 1792.
a. Elevation.
Maryland Historical Society, Baltimore.
b. *White House.*
Front view. 1997.
Photograph: Antonio M. Rosario/Getty Images Inc. – Image Bank.

Balance is the achievement of equilibrium, in which acting influences are held in check by opposing forces. We strive for balance in life and in art, and we may lack peace of mind in its absence. In art, our instinct for physical balance finds its parallel in a desire for visual balance. The two general types of balance are symmetrical (formal) and asymmetrical (informal).

Symmetrical Balance

Symmetrical balance is the near or exact matching of left and right sides of a three-dimensional form or a two-dimensional composition. Such works have **symmetry**.

Architects often employ symmetrical balance to give unity and formal grandeur to a building's facade or front side. For example, in 1792 James Hoban won a competition for his *Design for the President's House*, a drawing of a symmetrical, Georgian-style mansion. Today, two centuries and several additions later, we know it as the *White House*.

Symmetrical design is useful in architecture because it is easier to comprehend than asymmetry. Symmetry imposes a balanced unity, making large complex buildings comprehensible in a glance.

Symmetry connotes permanence and poise. We generally want our symbolically important buildings to seem motionless and stable. All the qualities that make symmetry desirable in architecture make it generally less desirable in sculpture and two-dimensional art. Too much symmetry can be boring. Although artists admire symmetry for its formal qualities, they rarely use it rigidly. Artists usually do not want their work to seem static.

Few works of art are perfectly symmetrical, but *Posterity—The Holy Place* by Damien Hirst is one.

3.8 Damien Hirst.
Posterity—The Holy Place. 2006.
Butterflies and household gloss on canvas, 89⅝″ × 48″.
© Damien Hirst. Courtesy of Gagosian Gallery.
Photograph: Purcence Cuming Associates, Inc. © 2010 Hirst Holdings Limited and Damien Hirst. All rights reserved, ARS, New York/DACS, London.

The artist formed it entirely out of butterflies, and it is symmetrical at every level: each butterfly, each unit of the composition, and the work as a whole. It resembles a stained-glass window, but is even more symmetrical than most of those. The stability of symmetry is a useful tool for religious art, which suggests the divine. But the sheer luminosity of *Posterity— The Holy Place* exceeds even that of a stained-glass window because butterfly wings do not depend on direct sunlight to show brilliance. (The artist bought the butterflies from a dealer who raises them.) Because the work is made up of so many small parts, the levels of symmetry help to structure the composition. We can prove this by merely imagining a work of similarly large size without a symmetrical arrangement.

Asymmetrical Balance

With **asymmetrical balance**, the left and right sides are not the same. Instead, various elements are balanced, according to their size and meaning, around a felt or implied center of gravity. For example, in *Noli Me Tangere* by Lavinia Fontana, the composition as a whole seems balanced, but only because dramatic imbalances are held in check. The painting illustrates a New Testament story in which Mary Magdalene went to the empty tomb of Jesus and saw the risen Christ, whom she at first took for the gardener. The story thus requires two people in the foreground, one of them prostrate.

This presents a difficult balancing problem, but Fontana solved it with a few ingenious steps. First, she gave the center of the composition strong weight, with Mary's large figure dressed in warm colors; above Mary is a glow in the sky. These anchor the composition. Christ occupies the right foreground, but he does not disrupt the equilibrium of the whole, because he is balanced by the higher and more massive tomb on the left. The small figure in red just outside the tomb also helps balance the strong figure of Christ.

What exactly are the visual weights of colors and forms, and how does an artist go about balancing them? As with design itself, there are no rules, only principles. Here are a few about visual balance:

- A large form is heavier, more attractive, or more attention-getting than a small form. Thus, two or more small forms can balance one large form.
- A form gathers visual weight as it nears the edge of a picture. In this way, a small form near an edge can balance a larger form near the center.
- A complex form is heavier than a simple form. Thus, a small complex form can balance a large simple form.

The introduction of color complicates these principles. Here are three color principles that counteract the three principles of form just given:

- Warm colors are heavier than cool colors. A single small yellow form can therefore balance a large dark blue form.

3.9 Lavinia Fontana.
Noli Me Tangere. 1581.
Oil on canvas. 47⅜″ × 36⅝″.
Erich Lessing/Art Resource, NY.

3.10 Nicolas Poussin (French, 1594–1665).
The Holy Family on the Steps. 1648.
Oil on canvas. 72.4 × 111.7 cm.
© The Cleveland Museum of Art, 2001, Leonard C. Hanna, Jr., Fund, 1981.18.

- Related to the point above, warm colors tend to advance toward the viewer, while cool colors tend to recede. This means that when considering two similar forms of opposing temperature, the warmer will be visually heavier because it seems closer to the viewer.

- Intense colors are heavier than weak or pale colors (tints and shades). Hence, a single small bright blue form near the center can balance a large pale blue form near an edge.

- The intensity, and therefore the weight, of any color increases as the background color approaches its complementary hue. Thus, on a green background, a small simple red form can balance a large complex blue form.

Although guidelines such as these are interesting to study and can be valuable to an artist if she or he gets "stuck," they are really "laboratory" examples. The truth is that most artists rely on a highly developed sensitivity to what "looks right" to arrive at a dynamic balance. Simply put, a work of art is balanced when it feels balanced.

A classic example of balance in Western art is Nicolas Poussin's *Holy Family on the Steps*, where he combined both asymmetrical and symmetrical elements in a complex composition. He grouped the figures in a stable, symmetrical pyramidal shape. The most important figure, the infant Jesus, is at the center of the picture, the strongest position. In case we don't notice that immediately, Poussin guided our attention by making the traditional red and blue of Mary's robes both light and bright, and by placing Jesus' head within a halo-like architectural space.

But then Poussin offset the potential inertness of this symmetry with an ingenious asymmetrical color balance. He placed Joseph, the figure at the right, in deep shadow, undermining the clarity of the stable pyramid. He created a major center of interest at the far left of the picture by giving St. Elizabeth a bright yellow robe. The interest created by the blue sky and clouds at the upper right counterbalances the figures of St. Elizabeth and the infant John the Baptist. But the final master stroke that brings complete balance is Joseph's

foot, which Poussin bathed in light. The brightness of this small, isolated shape with the diagonal staff above it is enough to catch our eye and balance the color weights of the left half of the painting.

An extreme case of dynamic balancing is *Jockeys Before the Race* by Edgar Degas. The artist boldly located the center of gravity on the right. To reinforce it, he drew it in as a pole. At first glance, all our attention is drawn to our extreme right, to the nearest and largest horse. But the solitary circle of the sun in the upper left exerts a strong fascination. The red cap, the pale pink jacket of the distant jockey, the subtle warm/cool color intersection

3.11 Edgar Degas (1834–1917).
Jockeys Before the Race. c. 1878–1879.
Oil essence, gouache, and pastel.
42½″ × 29″.
The Barber Institute of Fine Arts, University of Birmingham.
Bridgeman Art Library.

at the horizon, and the decreasing sizes of the horses all help to move our eyes over to the left portion of the picture, where a barely discernible but very important vertical line directs our attention upward.

In this work, a trail of visual cues moves our attention from right to left. If we are sensitive to them, we will perform the act of balancing the painting. If we are not, the painting will seem forever unbalanced. Degas, who was known for his adventurous compositions, relied on the fact that seeing is an active, creative process and not a passive one.

A good way to explore a picture's balance is to imagine it painted differently. Block out Joseph's light-bathed foot in the Poussin, then see how the lack of balance affects the picture. Cover the jockey's red cap in the Degas, and you'll see a spark of life go out of the painting.

Besides whatever visual balance the creator may seek, works of sculpture and architecture need structural balance or they will not stand up. Mark di Suvero's *Declaration* was erected in 2001 on a spot near the beach in Venice, California. As a work of public art, *Declaration* required a building permit and official structural checks to ensure its safety in earthquakes and tsunamis. The artist used his engineering ability to balance the long V-shaped wings that seem to leap out from the three-legged base. The artist described the work as "a painting in three dimensions with the crane as my paintbrush." Originally intended for a four-month viewing period, the dynamic geometries of *Declaration* have remained on the site ever since.

EMPHASIS AND SUBORDINATION

Artists use **emphasis** to draw our attention to an area. If that area is a specific spot or figure, it is called a **focal point**. Position, contrast, color intensity, and size can all be used to create emphasis.

Through **subordination**, an artist creates neutral areas of lesser interest that keep us from being distracted from the areas of emphasis. We have seen them at work in the two paintings we have just examined.

3.12 Mark di Suvero.
Declaration. 1999–2001.
Steel beams. Height 60′.
Copyright Mark di Suvero. Courtesy L.A. Louver, Venice, CA.

In *Holy Family on the Steps* (page 65), Poussin placed the most important figure in the center, the strongest location in any visual field. In *Jockeys Before the Race*, Degas took a different approach, using size, shape, placement, and color to create areas of emphasis *away* from the center. The sun is a separate focal point created through contrast (it is lighter than the surrounding sky area and the only circle in the painting) and through placement (it is the only shape in that part of the painting). Sky and grass areas, however, are muted in color with almost no detail so that they are subordinate to, and thus support, the areas of emphasis. Generally, using emphasis and subordination, the artist shows us where to look in a work.

DIRECTIONAL FORCES

Like emphasis and subordination, artists use **directional forces** to influence the way we look at a work of art. Directional forces are "paths" for the eye to follow, provided by actual or implied lines. Implied directional lines may be suggested by a form's axis, by the imagined connection between similar or adjacent forms, or by the implied continuation of actual lines. Studying directional lines and forces often reveals a work of art's underlying energy and basic visual structure.

Looking at *Jockeys Before the Race*, we find that our attention is pulled to a series of focal points: the horse and jockey at the extreme right, the vertical pole, the red cap, the pink jacket, and the blue-green at the horizon. The dominant directional forces in this work are diagonal. The focal points mentioned above create an implied directional line. The face of the first jockey is included in this line.

The implied diagonal line created by the bodies of the three receding horses acts as a related directional force. As our eyes follow the recession, encouraged by the attraction of the focal points, we perform the act of balancing the composition by correcting our original attraction to the extreme right.

Just as our physical and visual feelings for balance correspond, so do our physical and visual feelings about directional lines and forces. The direction of lines produces sensations similar to

standing still (|), being at rest (—), or being in motion (/). Therefore, a combination of vertical and horizontal lines provides stability. For example, columns and walls and horizontal steps provide a stable visual foundation for *Holy Family on the Steps*. The vertical pole and horizon provide stability in *Jockeys Before the Race*.

Francisco Goya's print *Bullfight* provides a fascinating example of effective design based on a dramatic use of directional forces. To emphasize the drama of man and bull, Goya isolated them in the foreground as large, dark shapes against a light background. He created suspense by crowding the spectators into the upper left corner.

Goya evoked a sense of motion by placing the bullfighter exactly on the diagonal axis that runs from lower left to upper right (diagram a). He reinforced the feeling by placing the bull's hind legs along the same line.

Goya further emphasized two main features of the drama by placing the man's hands at the intersection of the image's most important horizontal and vertical lines. He also directed powerful diagonals from the bull's head and front legs to the pole's balancing point on the ground (a). The resulting sense of motion to the right is so powerful that everything in the rest of the etching is needed to balance it.

By placing the light source to the left, Goya extended the bull's shadow to the right, to create a relatively stable horizontal line. The man looks down at the shadow, creating a directional force that

a.

b.

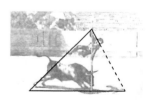

c.

3.13 Francisco Goya.
Bullfight: The Agility and Daring of Juanito Apiñani.
Plate 20. Etching with aquatint. 9½″ × 14″.
Ashmolean Museum, Oxford, England, UK.

causes us also to look. When we do, we realize that the implied lines reveal the underlying structure to be a stable triangle (diagram b). Formally, the triangle serves as a balancing force; psychologically, its missing side serves to heighten the tension of the situation.

The dynamism of the man's diagonal axis is so strong that the composition needed additional balancing elements; thus, Goya used light to create two more diagonals in the opposite direction (diagram c). The area of shadow in the background completes the balance by adding visual weight and stability to the left.

It has taken many words and several diagrams to describe the visual dynamics that make the design of Goya's etching so effective. However, our eyes take it in instantly. Good design is efficient; it communicates its power immediately.

CONTRAST

Contrast is the juxtaposition of strongly dissimilar elements. Dramatic effects can be produced when dark is set against light, large against small, bright colors against dull. Without contrast, visual experience would be monotonous.

Contrast can be seen in the thick and thin areas of a single brush stroke. It can also be seen in the juxtaposition of regular geometric and irregular organic shapes, or in hard (sharp) and soft (blurred) edges. Contrast can provide visual interest, emphasize a point, and express content.

In the *Luster-Painted Bowl*, for example, the gold luster contrasts strongly with the blue accents. There is also a great deal of contrast among the eight petal-shaped segments that radiate from the central starburst. These segments are divided and decorated quite differently, creating a richly varied surface. Four of the petals have a blue tree shape,

which evokes the idea of paradise described in the Koran, the Muslim holy book. They provide the major **rhythm** of the composition, while the other four petals alternate between a simple zigzag and a doubled tree separated by a band. After a moment's look, we realize that the vivid and rich contrasts of this piece are subjected to a rigorous balancing scheme based on the repetition of radiating shapes. This discovery soon gives way to admiration for the designer's ability to harmonize such disparate elements.

REPETITION AND RHYTHM

The repetition of visual elements gives a composition unity, continuity, flow, and emphasis. As we saw earlier, *Interior of a Dutch House* (page 61) is

3.14 *Luster-Painted Bowl.*
Hispano-Moresque, Manises. Spain. c. 1400.
Tin-glazed earthenware painted in cobalt blue and luster.
Height 5½", diameter 17⅝". (E643)
Courtesy of The Hispanic Society of America, New York.

organized around the repetition of rectangular shapes.

In Liubov Popova's *The Pianist*, the white shape at the center (the pianist's shirt front) is related visually to the pages of music, which form a strong rhythm leading the eye rightward and toward the keyboard. Likewise, the gray area of his face is repeated in organic shapes to the right and upward. (Both of these rhythmic sequences lead the eye in the same left-to-right direction that Westerners normally use in reading either music or books.) The angled shapes of the fingers suggest rhythmic motion across the keyboard just above. Indeed, the fragmentary shapes that dominate this painting suggest the rapidly ticking rhythm of the composition that *The Pianist* seems to play.

3.15 Liubov Popova.
The Pianist. 1915.
Oil on canvas. 106.5 × 88.7 cm.
National Gallery of Canada, Ottawa.
Photo: © NGC.

3.16 Ogata Korin (1658–1716).
   Cranes. c. 1700. Japanese, Edo period (1615–1868).
   Ink, color, gold, and silver on paper. 166 H × 371 cm (65⅜″ × 146⅛″).
   Freer Gallery of Art, Smithsonian Institution, Washington, DC: Purchase, F1956.20.

In the visual arts, rhythm is created through the regular recurrence of elements with related variations. Rhythm refers to any kind of movement or structure of dominant and subordinate elements in sequence. We generally associate rhythm with temporal arts such as music, dance, and poetry. Visual artists also use rhythm, as an organizational and expressive device.

Japanese artist Ogata Korin used repetition and rhythm to charming effect in *Cranes,* one of a pair of folding screens. The landscape is a flat yet opulent background of gold leaf, interrupted only by a suggestion of a curving stream at the right. The birds are severely simplified, their bodies and legs forming a pattern that is repeated with variations. The heads and beaks of the cranes create a strong directional force toward our left, leading the eye to an ironically empty rectangle. The heads are held high, and their location near the top of the composition enhances this loftiness, making the birds seem just a bit pretentious. Their procession in marching steps in a seemingly straight line supports this note of humor.

Strong rhythm dominates José Clemente Orozco's *Zapatistas.* The line of similar, diagonally placed figures grouped in a rhythmic sequence expresses the determination of oppressed people in revolt. The rhythmic diagonals of their hat brims, bayonets, and swords all contribute to a feeling of action. In fact, diagonal lines dominate the entire composition.

3.17 José Clemente Orozco.
   Zapatistas. 1931.
   Oil on canvas. 45″ × 55″ (114.3 × 139.7 cm).
   The Museum of Modern Art, New York. Given Anonymously. Photograph © 2002 The Museum of Modern Art, New York. © Clemente V. Orozco. Reproduction authorized by the Instituto Nacional de Bellas Artes.

3.18 *Scale Relationships.*

SCALE AND PROPORTION

Scale is the size relation of one thing to another. **Proportion** is the size relationship of parts to a whole.

Scale is one of the first decisions an artist makes when planning a work of art. How big will it be? We experience scale in relation to our own size, and this experience constitutes an important part of our response to works of art.

We see many relationships in terms of scale. You have probably noticed that when a short person stands next to a tall person, the short one seems shorter and the tall one taller. Their relationship exaggerates the relative difference in their heights. In the diagram *Scale Relationships*, the

inner circles at the center in both groups are the same size, but the center circle at the right seems much larger.

Many artists since the twentieth century have distorted scale for visual effect. Claes Oldenburg and Coosje van Bruggen's *Shuttlecocks* used distortion in a humorous way. The artists arrayed four huge metal shuttlecocks on the lawns outside the north and south façades of the Nelson-Atkins Museum of Art in Kansas City, Missouri. Each *Shuttlecock* is an outlandish seventeen feet high and weighs over five thousand pounds. Because badminton is played on grass, it appears that the shuttlecocks fell during a game between giants who used the museum as a net. *Shuttlecocks* thus uses distortion of scale to poke gentle fun at the museum, mocking its rather prim look with a playfully irreverent attitude.

When the size of any work is modified for reproduction in a book, its character changes. This is true of every picture in this book, with this exception: Rembrandt's *Self-Portrait in a Cap*. This tiny etching, which the artist created when he was

EXPLORE MORE: To see the entire lawn with all of the *Shuttlecocks*, go to Google Earth and enter "Nelson-Atkins Museum, Kansas City."

3.20 Rembrandt van Rijn. *Self-Portrait in a Cap, Open-Mouthed and Staring.* 1630. Etching. 2″ × 1⅞″. © The Trustees of The British Museum.

3.19 Claes Oldenburg and Coosje van Bruggen. *Shuttlecocks.* 1994. One of four. Aluminum, fiberglass-reinforced plastic, and paint. 215¾″ × 209″ × 191¾″.
North façade of The Nelson-Atkins Museum of Art, Kansas City, Missouri including one of four "Shuttlecocks," 1994, by Claes Oldenburg and Coosje van Bruggen. Purchase; acquired through the generosity of the Sosland Family. © Claes Oldenburg and Coosje van Bruggen. F94-1/1 Photograph by Jamison Miller.

twenty-four years old, is reproduced here at the actual size of the original. It captures a fleeting expression of intense surprise. At this scale, it reads as an intimate notation of human emotion. On the other hand, many large-sized works have been reduced in this book to tiny fractions of their actual sizes, thereby altering their impact. Because works of art are distorted in a variety of ways when they are reproduced, it is important to experience original art whenever possible.

The term **format** refers to the size and shape—and thus to the scale and proportion—of a two-dimensional picture plane, such as a piece of paper, a canvas, a book page, or a video screen. For example, the format of this book is a vertical 8½ by 11–inch rectangle, the same format used for computer paper and most notebooks. Rembrandt's etching uses a tiny format; some modern artists have used huge ones.

The format an artist chooses strongly influences the total composition of a particular work. Henri Matisse made this clear in his *Notes of a Painter*:

Composition, the aim of which should be expression, is modified according to the surface to be covered. If I take a sheet of paper of a given size, my drawing will have a necessary relationship to its format. I would not repeat this drawing on another sheet of different proportions, for example, rectangular instead of square.[3]

Change in proportion can make a major difference in how we experience a given subject. This becomes apparent when we compare two *pietàs* (*pietà*, Italian for "pity," refers to a depiction of Mary holding and mourning over the body of Jesus).

Creating a composition with an infant on its mother's lap is much easier than showing a fully grown man in such a position. In his most famous *Pietà*, Michelangelo solved the problem by dramatically altering the human proportions of Mary's figure. Michelangelo made the heads of the two figures the same size but greatly enlarged Mary's body in relation to that of Christ, disguising her immensity with deep folds of drapery. Her seated figure spreads out to support the almost horizontal curve of

3.21 Michelangelo Buonarroti.
Pietà, 1501.
Marble. Height 6′8½″.
Canali Photobank.

Christ's limp body. Imagine how the figure of Mary would appear if she were standing. Michelangelo made Mary's body into that of a giant; if she were a living human being rather than a work of art, she would stand at least eight feet tall!

Because the proportions of the figure of Christ are anatomically correct and there are abundant naturalistic details, we overlook the proportions of Mary's figure, yet the distortion is essential to the way we experience the content of the work.

LEARN MORE: For a Closer Look at Michelangelo's *Pietà*, go to **www.myartslab.com**

Compare Michelangelo's work with the *Roettgen Pietà*, created about two centuries earlier. Unlike the Renaissance work, the German sculptor carved both figures of similar height. Making Christ bony and emaciated helped to alleviate the problem of how Mary can support a person of similar size; Christ's gaunt body also expresses the truth of his suffering in a way that Michelangelo avoided. The anonymous creator of *Roettgen Pietà* also carved both heads larger, out of proportion to the sizes of their bodies. These distortions help to heighten the expressiveness of the work.

3.22 *Roettgen Pietà.* 1300–1325.
Painted wood, height 34½″.
LVR-Landesmuseum Bonn.

DESIGN SUMMARY

A finished work affects us because its design seems inevitable. However, design is not inevitable at all. Faced with a blank piece of paper, an empty canvas, a lump of clay, or a block of marble, an artist begins a process involving many decisions, false starts, and changes in order to arrive at an integrated whole. This chapter has presented some of the principles of design that guide the creation of artworks.

By photographing the progress of his painting *Large Reclining Nude*, Henri Matisse left us a rare record of the process of designing. He took twenty-four photographs over a period of four months; three of them are reproduced here.

The first version (State I) is by far the most naturalistic: the proportions of the model's body on the couch and the three-dimensional space of the room seem ordinary. This stage of the work shows the traditional rules of picture construction, but this is only the start of a fascinating journey.

By State IX, Matisse had introduced a number of bold changes. Because the model's head and crooked right arm did not give the proper weight to that side of the composition, he greatly enlarged the arm. He added more curves to the torso, and he put the legs together to provide a balancing element on the left side. The space of the room now has a new look because he removed the diagonal; this change flattened the composition, highlighting its two-dimensional design. The model's left arm is now closer to a ninety-degree angle, which makes it seem to support more weight; this is a stronger effect than that of the rubbery arm in the first photo. The boldest change regards the couch. Now it is far larger, with vertical white stripes in a rhythmic pattern. Because the stripes are parallel, they do not function as perspective lines; rather, the couch appears to be tipped toward us. Matisse kept the potted flowers and the chair, but he simplified the chair and placed the flowers on the couch.

By the time the artist took our third photograph (State XIII), he had introduced even more changes, to compensate for some of the bold effects he had introduced earlier. The model's head is larger and placed upright, so that it fits better into the shape of the raised arm. He simplified the curves of the torso and created a new position for the left arm, a compromise between its position in the first photo and the second one. The legs are now almost a unit, their bulky mass balancing the verticals and diagonals on the right. He added horizontal lines to the couch, making a pattern of squares that parallel the framing edges of the painting. This netlike motif is repeated in the larger squares on the back wall of the room. The composition is already interesting, but Matisse did not stop here.

The final version (on the following page) shows further refinements and a few discoveries. Because the model's left arm probably still seemed weak, Matisse finally fixed it in the corner of the work at a strong angle aligned with the picture frame. The head is smaller, because the new position of the arms provides enough visual weight on that side of the work. He intensified the pattern on the back wall, so that it now serves as a variation of the motif on the couch. He gave new functions to the shapes and lines of the chair back and flowers by emphasizing their curves. They now echo the shapes of the body and balance the rigidity of the squares in the couch and wall. The position of the legs is the biggest change. By moving one of them down, he created a "pinwheel" effect that the arms carry through, adding a new circular element to the design of the whole. Finally, he repositioned the model's entire body at a slight angle from the horizontal.

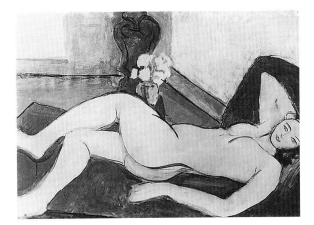

3.23 Henri Matisse (French, 1869–1954).
Photographs of three states of *Large Reclining Nude*.
a. State I, May 3, 1935.
b. State IX, May 29, 1935.
c. State XIII, September 4, 1935.

3.24 Henri Matisse (French, 1869–1954).
Large Reclining Nude. 1935.
Oil on canvas. 26″ × 36½″ (66 × 92.7 cm).
The Baltimore Museum of Art: The Cone Collection, formed by Dr. Claribel Cone and Miss Etta Cone of Baltimore, Maryland. BMA 1950.258. ⓒ2010 Succession H. Matisse/Artists Rights Society (ARS), New York.

Matisse's keen sense of design and restless experimentation produced a work in which powerful forces in the composition are balanced with seemingly simple means. He wrote that the expressiveness of a work does not rest merely on facial expressions or gestures of figures:

The entire arrangement of my picture is expressive: the place occupied by the figures, the empty spaces around them, the proportions, everything has its share.[4]

Now that we have discussed how artworks are constructed, we will spend the next several chapters on the media that artists use.

PRACTICE MORE: Get flashcards for images and terms and review chapter material with quizzes at **www.myartslab.com**

HENRI MATISSE

Expression Is Foremost

IF HENRI MATISSE had not had an attack of appendicitis, the history of art would have been different. After earning his law degree and working as a clerk, he fell gravely ill. During the long convalescence at his parents' home, his mother tried to amuse him with a gift of a box of paints, brushes, and a do-it-yourself book on painting. The result was extraordinary.

By the age of twenty-one, Matisse knew he wanted to be a painter. He returned to Paris and became a full-time art student. In the methodical manner of a lawyer, he began his artistic career by becoming thoroughly proficient in the traditional techniques of French art. Throughout his life he worked at adding to both his knowledge and his skills, while being careful to preserve his original freshness of vision.

For Matisse, a painting was a combination of lines, shapes, and colors before it was a picture of any object. His personal style was based on intuition, yet he acknowledged the importance of his years of study. He carefully assimilated influences from the arts of the Near East and Africa and from other painters.

Matisse's primary interest was to express his passion for life through the free use of visual form, with the human figure his main subject.

What interests me most is neither still life nor landscape but the human figure. It is through it that I best succeed in expressing the nearly religious feeling that I have towards life.[5]

His search for expressive means caused him to question or abandon many of the "rules" of art as it was then understood. For example, he often used colors that did not correspond to what the eye sees, but rather to what he felt inside. He also simplified and flattened his compositions, because he felt that adding too much detail took away feeling. For these and other innovations in painting style, he was once called a "wild beast"—*fauve* in French. The name stuck, and Fauvism took its place among the most important modern art movements.

Matisse sought to hide his own artistic struggles so that his work would appear effortless and light. He was concerned, however, that young people would think he had created his paintings casually—even carelessly—and would mistakenly conclude that years of disciplined work and study were unnecessary.

The dominant qualities in Matisse's art are lyric color and vitality. Behind the playful appearance lie radiant

3.25 André Derain (1880–1954). *Portrait of Henri Matisse.* 1905. Oil on canvas. 46.0 × 34.9 cm. Tate Gallery, London, Great Britain. Art Resource, NY. © 2010 Artists Rights Society (ARS), New York/ADAGP, Paris; © 2010 Succession H. Matisse/Artists Rights Society (ARS), New York.

big-heartedness, grace, and wisdom. Although he lived through both world wars and was aware of acute suffering, Matisse chose to express joy and tranquility in his art.

What I dream of is an art of balance, of purity and serenity, devoid of troubling or depressing subject matter, an art which might be for every mental worker ... businessman or writer, like an appeasing influence, like a mental soother, something like a good armchair in which to rest from physical fatigue.[6]

4

DRAWING

When my daughter was about seven years old, she asked me one day what I did at work. I told her that I worked at the college—that my job was to teach people to draw. She stared back at me, incredulous, and said, "You mean they forget?"

HOWARD IKEMOTO[1]

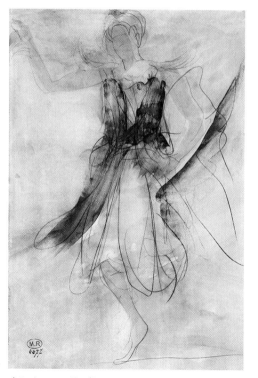

4.1 Auguste Rodin.
Cambodian Dancer. 1906.
Graphite, watercolor, gouache, and crayon on cream vellum paper. 11¾" × 7⅞".
Rodin Museum, Paris, France.

The desire to draw is as natural as the desire to talk. As children, we draw long before we learn to read and write. In fact, making letter forms is a kind of drawing—especially when we first learn to "write." Some of us continue to enjoy drawing; others return to drawing as adults. Those who no longer draw probably came to believe they did not draw well enough to suit themselves or others. Yet drawing is a learned process. It is a way of seeing and communicating, a way of paying attention.

In the most basic sense, to draw means to pull, push, or drag a marking tool across a surface to leave a line or mark. Most people working in the visual arts use drawing as an important tool for visual thinking—for recording and developing ideas.

Drawing is an immediate and accessible way to communicate through imagery. Through drawing we can share ideas, feelings, experiences, and imaginings. Sometimes a drawing does several of these things simultaneously.

When French sculptor Auguste Rodin saw a troupe of Cambodian folk dancers in 1906, he was so transfixed by their graceful movements that he went to their rehearsals and made dozens of drawings. His *Cambodian Dancer* is one of these,

HEAR MORE: Listen to an audio file of your chapter at **www.myartslab.com**

heightened with washes of watercolor and crayon. The drawing seems almost as spontaneous and fluid as the dancer's movements that inspired it.

Many people find it valuable to keep a sketchbook handy to serve as a visual diary, a place to develop and maintain drawing skills and to note whatever catches the eye or imagination. From sketchbook drawings, some ideas may develop and reach maturity as finished drawings or complete works in other media. Leonardo da Vinci, for example, was a restless draftsman who used sketches as a type of scientific research. His drawing *Three Seated Figures and Studies of Machinery* shows his effort to capture both human and mechanical motion.

Guillermo del Toro, director and producer of *Hellboy, Don't Be Afraid of the Dark*, and other films, keeps a *Sketchbook* for jotting notes and ideas. The pages here show his musings about the desire for fame, meeting other directors, and sketches of some strange beings that found their way into his 2006 feature *Pan's Labyrinth*. (This film is discussed on page 141.)

A great deal of drawing is receptive; that is, we use it to attempt to capture the physical appearance of something before us. Many people use drawing in this way, as they take up a pencil or pen or chalk to render the fall of light on a jar, the leaves of a tree, arrangement of a landscape, the roundness of a body, or their own reflection in a mirror. This was Rodin's goal in his drawing of the *Cambodian Dancer*. Such drawings can be a professional necessity for an artist, or recreation for the rest of us.

4.2 Leonardo da Vinci.
Three Seated Figures and Studies of Machinery.
Silverpoint and pale ink on prepared surface.
Ashmolean Museum, Oxford, England, U.K.

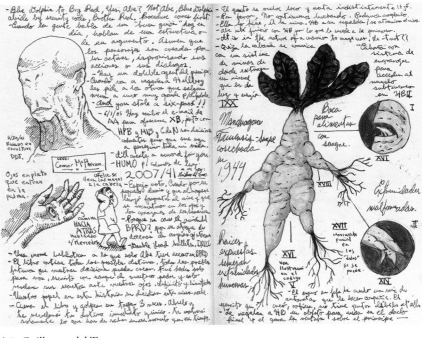

4.3 Guillermo del Toro.
Pages from *Sketchbook*. 2006 *Pan's Labyrinth*.

LEARN MORE: For a Closer Look at Guillermo del Toro's *Sketchbook* pages, go to **www.myartslab.com**

Other drawings, in contrast, are projective: We may draw something that exists only in our minds, either as a memory of something we have seen or a vision of something we imagine. Artists whose work is based on imagination often use this sort of drawing, as do architects when they plan new structures. Leonardo's drawings of *Studies of Machinery* are more projective than receptive; Del Toro's *Sketchbook* likewise combines projective and receptive approaches. The general tendency among today's artists in Europe and the United States seems to be toward projective types of drawing.

Drawing from direct observation is neither more nor less important than drawing from imagination or memory. However, the process of drawing from observation helps people learn to see more attentively and develops the ability to draw from either memory or imagination. In *The Zen of Seeing,* medical doctor Frederick Franck describes drawing as a means to heighten visual awareness:

I have learned that what I have not drawn, I have never really seen, and that when I start drawing an ordinary thing I realize how extraordinary it is, sheer miracle: the branching of a tree, the structure of a dandelion's seed puff.[2]

Learning to draw to your own satisfaction can transform your outlook on life. Elizabeth Layton was in her late sixties and had been suffering from depression for many years when she took a drawing course that changed her life. She began drawing by setting down outlines in black, as most of us do. After learning a few more sophisticated techniques, Layton drew with enthusiasm and gained wide recognition for the quality of her drawings.

Her most common subject was herself and her experiences, which she learned to depict with a keen and sometimes ironic visual sense. Her 1985 drawing *The Eyes of the Law* shows her aged face reflected in a crowd of policemens' mirrored sunglasses.

Some artists, such as Picasso, demonstrated exceptional drawing ability as young children. Others, such as Paul Cézanne and Vincent van Gogh, did not start out with obvious drawing ability; they developed skills through diligent effort. In spite of early difficulties, they succeeded in teaching themselves to draw. Their examples show that seeing and drawing are learned processes, not just inborn gifts.

4.4 Elizabeth Layton.
The Eyes of the Law. 1985.
Crayon, colored pencil on paper.
Spencer Museum of Art: Gift of Don Almbert and the Artist.

4.5 Vincent van Gogh.
Carpenter. c. 1880.
Black crayon. 22″ × 15″.
Kröller-Müller, Otterlo, Netherlands.

Van Gogh learned a great deal about both seeing and painting through his practice of drawing. He was just beginning his short career as an artist when he made the drawing of a *Carpenter*. Although stiff, and clumsy in proportion, the drawing reveals van Gogh's careful observation and attention to detail. His letters to his brother Theo show how he struggled to render the world with pencil and crayon. In one of these notes, he recalled the difficulty and a breakthrough:

I remember quite well, now that you write about it, that at the time when you spoke of my becoming a painter, I thought it very impractical and would not hear of it. What made me stop doubting was reading a clear book on perspective ... and a week later I drew the interior of a kitchen with stove, chair, table, and window—in their places and on their legs—whereas before it had seemed to me that getting depth and the right perspective into a drawing was witchcraft or pure

chance. If only you drew one thing right, you would feel an irresistible longing to draw a thousand other things.[3]

Old Man with His Head in His Hands, made two years after *Carpenter*, shows that van Gogh made great progress in seeing and drawing during those two years. By this time, van Gogh was able to portray the old man's grief, as well as the solidity of the figure, and to give a suggestion of his surroundings. The groups of parallel lines appear to have been drawn quickly, with sensitivity and self-assurance.

4.6 Vincent van Gogh.
Old Man with His Head in His Hands. 1882.
Pencil on paper. 19¹¹⁄₁₆″ × 12³⁄₁₆″.
Amsterdam, Van Gogh Museum (Vincent van Gogh Foundation).

EXPLORE MORE: To see a video on figure drawing, go to **www.myartslab.com**

VINCENT VAN GOGH
A Life's Work in Ten Years

TODAY THE ART of Vincent van Gogh is internationally known and admired, but it is hard to believe that van Gogh worked as an artist for only ten years. During his lifetime his art was known only to a few; in fact, he sold only one painting.

Van Gogh was born in the Netherlands to a middle-class family: His father was a minister, his grandfather a famous preacher; three uncles, and later his brother, were art dealers—a background that paved the way for Vincent's lifelong concern with both art and religion.

After six years working in the art business in Paris and London, he returned to the Netherlands to study theology. In 1878, at age twenty-five, he became a lay preacher among impoverished miners in Belgium. Although not successful at preaching, van Gogh was effective at aiding the victims of mining disasters and disease. When his compassion spurred him to give most of his possessions to the poor, the missionary society that had hired him dismissed him because they thought he interpreted Christ's teachings too literally.

He then decided to take up art, not because he possessed any obvious talent, but because he saw art as the means through which he could communicate with others. Although determined to be a painter, van Gogh believed that he had to master drawing before he allowed himself to use color. The miners and farm

laborers that he helped with his social work were his first models. As he developed his skill, Vincent was supported by his brother Theo, who regularly sent money and provided encouragement through his letters.

Van Gogh studied briefly at the art academy in Antwerp, Belgium, but he was largely self-taught. In 1886 he joined his brother in Paris, where he met the leading French Impressionist and Post-Impressionist painters. Under their influence van Gogh's paintings, which had been limited to the somber tones of traditional Dutch painting, became much lighter and brighter in color, as we see in *Self-Portrait with Gray Hat*.

In 1888 he moved to southern France, where in less than two years he produced most of the paintings for which he is known. There, armed with the Impressionists' bright, free color, and inspired by the intense semitropical light, van Gogh took color even further. He developed a revolutionary approach to color based on the way colors and color combinations symbolize ideas and emotional content. His new understanding of expressive color led him to write that "the painter of the future will be a colorist such as has never existed."[4]

Van Gogh's use of pure colors and his bold strokes of thick paint created images of emotional intensity that had a great impact on artists of the twentieth

4.7 Vincent van Gogh.
Self-Portrait with Gray Hat. 1887.
Oil on canvas. 17¼″ × 14¾″.
Amsterdam, Van Gogh Museum (Vincent van Gogh Foundation).

century. Before van Gogh, most Western painters used color to describe the appearance of their subjects. After van Gogh, painters began to realize that color and brushwork could make visible feelings and states of mind.

Beginning in his teenage years, van Gogh suffered episodes of mental breakdown. With passing years, these increased in duration. Spells of fervent painting were interrupted by periods of illness and depression. Contrary to popular belief, these episodes contributed nothing to his development as an artist.

Increasing illness led him voluntarily to enter a mental hospital for several months. After leaving the hospital,

he returned to Paris, then settled in a nearby town under the watchful eye of a doctor known to be a friend of artists. However, his increasing despair over his mental state drove him to suicide at age thirty-seven.

An emphasis on the tragic aspects of van Gogh's now legendary life has produced a popular view of the man that tends to obscure his great contribution to art. In spite of his difficulties, van Gogh produced almost two thousand works of art within a mere ten years. Although most of his contemporaries could not see the value of his art, his paintings and drawings are displayed today in major museums worldwide, and exhibitions of his works attract record crowds.

Good drawing may appear deceptively simple, yet it can take years of patient work to learn to draw easily and effectively. According to one account, a person viewing a portrait drawn by Matisse with only a few quick lines asked the artist with some disgust, "How long did it take you to do this?" "Forty years," replied Matisse.

PURPOSES OF DRAWING

A drawing can function in three ways:

- as a notation, sketch, or record of something seen, remembered, or imagined
- as a study or preparation for another, usually larger and more complex work
- as an end in itself, a complete work of art

We see examples of the first case in Rodin's *Cambodian Dancer* that began this chapter, and in the Vincent van Gogh drawings just examined. The second case, drawing as preparatory tool, is traditional in Western art. For example, Michelangelo made detailed studies of the *Libyan Sybil* for his finished painting of the figure on the ceiling of the Sistine Chapel.

This magnificent drawing of a mythical female figure was drawn from a male model. The studies are a record of search and discovery as Michelangelo carefully drew what he observed. His knowledge of anatomy helped him to define each muscle. The flow between the head, shoulders,

and arms of the figure is based on Michelangelo's feeling for visual continuity as well as his attention to detail. The parts of the figure that he felt needed further study he drew repeatedly. To achieve the dark reds, Michelangelo evidently licked the point of the chalk.

A simple, tiny sketch, quickly done, is often the starting point for a far larger and more complex work. In such drawings an artist can work out problems of overall design or concentrate on small details. For example, Picasso did many studies in

4.8 Michelangelo Buonarotti.
Studies for the Libyan Sibil. c. 1510.
Red chalk on paper. 11⅜″ × 8⁷⁄₁₆″
(28.9 × 21.4 cm).
The Metropolitan Museum of Art, Purchase, Joseph Pulitzer Bequest, 1924. (24.197.2) Photograph © 1995 The Metropolitan Museum of Art/Art Resource, NY.

preparation for his major painting, *Guernica*, a huge work measuring more than 11 by 25 feet (a larger reproduction appears on page 383). Forty-five of Picasso's studies are preserved and dated; they show the evolution of this important work.

The first drawing for *Guernica* shows a dark form at the top center; this later became a woman with a lamp, apparently an important symbol to Picasso. The woman leans out of a house in the upper right. On the left appears a bull with a bird on its back. Both the bull and the woman with the lamp are major elements in the final painting. The first drawing was probably completed in a few seconds, yet its quick gestural lines contain the essence of the large, complex painting.

Although artists do not generally consider their preliminary sketches as finished pieces, studies by leading artists are often treasured both for their intrinsic beauty and for what they reveal about the creative process. Picasso recognized the importance of documenting the creative process from initial idea to finished painting:

It would be very interesting to preserve photographically, not the stages, but the metamorphoses of a picture. Possibly one might then discover the path followed by the brain in materializing a dream. But there is one very odd thing to notice, that basically a picture doesn't change, that the first "vision" remains almost intact, in spite of appearances.[5]

Another type of preparatory drawing is the **cartoon**. The original meaning of cartoon, still used by art professionals, is a full-sized drawing made as a guide for a large work in another medium, particularly a fresco painting, mosaic, or tapestry. In making the final work, artists often use such cartoons as overlays for tracing.

4.10 Pablo Picasso.
Composition Study for Guernica. May 9, 1937.
Pencil on white paper. 9½″ × 17⅞″.
Museo Nacional Centro de Arte Reina Sofia/© 2010 Estate of Pablo Picasso/Artists
Rights Society (ARS), New York.

4.11 Pablo Picasso.
Guernica. 1937.
Oil on canvas. 350 × 782 cm.
Museo Nacional Centro de Arte Reina Sofia, Madrid, Spain. Copyright John Bigelow Taylor/
Art Resource, NY. © 2010 Estate of Pablo Picasso/Artists Rights Society (ARS), New York.

4.12 *Drawing Tools and Their Characteristic Lines.*

In today's common usage, the word cartoon refers to a narrative drawing emphasizing humorous or satirical content. Cartoons and comics are among the most widely enjoyed drawings, and will be discussed later in this chapter.

Many artists today view drawing as a medium in itself, and drawings as finished works of art. Among these are several in this chapter, such as the works by Charles White, Nancy Spero, and Julie Mehretu.

TOOLS AND TECHNIQUES

Each drawing tool and each type of paper has its own characteristics. The interaction between these materials and the technique of the artist determines the nature of the resulting drawing. The illustration *Drawing Tools* shows the different qualities of marks made by common drawing tools. Some of these tools give a dry, refined line; others are wet and more expressive. Note also how each tool responds to varying degrees of pressure; the ink brush in the middle is most responsive, the pen at the bottom, the least.

Artists often use rows of parallel lines to suggest shadows or volumes. These parallel lines are called **hatching**; each method is illustrated in the accompanying diagram, titled *Types of Hatching*. Charles White used crosshatched ink lines in *Preacher* to build up the figure's mass and

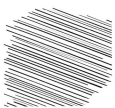

a. Hatching

b. Crosshatching.

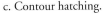

c. Contour hatching.

4.13 *Types of Hatching.*

4.14 Charles White (1918–1979). *Preacher.* 1952. Pen and black ink, and graphite pencil on board, Sheet: 22¹³⁄₁₆″ × 29¹⁵⁄₁₆″ × ³⁄₁₆″ (57.9 × 76 × 0.5 cm). Collection of Whitney Museum of American Art, New York. Purchase. 52.25. Photo by Geoffrey Clements, New York © 2001: Whitney Museum of American Art.

gesture in a forceful manner. Through the use of contour hatching, White gave the figure a feeling of sculptural mass. The foreshortened right hand and forearm add to the drawing's dramatic impact. Printmakers often use hatching to suggest mass and shadow, as we shall see in Chapter 6.

The quality and type of paper that an artist uses also have an important impact on the drawing. Most drawing surfaces are smooth, but some papers have **tooth**, a quality of roughness or surface grain that gives texture to a drawing. The drawing by Georges Pierre Seurat, *L'Echo*, was done on toothy paper and it shows its texture as a result.

Dry Media

Dry drawing media include pencil, **charcoal**, **conté crayon**, and **pastel**. Most drawing pencils are made of graphite (a crystalline form of carbon). They are available in varying degrees of hardness; softer pencils give darker lines, and harder pencils give lighter ones.

Darkness and line quality are determined both by the degree of hardness of the pencil and by the texture of the surface to which it is applied. Pencil lines can vary in width or length, can be made by using the side of the pencil point in broad strokes, and can be repeated as hatching. Artists create a considerable range of values by varying the pressure on a medium-soft drawing pencil.

A rich variety of values and inventive shapes made with light and dark grades of drawing pencils fills Judith Murray's drawing *Obsidian*.

The sticks of charcoal used today are similar to those used by prehistoric people to draw on cave walls: Both are simply charred sticks of wood. With charcoal, dark passages can be drawn quickly. The various hard-to-soft grades of charcoal provide a flexible medium for both beginning and advanced artists. Because not all charcoal particles bind to the surface of the paper, charcoal is easy to smudge, blur, or erase. This quality is both an advantage and a drawback: it enables quick changes, but finished works can easily smear. A completed charcoal drawing may be set or "fixed" with a thin varnish called a **fixative**, which is sprayed over it to help seal the charcoal onto the paper and prevent smudging. Charcoal produces a wide range of light to dark values from soft grays to deep velvety blacks.

Georgia O'Keeffe took full advantage of charcoal in her drawing of a *Banana Flower*. The potential for showing gradations of shade in charcoal provided her with the means to draw with powerful precision. Here she dramatized the structure of her subject as a monumental sculptural mass. Although O'Keeffe is best known for her colorful paintings of enlarged close-up views of flowers (see page 53), in this drawing she achieved a comparable impact with just black and white.

4.15 Judith Murray.
Obsidian. 1988.
Pencil on Arches paper. 17½″ × 19¼″.
Courtesy of the artist and Howard and Terry Walters, Summit, NJ.

4.16 Georgia O'Keeffe.
Banana Flower. 1933.
Charcoal and black chalk on paper. 21¾″ × 14¾″
(55.2 × 37.7 cm).
The Museum of Modern Art/Licensed by Scala-Art Resource, NY. Given
anonymously (by exchange). Photograph © 2002 the Museum of Modern
Art, New York. © 2010 Georgia O'Keeffe Museum/Artists Rights Society
(ARS), New York.

obscured by the total effect of finely textured light and dark areas. He selected conté crayon on rough paper as a means of concentrating on basic forms and on the interplay of light and shadow.

Natural chalks of red, white, and black have been used for drawing since ancient times. Pastels, produced since the seventeenth century, have characteristics similar to those of natural chalk. They have a freshness and purity of color because they are comprised mostly of pigment, with very little binding material. Because no drying is needed, there is no change in color, as occurs in some paints when they dry. Soft pastels do not allow for much detail; they force the user to work boldly. Blending of strokes with fingers or a paper stump made for the purpose produces a soft blur that lightly mixes the colors. Pastels yield the most exciting results when not overworked.

4.17 Georges Pierre Seurat.
L'Echo. Study for *Une Baignade, Asnières.*
1883–1884. Black conté crayon on Michallet paper.
31.2 × 24 cm (12⅚″ × 9⅞″).
Bequest of Edith Malvina K. Wetmore. Yale University Art Gallery, New
Haven, Connecticut, USA.

Conté crayon is made from graphite that is mixed with clay and pressed into sticks. It can produce varied lines or broad strokes that resist smudging far more than charcoal. Wax-based crayons, such as those given to children, are avoided by serious artists; they lack flexibility, and most fade over time. Because the strokes do not blend easily, it is difficult to obtain bright color mixtures with wax crayons.

Georges Seurat used conté crayon to build up the illusion of three-dimensional form through value gradations (**chiaroscuro**) in his drawing *L'Echo*. Seurat actually drew a multitude of lines, yet in the final drawing the individual lines are

Venetian portraitist Rosalba Carriera made dozens of works with pastels in the early eighteenth century. Her *Portrait of a Girl with a Bussolà* shows her sensitivity to the medium. The hard, fine-grained pastels in common use at that time give the finished work a smooth surface that makes possible fine color shadings. Because of the artist's light, deft touch with short strokes of the pastel, the work resembles an oil painting in its appearance, an effect promoted by the very smooth paper.

French artist Edgar Degas shifted from oil painting to pastels in his later years, and occasionally he combined the two. He took advantage of the rich strokes of color and subtle blends possible with pastel. Although carefully constructed, his compositions look like casual, fleeting glimpses of everyday life. In *Le Petit Déjeuner après le Bain* (*Breakfast after the Bath*), bold contours give a sense of movement to the whole design.

Liquid Media

Black and brown inks are the most common drawing liquids. Some brush drawings are made with **washes** of ink thinned with water. Such ink drawings are similar to watercolor paintings. Felt- and fiber-tipped pens are widely used recent additions to the traditional pen-and-ink media.

4.19 Edgar Degas.
Le Petit Déjeuner après le Bain (Jeune Femme S'Essuyant). c. 1894. Pastel on paper. 99.7 × 59.7 cm.
© 2002. Courtesy Christie's Images, New York.

4.18 Rosalba Carriera.
Portrait of a Girl with a Bussolà. 1725–1730.
Pastel on paper. 13⅜″ × 10½″.
Cameraphoto/Art Resource, N.Y.

4.20 Vincent van Gogh.
The Fountain in the Hospital Garden. 1889.
Pen and ink. 18⅞″ × 17¾″.
Amsterdam, Van Gogh Museum
(Vincent van Gogh Foundation).

In *The Fountain in the Hospital Garden*, van Gogh used a Japanese bamboo pen and ink for his vigorous lines, varying the darkness of lines by using both full strength and diluted ink. Rhythmic line groups suggest the play of light and shadow on the various surfaces.

Nancy Spero used mostly liquid media to make drawings that she considered finished works. One of these is *Peace*, a protest against the Vietnam war made at the height of that conflict. She used black ink and white **gouache**, a type of opaque watercolor, to sketch a jubilant figure standing on a flattened helicopter. She smudged the ink around the figure before it dried, creating an aura. The quick execution and casual composition of this work reveal its exuberant, impulsive force.

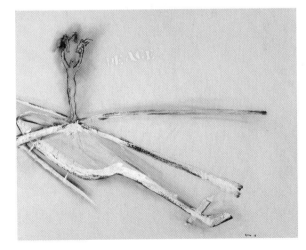

4.21 Nancy Spero.
Peace. 1968.
Gouache and ink on paper. 19″ × 23¾″.
©The Estate of Nancy Spero. Courtesy Galerie Lelong, New York.

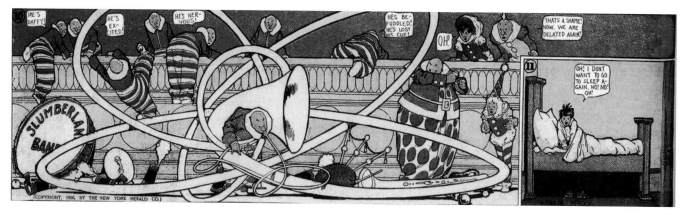

4.22 Windsor McCay.
Little Nemo in Slumberland (detail).
New York Herald, 4 April 1906.

GRAPHIC NOVELS/COMICS

A comic is a sequential art form based on drawing. Comics have been a popular feature in newspapers since the early twentieth century. One of the most imaginative of these was *Little Nemo in Slumberland*, which narrated and illustrated a child's fantastic

4.23 Gilbert Hernandez.
Cover of *Fear of Comics.* 2000.
Courtesy Fantagraphics Books. © Gilbert Hernandez, 2007.

dreams. In our example a tuba player loses control of his instrument as it lengthens with every note that he plays.

In recent years, comics have become a much more serious art form, as their creators take up unusual or important subjects. Because of the serial nature of comics, showing a complete work is difficult. A complete, if brief, work by Gary Panter is illustrated on page 35.

Los Angeles-based Gilbert Hernandez drew highly imaginative short stories that were collected into the anthology *Fear of Comics* in 2000. These stories show a wide range of characters and themes (not all of them printable in a book such as this). In one story, for example, a handicapped Mexican laborer gains wisdom from conversing with trees. Another takes Herman Melville's classic novel *Moby Dick* and boils it down to six crisply drawn frames. In another, a wind-up ballerina doll and a jack-in-the-box argue about the meaning of life. All the stories, drawn in the artist's concise and ironic style, could help any reader get over a *Fear of Comics.*

The increasing acceptance of graphic novels has led major publishers to seek out artists and produce their work in book form for national distribution. Among the most successful of these was *Persepolis* by Marjane Satrapi, a story of a girl growing up in a progressive family in Tehran, Iran, in the years surrounding the Iranian revolution of 1979. The bold and simple drawing style parallels the crystal-clear narration of an intelligent young person. In the present frame (published first in France), we see the artist reflecting with regret on how the revolutionary fundamentalist regime justified its existence with the Iran–Iraq war, thereby wasting a million lives. Through it all, we see not only the artist's uneasiness under the new regime, but also her love for her country. "Iran is my mother," she once told an interviewer, "My mother, whether she's crazy or not, I would die for her; no matter what, she is my mother."

She could have written *Persepolis* as a narrative without pictures, but for Satrapi as for other graphic novelists, combining word and drawn image adds to the power of each. She said, "Images are a way of writing. When you have the talent to be able to write and to draw it seems a shame to choose one. I think it's better to do both."[6]

CONTEMPORARY APPROACHES

Today's artists have considerably expanded the definitions and uses of drawing. Many use it in combination with other media in finished works. Some artists create works in new ways using new media and label them drawings because no other name quite describes what they do. Julie Mehretu, for example, uses media from both drawing and painting in the same large works. Her *Back to Gondwanaland* from 2000 includes colored swatches of cut paper along with drawn ink lines. She makes abstract drawings, but the shapes she uses generally suggest the impersonal public spaces of today's mass-produced world: offices, classrooms, airports, and stadiums. If drawing has been traditionally an organic process, her works do not look entirely handmade. Rather, they exist in a gap between the natural and the manufactured.

4.24 Marjane Satrapi.
Page from *Persepolis*. 2001.
L'association, Paris.

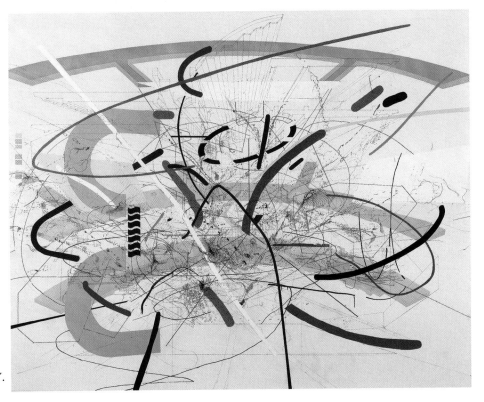

4.25 Julie Mehretu.
Back to Gondwanaland. 2000.
Ink and acrylic on canvas. 8″ × 10″.
Collection A & J Gordts-Vanthournout, Belgium.

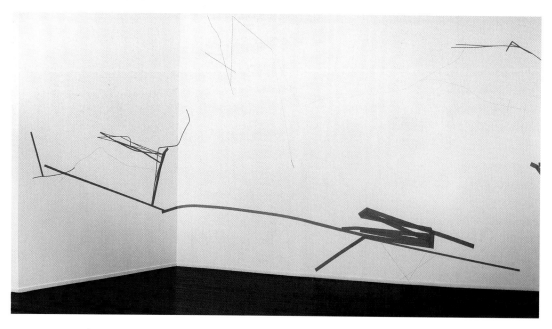

4.26 Christine Hiebert. *Wall Drawing* (Detail). 2004. Margarete Roeder Gallery, New York. Blue adhesive tape on wall, full drawing; running wall length 36'7", wall height 11'6".
Courtesy of the artist.

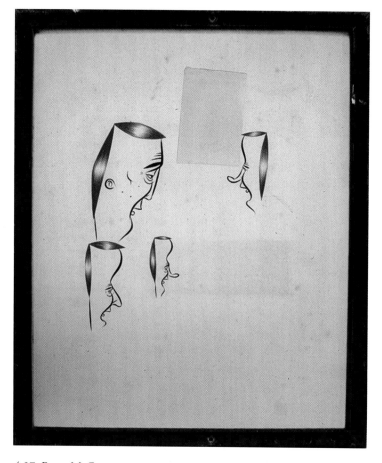

4.27 Barry McGee. *Untitled*. 2006. Ink on found paper in found frame. 10¾" × 8¾".
Gallery Paule Anglim, San Francisco.

Christine Hiebert makes lines directly on walls with the blue tape that painters use to mask negative spaces. In works that she creates specifically for each exhibition, her lines affect our perception of the space. In her work, *Wall Drawing*, from 2004, for example, she interrupted the clean horizontals and verticals of a gallery with diagonals of varying thickness. Her lines resemble drawn lines, but in fact she has "drawn" the tape across the walls. When the show is over, the tape comes off without leaving a trace.

Barry McGee takes drawing out of the realm of "fine art" and brings it to everyone's level. He made his 2006 *Untitled* work using pens bought at a drug store, "The same pens everyone has on the dashboard of their cars or in the office," he said. The four heads resemble doodles that we might make while talking on the phone or waiting in line. He used paper that he found in a dumpster, and a frame bought at a thrift store. He creates these works in bursts of 20 to 30 and then exhibits them in overlapping constellations, casually nailed to the wall. The work thus embodies an unpretentious "street art" style similar to the graffiti that he also makes. We will consider works by other street artists in Chapter 25.

PRACTICE MORE: Get flashcards for images and terms and review chapter material with quizzes at **www.myartslab.com**

SEE MORE: To see a video interview with Christine Hiebert, go to **www.myartslab.com**

PAINTING

For many people in the Western world, the word "art" means painting. The long, rich history of painting, the strong appeal of color, and the endless image-making possibilities have made painting a preferred medium for both artists and viewers for centuries.

Drawing is often a natural prelude to painting, and painting is often drawing with paint. In Gerhard Richter's *Abstract Painting* (on the following page), the medium (paint) and the process of its application are a major part of the message. Richter's invented landscape suggests rugged forms in the foreground and an open, distant sky. Large brushstrokes of thickly applied oil paint contrast with the smooth gradations of paint in the sky area.

Painting far predates human history. The people who made the earliest cave paintings used natural pigments obtained from plants and nearby deposits of minerals and clays. Pigments used in cave paintings at Pont d'Arc, France—including blacks from charred woods and earth colors—have lasted more than 30,000 years.

By Rembrandt's time, the seventeenth century, painters or their assistants mixed finely ground pigments with oil by hand until the paint reached a desirable fineness and consistency. Today high-quality paints are conveniently packaged in tubes or jars, ready for immediate use.

INGREDIENTS AND SURFACES

All paints consist of three ingredients: **pigment**, **binder**, and **vehicle**. The pigment provides color, usually in the form of a powder. Pigment colors must be stable while drying and resist fading over time. Ground minerals and dried plant juices were the most common pigment sources in ancient times. More exotic pigments have included powdered animal urine and even dried insect blood. In the nineteenth and twentieth centuries, major advances in the chemical industry made it possible to produce synthetic pigments that extend the available range of stable colors. Since then, the durability of both natural and synthetic pigments has improved. Most of the same pigments are used in manufacturing the various painting and drawing media.

The binder is a sticky substance that holds the pigment particles together and attaches the pigment to the surface. Binders vary with the type of paint: Oil paint, for example, contains linseed oil as a binder, while traditional tempera uses egg yolk.

The vehicle makes the paint a liquid, and can be added to the paint for thinning. In traditional oil paint, turpentine is the vehicle; watercolors, of course, use water.

HEAR MORE: Listen to an audio file of your chapter at **www.myartslab.com**

5.1 Gerhard Richter.
Abstract Painting (551–4). 1984.
Oil on canvas. 17″ × 23⅝″.
© Gerhard Richter.

Paint surfaces require a **support**, or structure to hold them. Wood panel, stretched canvas, and paper are common supports. Many of these supports require sealing, to limit their absorptive qualities and to smooth them. Such sealing is usually called **size** or **sizing**, and is generally made from liquid clay, wax, or glue. Wood and canvas usually require sizing, while paper used for watercolor generally does not. Atop the sizing (or instead of it), artists often apply a **primer** in order to create a uniform surface. Primers are generally white. The sizing plus the primer equals the **ground** of a painting, and constitutes the surface preparation that artists generally do.

Each type of paint has unique characteristics, advantages, and disadvantages. In the remainder of this chapter, we will consider the most common types, beginning with the simplest.

WATERCOLOR

In **watercolor**, pigments are mixed with water as a vehicle and gum arabic (sap from the acacia tree) as a binder. The most common support is white rag paper (made from cotton rag), because of its superior absorbency and long-lasting qualities. Such paper requires neither sizing nor priming; the paper itself is both the ground and support. Watercolor was traditionally sold in solid blocks that the painter mixed with water to reach the desired thickness; today most professional watercolor is sold in tubes.

Watercolor is basically a staining technique. The paint is applied in thin, translucent washes that allow light to pass through the layers of color and to reflect back from the white paper. Highlights are obtained by leaving areas of white paper unpainted.

EXPLORE MORE: To see a studio video about watercolor technique, go to **www.myartslab.com**

Opaque (nontranslucent) watercolor is sometimes added for detail. Watercolors are well suited to spontaneous as well as carefully planned applications. Despite the simple materials involved, watercolor is a demanding medium because it does not permit easy changes or corrections. If you overwork a watercolor, you lose its characteristic freshness.

Watercolor's fluid spontaneity makes it a favorite medium for painters who want to catch quick impressions outdoors. The translucent quality of watercolor washes particularly suits depictions of water, atmosphere, light, and weather.

American artist Winslow Homer was one of the best watercolorists. In *Sloop, Nassau*, Homer used the bright whiteness of the bare paper to form the highlights of ocean waves, boat, and sails. From light pencil lines to finished painting, his whole process is visible. Homer captured the mood of weather—in this case, the particular qualities of light and color in the calm just before a storm. For Homer, a keen observer of nature, a quick impression made with watercolor was visually stronger than a painting filled with carefully rendered details.

Homer's spontaneous technique was well suited to watercolor; because it dries so quickly, watercolor does not allow for easy changes if the artist makes a mistake or decides to alter the composition.

Opaque watercolor (also called **gouache**) has been widely used for centuries. It was common in book illustration during the European Middle Ages, and also in traditional Persian art (see Chapter 18 for an example). Gouache is like watercolor except that the vehicle includes small amounts of fine chalk powder that make it opaque. It is popular in our times with designers and illustrators because of its ease of use and low cost. Jacob Lawrence used

5.2 Winslow Homer.
Sloop, Nassau. 1899.
Watercolor and graphite on off-white wove paper. 14⅞″ × 21⅞₆″ (37.8 × 54.3 cm).
The Metropolitan Museum of Art, New York, NY. Image copyright © The Metropolitan Museum of Art. Art Resource, NY.

5.3 Zhang Daqian.
Hidden Valley, After Guo Xi. 1962. Ink and color on paper. 76¼" × 40⅛".
Arthur M. Sackler Gallery, Smithsonian Institution, Washington D.C.: Gift of the Arthur M. Sackler Foundation, S1999.119.

TEMPERA AND ENCAUSTIC

Tempera was used by the ancient Egyptians, Greeks, and Romans. Artists perfected it during the Middle Ages, when it was used for small paintings on wood panels. Most traditional tempera use egg yolk as a binder, mixed in equal parts with pigment powder and then thinned with water. Tempera is little used today, and as a result the word has changed its meaning. Today, the word "tempera" is often used for the water-based paints such as poster paints or paints with binders of glue or **casein** (milk protein).

Traditional egg tempera has a luminous, slightly matte (not shiny) surface when dry. Because it cannot be mixed after it is applied, artists generally apply tempera in thin layers to build up desired shades of color. The preferred ground for egg tempera is **gesso**, a chalky, water-based liquid that dries to a bright white.

Egg tempera is good for achieving sharp lines and precise details, and it does not darken with age. However, its colors change during drying, and blending and reworking are difficult because tempera dries rapidly. Traditional tempera painting requires complete preliminary drawing and pale underpainting because of its translucency and the difficulty in making changes. Overpainting consists of applying layers of translucent paint in small, careful strokes. Because tempera lacks flexibility, movement of the support may cause the gesso and pigment to crack. Thus, a rigid support, such as a wood panel, is required.

In *Madonna and Child*, Filippo Lippi methodically built up thin layers of color, creating a smooth, almost luminous surface. Tempera is well suited for depicting translucencies such as those he created in the halo and the sheer neck scarf. His naturalistic yet poetic portrayal brought a worldly dimension to religious subject matter.

Like egg tempera, **encaustic** is little used today, though it too was popular in the ancient world. Pigments are dissolved in a binder of molten beeswax; there is no vehicle, as the wax is sufficiently fluid. Encaustic creates cumbersome work-

gouache to good advantage in his work *Going Home* (see page 60). Here we see the typical opaque appearance of the colors.

In traditional Chinese watercolor technique, the artist employs water-based black ink as well as color, and often uses the ink without color. The Chinese regard painting as descended from the art of calligraphy, which is also done with black ink. In Asia, black ink painting is a fully developed art form, accorded at least as much honor as painting with color.

A modern Chinese artist who updated the ancient traditions was Zhang Daqian, and we see his skillful use of water-based media in *Hidden Valley, After Guo Xi.* Zhang used black ink for outlining, for trees, and for the darkest areas of this large landscape painting, which is over six feet tall. Opaque watercolors gave the earthy tones for the rocks, and the red accents near the base. This work borrows the dramatic style of Guo Xi, an important artist from the 12th century.

5.4 Filippo Lippi.
Madonna and Child. c. 1440–1445.
Tempera on panel. .797 × .511 cm (31⅜″ × 20⅛″).
Samuel H. Kress Collection, Photograph © 2001 Board of Trustees, National Gallery of Art, Washington. 1939.1.290.(401)/PA.

ing conditions for artists because the paint must be kept hot during application. The resulting colors have a deep, resonant glow, however.

We see encaustic to good advantage in the work of the San Francisco-based painter Anne Appleby. Her two-panel work *Mother E* shows some of the translucency of wax in the deep colors that she achieves. This work evokes the blue of sky and the green of earth. Another modern artist who used encaustic was Jasper Johns, whose *Target with Four Faces* is pictured in Chapter 23.

OIL

In Western art, oil paint has been a favorite medium for five centuries. Pigments mixed with various vegetable oils, such as linseed, walnut, and poppyseed, were used in the Middle Ages for decorative purposes, but not until the fifteenth century did Flemish painters fully develop the use of paint made with linseed oil pressed from the seeds of the flax plant. In this early period, artists applied oil paint to wood panels covered with smooth layers of gesso, as in the older tradition of tempera painting.

The brothers Hubert and Jan van Eyck are credited with developing oil painting techniques and bringing them to their first perfection. They achieved glowing, jewel-like surfaces that remain amazingly fresh to the present day.

5.5 Anne Appleby.
Mother E. 2009.
Encaustic on canvas. Each panel, 72″ × 34″.
Gallery Paule Anglim.

5.6 Jan van Eyck.
*Madonna and Child with the
Chancellor Rolin.*
c. 1433–1434.
Oil and tempera on panel.
66 × 62 cm.
Louvre, Paris, France. Copyright Erich
Lessing/Art Resource, NY.

Jan van Eyck's *Madonna and Child with the Chancellor Rolin* is an example of his early mastery of the oil technique. Jan painted it on a small gesso-covered wood panel. After beginning with a brush drawing in tempera, he proceeded with thin layers of oil paint, moving from light to dark and from opaque to translucent colors. The luminous quality of the surface is the result of successive oil glazes. A **glaze** is a very thin, transparent film of color applied over a previously painted surface. To produce glazes, oil colors selected for their transparency are diluted with a mixture of oil and varnish. Glazes give depth to painted surfaces by allowing light to pass through and reflect from lower paint layers.

Here the sparkling jewels, the textiles, and the furs each show their own refined textures. Within the context of the religious subject, the artist demonstrated his enthusiasm for the delights of the visible world. Veils of glazes in the sky area provide atmospheric perspective and thus contribute to the illusion of deep space in the enticing view beyond the open window. The evolution in the new oil painting technique made such realism possible.

Oil has many advantages over other traditional media. Compared to tempera, oil paint can provide both increased opacity—which yields better covering power—and, when thinned, greater transparency. Its slow drying time is a distinct advantage, allowing artists to blend strokes of color and make changes during the painting process. Pigment colors in oil change little when drying; however, the binder (usually linseed oil) has a tendency to darken and yellow slightly with age. Because layers of dried oil paint are flexible, sixteenth-century Venetian painters who wished to paint large pictures could replace heavy wood panels with canvas stretched on wood frames. A painted canvas not only is light in weight but also can be unstretched and rolled for transporting. Most oil painters today still prefer canvas supports.

5.7 Rembrandt van Rijn.
Detail from *Self-Portrait.* 1663.
Oil on canvas. Full painting 45″ × 38″.
Kenwood House The Iveagh Bequest, © English Heritage Photo Library.

Oil can be applied thickly or thinly, wet onto wet or wet onto dry. When applied thickly, it is called **impasto** (only oil paint has this capacity). When a work is painted wet into wet and completed at one sitting, the process is called the direct painting method.

Rembrandt used this method in his *Self-Portrait.* The detail here shows how the impasto of light and dark paint both defines a solid-looking head and presents the incredible richness of Rembrandt's brushwork.

In Rembrandt's *Self-Portrait* and in Frank Auerbach's *Head of Michael Podro,* we see the artists' responsiveness to both the reality of their subjects and the physical nature of paint. Because the thick, paste-like quality of oil paint is celebrated rather than hidden, viewers participate in the process of conjuring up images when viewing Rembrandt's rough strokes and Auerbach's smears and globs of paint. Both paintings project strong images when seen at a distance and show rich tactile surfaces when viewed close up.

The wide range of approaches possible with oil paint becomes apparent when we compare Jan van Eyck's subtly glazed colors with the impasto surfaces of Rembrandt and Auerbach.

EXPLORE MORE: To see a studio video about oil painting technique, go to **www.myartslab.com**

5.8 Frank Auerbach.
Head of Michael Podro. 1981.
Oil on board. 13″ × 11″.
Marlborough Fine Art, Ltd., London.

5.9 Joan Mitchell.
Border. 1989.
Oil on canvas. 45½″ × 35″.
© The Estate of Joan Mitchell. Courtesy Robert Miller Gallery.

In one sense, the story of painting is about the visual magic that people around the world have been able to conjure up with various paint media.

Joan Mitchell used oil paint to spontaneously recreate emotional states in abstract visual form. *Border* is painted very loosely in a complex mix of rich, sensuous colors. The composition is subtly symmetrical (note the light vertical green stripe near the top center), and colors are applied with a combination of care and abandon. To arrive at the bright and lush yellows, blues, greens, and reds, the artist avoided overmixing her colors. The varying textures of the work show spontaneous, expressive execution. She made the yellow strokes with a dry brush; she allowed some of the blues to run; reds give accents at carefully selected points. We can actually follow the creation of this work, layer by layer and color by color, as we look at this embodiment of a warm, even excited, mood.

Some contemporary artists use oil in ways that show the influence of digital arts and animation. Inka Essenhigh's 2003 work *Escape Pod*, for example, resembles a still from an animated science fiction film. The work's title refers to the small craft that space travelers use in case of disaster, and some kind of accident seems to have happened here. The slick surfaces and subtle gradations of tone in this work make good use of the characteristics of oil paint. Digital painting applications have found little favor with contemporary painters; they generally prefer to manipulate colors directly.

5.10 Inka Essenhigh.
Escape Pod. 2003.
Oil on canvas. 50″ × 50″.
Courtesy 303 Gallery, New York.

ACRYLIC

Many artists today use **acrylic** paint, an invention of the late twentieth century. The binder that holds the pigment is acrylic polymer, a synthetic resin which provides a fast-drying, flexible film. The vehicle is water. These relatively permanent paints can be applied to a wider variety of surfaces than traditional painting media. Because the acrylic resin binder is transparent, colors can maintain a high degree of intensity. Unlike oils, acrylics rarely darken or yellow with age. Their rapid drying time restricts blending and limits reworking, but it greatly reduces the time involved in layering processes such as glazing. Water thinning is also more convenient in the studio than the volatile and toxic turpentine of oil paint.

Acrylics work well when paint is applied quickly with little blending, as we see in the splash in David Hockney's painting *A Bigger Splash*. Acrylic also works well when it is brushed on in flat areas, as in the sky at the top. The strong contrast between the dramatic freedom of the paint application of the splash and the thinly painted, geometric shapes of house, chair, pool rim, and diving board gives lively energy to the suburban scene.

In recent years many painters have used **airbrushes** to apply acrylics and other types of paint. An airbrush is a small-scale paint sprayer capable of projecting a fine, controlled mist of paint. It provides an even paint application without the personal touch of individual brush strokes, and it is therefore well suited to the subtle gradations of color values found in many paintings of the 1960s and 1970s, such as Audrey Flack's *Wheel of Fortune*. Graffiti artists, of course, also favor airbrushes or spray cans because of the quickness of execution.

5.11 David Hockney.
A Bigger Splash. 1967.
Acrylic on canvas. 96″ × 96″.
© David Hockney
Photo: Tate, London/Art Resource, NY.

5.12 Audrey Flack.
Wheel of Fortune. 1977–1978.
Oil over acrylic on canvas. 96″ × 96″.
Louis K. Meisel Gallery, New York.

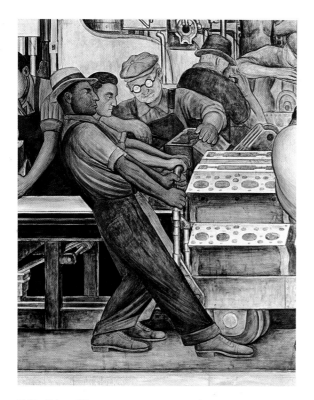

5.13 Diego Rivera.
Detail from *Detroit Industry.* 1932–1933.
Fresco.
The Detroit Institute of Arts. Gift of Edsel B. Ford/The Bridgeman Art Library/© Banco de Mexico Diego Rivera & Frida Kahlo Museums Trust, Mexico, D.F. / Artists Rights Society (ARS), New York.

FRESCO

True **fresco**, or *buon fresco*, is an ancient wall-painting technique in which very finely ground pigments suspended in water are applied to a damp lime-plaster surface. The vehicle is water, and the binder is the lime already present in the damp plaster. Most fresco painters prepare a full-size drawing called a cartoon first, then transfer the design to the freshly laid plaster wall before painting. Because the plaster dries quickly, only the portion of the wall that can be painted in one day is prepared; joints are usually arranged along the edges of major shapes in the composition.

The painter works quickly in a rapid staining process similar to watercolor. Lime, in contact with air, forms transparent calcium crystals that chemically bind the pigment to the moist lime-plaster wall. The lime in the plaster thus becomes the binder, creating a smooth, extremely durable surface. Once the surface has dried, the painting is part of the wall. Notice the texture of the plaster in the detail from Diego Rivera's *Detroit Industry.* Completion of the chemical reaction occurs slowly, deepening and enriching the colors as the fresco ages. Colors reach their greatest intensity fifty to one hundred years after a fresco is painted, yet the hues always have a muted quality.

The artist must have the design completely worked out before painting, because no changes can be made after the paint is applied to the fresh plaster. It may take twelve to fourteen straight hours of work just to complete two square yards of a fresco painting. Fresco technique does not permit the delicate manipulation of transitional tones; but the luminous color, fine surface, and permanent color make it an ideal medium for large murals. (A mural is any wall-sized painting; fresco is one possible medium for such a work.)

Fresco secco (dry fresco), another ancient wall-painting method, is done on finished, dried lime-plaster walls. With this technique, tempera paint is applied to a clean, dry surface or over an already dried true fresco to achieve greater color intensity than is possible with true fresco alone. Fresco painters often retouch their work, or put on finishing details, in fresco secco over the true fresco.

Fresco has been used in Asian and Western cultures for at least four thousand years. In Renaissance Italy it was the favored medium for painting on church walls. Probably the best known fresco paintings are those by Michelangelo on the Sistine Chapel ceiling in the Vatican in Rome. After the Renaissance and Baroque periods, fresco became less popular, eclipsed by the more flexible oil medium. However,

5.14 Diego Rivera.
   Mural depicting *Detroit Industry*. 1932–1933.
   Fresco.
   The Detroit Institute of Arts. Gift of Edsel B. Ford/The Bridgeman Art Library/© Banco de Mexico Diego Rivera & Frida Kahlo Museums Trust/Artists Rights Society (ARS), NY. Av. Cinco de Mayo No. 2, Col. Centro, Del. Cuauhtemoc 06059, Mexico, D.F. Reproduction authorized by the Instituto Nacional de Bellas Artes y Literatura.

a revival of the fresco technique began in Mexico in the 1920s, encouraged by the new revolutionary government's support for public murals.

By leading the revival in fresco mural painting for public buildings, Diego Rivera broke away from the limited studio and gallery audience and made art a part of the life of the people. His style blends European and native art traditions with contemporary subject matter. He created *Detroit Industry* in the lobby of the Detroit Institute of Arts.

PRACTICE MORE: Get flashcards for images and terms and review chapter material with quizzes at **www.myartslab.com**

THE WORLD'S LARGEST painting is fourteen feet high and stretches for a half mile along the side wall of a drainage ditch in the San Fernando Valley. Not able to take it in all at once, viewers must contemplate it from a bike path or through the windows of their passing cars. This colossal project is the brainchild of Judy Baca, who for thirty years has combined art with community activism.

She was inspired by the mural paintings of Mexican artists of the 1920s and 1930s, who decorated public buildings with scenes of their country's history and life. They showed through their work how art could become, rather than a luxurious private possession, a vehicle of community awareness and empowerment.

The Great Wall presents a sweeping panorama of the history of California. Beginning with the Native American cultures of the area, it continues with the Roman Catholic missions and moves on to the Anglicization of the state when it became part of the United States with the Treaty of Guadalupe Hidalgo in 1848. The twentieth-century section includes the Dust Bowl migrants of the 1930s, the dawn of the movie and aviation industries, and the impact of World War II.

Many parts of the mural highlight histories that are often left untold. One panel tells graphically how the building of Dodger Stadium in 1962 dislodged a

5.15 Judith F. Baca.
View of *Great Wall of Los Angeles.* 1976–1983.
Social and Public Art Resource Center.

Mexican-American neighborhood. Another depicts the forced incarceration of Japanese Americans in "relocation" camps after the Pearl Harbor attack that started World War II in the Pacific. A third deals with the blacklisting of dozens of Hollywood writers for suspected Communist affiliations during the height of the Cold War. *The Great Wall*'s size parallels its expansive, inclusive vision of the history of California.

Getting it done was a monumental task. She recruited hundreds of young people from troubled communities over a period of seven summers. Many of the Mural Makers were former gang members, juvenile delin-

quents, or ex-offenders on parole; painting the mural was their first job. She organized the workers into crews, taking care that each unit was multi-ethnic. The mural's impact on the lives of those who painted it is well documented. Many disadvantaged youths got needed job skills. Social service referrals to counseling or drug treatment were readily available. For the first time, hundreds learned of their history and how

it related to the state as a whole. One participant recalled, "After my first year on the mural, I left with a sense of who I was and what I could do that was unlike anything I'd ever felt before."[1]

SEE MORE: To see a video with several views of the *Great Wall*, go to **www.myartslab.com**

PRINTMAKING

IF A WORK OF ART EXISTS IN MULTIPLE COPIES, IS IT STILL ART?

WHY DO ARTISTS MAKE PRINTS, WHEN THEY CAN SELL PAINTINGS FOR MORE MONEY?

HOW ARE TODAY'S ARTISTS VARYING THE TRADITIONAL TECHNIQUES?

The first thing we might notice about the print *Quiver* is its layering of images. A framed dragonfly hovers in a yellow-green square; a negative picture of a radio telescope seems to overlay a closer view of a similar device. At the base of all is a pattern of gray-green branches, silhouetted as if on a forest floor. Note that each layer has its color: gray, blue, brown, black, green. Overall, the work seems a meditation on fragile structures, which might *Quiver* in a strong wind.

This layering of images resembles in some ways the process of memory: Each of our memories inhabits a layer of our minds, and each probably has its "color" of feeling or association. Such are the goals of the artist, who said that she tries to make "visual poems." It's no mistake that she chose a print to realize this vision because this type of layering is a technique uniquely suited to printmaking.

In the visual arts, a **print** is a multiple work of art, a series of nearly identical pieces, usually printed on paper. Prints are made from a **matrix**, which an artist may create of metal, wood, or stone. The artist supervises the printing of a group of images from the same matrix, usually called an **edition**.

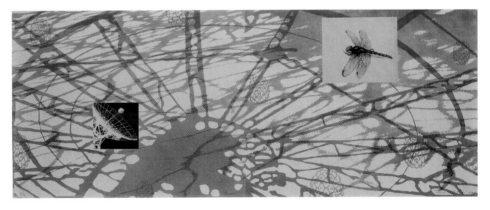

6.1 Tanja Softic.
Quiver. 2008.
Lithograph. 20″ × 52″.
University of Richmond.

Nearly all original prints are numbered to indicate the total number of prints pulled, or printed, in the edition, and to give the number of each print in the sequence. The figure 6/50 on a print, for example, would indicate that it was the sixth print pulled from an edition of fifty.

As part of the printmaking process, artists make prints called progressive proofs at various

HEAR MORE: Listen to an audio file of your chapter at **www.myartslab.com**

stages to see how the image on the matrix is developing. When a satisfactory stage is reached, the artist makes a few prints for his or her record and personal use. These are marked AP, meaning **artist's proof**.

One of the best definitions of an original print comes from artist June Wayne: "It is a work of art, usually on paper, which has siblings . . . They all look alike, they were all made at the same time from the same matrix, the same creative impulse, and they are all originals. The fact that there are many of them is irrelevant."[1] Artists generally make prints for one or more of these reasons:

- They wish to make multiple works that are less expensive than paintings or sculpture, so that their work will be available for purchase by a wider group of viewers.
- They may wish to influence social causes. Because prints are multiple works, they are easy to distribute far more widely than a unique work of art.
- They may be fascinated by the process of printmaking, which is an absorbing craft in itself.

In this chapter we will discuss various methods of printmaking, noting unique characteristics of each. Traditionally, these methods are divided into four basic categories: relief, intaglio, lithography, and stencil. In our time, artists are using the old methods in new ways, sometimes combining them with digital techniques; we will consider some of these new directions at the end of this chapter.

RELIEF

We already know what a **relief** print is, if we think of how fingerprints, rubber stamps, and wet tires leave their marks. In a relief process, the printmaker cuts away all parts of the printing surface not meant to carry ink, leaving the design "in relief" at the level of the original surface (see the *Relief* diagram on page 109). The surface is then inked, and the ink is transferred to paper with pressure.

The oldest relief prints are **woodcuts**. The woodcut process lends itself to designs with bold black-and-white contrast. The image-bearing block of (usually soft) wood is a plank cut along the grain. Because the woodcut medium does not easily yield shades of color, artists who use it are generally drawn by the challenge of working in black and white only. Others use woodcut because they enjoy the feel of carving a fresh block of wood. Woodcut editions are limited to a couple of hundred because the relief edges begin to deteriorate with repeated pressure.

The woodcut technique originated in China, where the desire to spread the Buddhist religion greatly influenced the type of prints produced. *The Diamond Sutra* is one of the world's oldest surviving documents. It opens with a woodblock print of the Buddha, surrounded by attendants and guardians,

6.2 Section of *The Diamond Sutra.*
Chinese Buddhist text, 868.
Scroll, woodblock print on paper.
Length of entire scroll 18′.
By permission of The British Library. OR.8210f2.

6.3 Katsushika Hokusai.
The Wave. c. 1830.
Color woodblock print.
10¼" × 15⅛".
Private Collection. Copyright Art
Resource, NY.

preaching to an old man seen in the lower left. (The swastika on the Buddha's chest is an ancient symbol of his enlightenment.) An inscription states that it was made in 868 for free distribution, an apparent act of religious goodwill. The relatively hard wood of this early print makes possible the many fine lines in the design, which is similar in style to stone carvings from the same time period. This scroll is in excellent condition despite its age, because it was hidden in a dry cave for many centuries.

Woodblock printing flourished in Japan in the seventeenth through the nineteenth centuries. Japanese woodblock prints were made through a complex process that used multiple blocks to achieve subtle and highly integrated color effects. Because they were much cheaper than paintings, these prints were the preferred art form for middle-class people who lived in the capital city of Edo (now known as Tokyo). Their subject matter included famous theater actors, nightlife, landscapes, and even erotic pictures. Japanese prints were among the first objects of Asian art to find favor among European artists, and

many Impressionist and Post-Impressionist painters were strongly influenced by them.

Color woodcuts are usually printed with multiple woodblocks. As with most printmaking techniques, when more than one color is used, individually inked blocks—one for each color—are carefully **registered** (lined up) to ensure that colors will be exactly placed in the final print.

Japanese artist Hokusai made some of the world's best color woodcuts. Hokusai worked in close collaboration with highly skilled carvers to realize the final prints. For each of his woodcuts, specialists transferred Hokusai's watercolor brush painting to as many as twenty blocks, cut the blocks, and then inked each one with a separate color. In Hokusai's print *The Wave*, a clawing mountain of water threatens tiny fishermen in their boats. The rhythmic curves of the churning sea even dwarf Mount Fuji, which nonetheless stands firm in the distance. This print is from a series of Hokusai's "Thirty-Six Views of Mount Fuji" seen from various locations.

it also makes large editions possible, facilitating the use of wood engraving in publishing.

One of the best wood engravers was the American artist Rockwell Kent, who made *Workers of the World, Unite* in 1937. We see here the fine detail in the body and the background cloud that the dense wood, placed on end, allows. This work is also an example of socially conscious printmaking, as it shows a farmer defending his territory against encroaching military bayonets. Kent was an agitator throughout his life on behalf of workers of all sorts, and frequently made prints to forward his favorite causes.

The **linoleum cut** is a modern development in relief printing. The artist starts with the rubbery, synthetic surface of linoleum, and just as in woodcut, gouges out the areas not intended to take ink.

6.4 Rockwell Kent.
Workers of the World, Unite. 1937.
Wood engraving. 8″ × 5⅛″.
Fine Arts Museums of San Francisco, Achenbach Foundation for the Graphic Arts. Gift of the American College Society of Print Collectors. 54959. Courtesy of the Plattsburgh State Art Museum, State University of New York, Rockwell Kent Gallery and Collection, Bequest of Sally Kent Gorton.

The detail in Hokusai's print is quite different from the roughness of the woodcut *Prophet* by German artist Emil Nolde. Each cut in this block is expressive of an old man's face, and reveals the character of the wood and the woodcut process. The simplified light-and-dark pattern of the features gives emotional intensity to the image. Nolde's direct approach is part of a long tradition of German printmaking.

A related method that was traditionally used for book illustration is **wood engraving**. In this method, the artist uses very dense wood (often boxwood) set on end rather than sideways. The hardness of the wood requires the use of metal engraving tools, but

6.5 Emil Nolde.
Prophet. 1912.
Woodcut (Schiefler/Mosel 1966 [W] 110.only),
image: .317 × .225 cm (12½″ × 8¹³⁄₁₆″).
Rosenwald Collection. Photograph © Board of Trustees, National Gallery of Art, Washington, D.C. 1943.3.6698.(B-9059)/PR. Stiftung Seebull Ada und Emil Nolde.

Linoleum is softer than wood, has no grain, and can be cut with equal ease in any direction. The softness of the matrix material makes fine detail impossible.

An example of a linoleum cut (or **linocut**) is *Sharecropper* by Elizabeth Catlett, in which the even, white gouges betray the soft material. This work also typifies Catlett's lifelong devotion to creating dignified images of African Americans.

INTAGLIO

Intaglio printing is the opposite of relief: areas below the surface hold the ink (see the *Intaglio* diagram). The word *intaglio* comes from the Italian *intagliare*, "to cut into." The image to be printed is cut or scratched or etched into a metal surface. To make an intaglio print, the printmaker first daubs the plate with printer's ink, then wipes the surface clean, leaving ink only in the etched or grooved portions. Damp paper is then placed on the inked plate, which then passes beneath the press roller. A print is made when the dampened paper picks up the ink in the grooves. The pressure of the roller creates a characteristic plate mark around the edges of the image. Intaglio printing was traditionally done from polished copper plates, but now zinc, steel, aluminum, and even plastic are often used. Engraving and etching are the two principal intaglio processes.

Engraving

To make an **engraving**, the artist cuts lines into the polished surface of a metal plate with a **burin**, or engraving tool. This exacting process takes strength and control. Lines are made by pushing the burin into the metal to carve a groove, removing a narrow strip of metal in the process. A clean line is preferable; thus, any rough edges of the groove must be

6.6 Elizabeth Catlett (Mexican, 1919).
Sharecropper. 1970.
Color linocut on cream Japanese paper. 54.5 × 51.3 cm.
Restricted gift of Mr. and Mrs. Robert S. Hartman. 1992.182 Photograph © 2002 The Art Institute of Chicago. All Rights Reserved. © Elizabeth Catlett/Licensed by VAGA, NY.

smoothed down with a scraper. Engraved lines cannot be freely drawn because of the pressure needed to cut the grooves. Darker areas are shaded with various types of cross-hatching. Thus, a successful engraving requires precise, smooth curves and parallel lines. To see a good example of engraving, look at the United States currency; all of our bills are engravings, made by experts.

EXPLORE MORE: To see a studio video of Intaglio technique, go to **www.myartslab.com**

6.7 *Relief.*

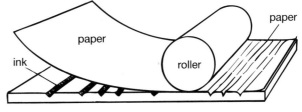

6.8 *Intaglio.*

6.9 Albrecht Dürer (1471–1528).
The Knight, Death and the Devil. 1513. Engraving. Page: 10″ × 7⅞″ (25.5 × 20 cm), Plate 9⅝″ × 7½″
(24.5 × 19 cm).
Brooklyn Museum of Art, Gift of Mrs. Horace Havemeyer. 54.35.6.

6.10 Rembrandt Harmensz van Rijn (1606–1669).
Christ Preaching. c. 1652.
Etching. 6¼" × 8⅛".
The Metropolitan Museum of Art. Bequest of Mrs. H. O. Havemeyer, 1929. The H. O. Havemeyer Collection. (29.107.18). Art Resource, NY.

We can also see the complex richness of engraved lines in Albrecht Dürer's engraving *The Knight, Death, and the Devil,* reproduced close to its actual size at the left. Thousands of fine lines define the shapes, masses, spaces, values, and textures of the depicted objects. The precision of Dürer's lines seems appropriate to the subject—an image of the noble Christian knight moving with resolute commitment, unswayed by the forces of chaos, evil, and death that surround him.

Etching

The process of making an **etching** begins with the preparation of a metal plate. The artist paints the surface of the copper or zinc plate with a coating of either wax or varnish that will resist acid. The artist then draws easily through this ground with a pointed tool, exposing the metal with each stroke.

An etching tool may be as thick as a pen, but is more often closer to a needle. Finally, the plate is immersed in nitric acid. Acid bites into the plate where the drawing has exposed the metal, making a groove that varies in depth according to the strength of the acid and the length of time the plate is in the acid bath.

Because they are more easily produced, etched lines are generally more relaxed or irregular than engraved lines. We can see the difference in line quality between an etching and an engraving— the freedom versus the precision—by comparing the lines in Rembrandt's etching *Christ Preaching* with the lines in Dürer's engraving *The Knight, Death, and the Devil.*

In *Christ Preaching,* Rembrandt's personal understanding of Christ's compassion harmonizes with the decisive yet relaxed quality of the artist's etched lines. This etching shows Rembrandt's typical use of a wide range of values, mostly created through hatching. Skillful use of light and shadow draws attention to the figure of Christ and gives clarity and interest to the whole image. In a composition in which each figure is similar in size, Rembrandt identified Jesus as the key figure by setting him off with a light area below, a light vertical band above, and implied lines of attention leading to him from the faces of his listeners.

Etching yields only lines, but there is a way to create shaded areas in intaglio. **Aquatint** is an etching process used to obtain gray areas in black-and-white or color prints. The artist sprinkles acid-resistant powder on the plate over parts that need a gray tone. When the plate is bathed in acid, the exposed areas between the paint particles are eaten away to produce a rough surface capable of holding ink. Values thus produced can vary from light to dark,

depending on how long the plate is in the acid and how thick the dusting of powder. Because aquatint is not suited to making thin lines, it is usually combined with a linear print process such as engraving or etching. Francisco Goya used such a combination in his print from the series *The Disasters of War* on page 9. Goya achieved the lightly colored sky and some of the shading on the ground by using aquatint along with etched lines.

American artist Mary Cassatt combined a few intaglio techniques in her work *The Letter*. She made the colored areas with aquatint; principal outlines were etched. For the finest lines, she used **drypoint**, an acid-free method in which she simply scratched the metal plate with a diamond-tipped tool, leaving a shallow groove and low ridge that would take the ink. A drypoint ridge (called a **burr**) is fragile, so prints made with drypoint are typically small editions.

LITHOGRAPHY

Etching and engraving date from the fifteenth and sixteenth centuries, respectively, but **lithography** was not developed until early in the nineteenth century.

Lithography is a surface or planographic printing process based on the mutual antipathy of oil and water. Lithography lends itself well to a direct manner of working because the artist draws an image on the surface of the stone or plate, without any cutting. Its directness makes lithography faster and somewhat more flexible than other methods. A lithograph is often difficult to distinguish from a crayon drawing.

Using litho crayons, litho pencils, or a greasy liquid called **tusche**, the artist draws the image on flat, fine-grained Bavarian limestone (or on a metal surface that duplicates its character). After the image is complete, it is chemically treated with

6.11 Mary Cassatt.
The Letter. 1891.
Drypoint, soft ground etching, and aquatint, printed in color. Third state, from a series of ten. H: 13⅜″ × 8¹⁵⁄₁₆″.
The Metropolitan Museum of Art, Gift of Paul J. Sachs, 1916. (16.2.9).
Photograph © 1991 The Metropolitan Museum of Art. Art Resource, NY.

6.12 Honoré Daumier.
Rue Transnonain, April 15, 1834. 1834.
Lithograph. 28.6 × 44 cm.
© The Cleveland Museum of Art, 2001. Gift of Ralph King. 1924.809.

gum arabic and a small amount of acid to "fix" it on the upper layer of the stone. The surface is then dampened with water and is inked. The oil-based ink is repelled by the water in the blank areas, but it adheres to the greasy area of the image. As in other print processes, when the surface is covered with

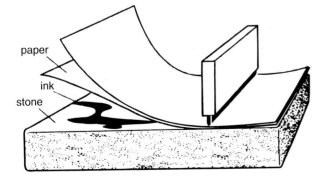

6.13 *Lithography.*

paper and run through a press, the image is transferred to the paper. Because the surface remains intact, lithographic stones or plates can be re-used after cleaning.

Although lithography was a new medium in the early 1800s, it had a major impact on society because prints could be produced quickly and easily. Before the development of modern printing presses, it provided the illustrations for newspapers, posters, and handbills. Honoré Daumier, one of the first great lithographic artists, made his living drawing satirical and documentary lithographs for French newspapers. His personal style was well suited to the direct quality of the lithographic process.

In *Rue Transnonain*, Daumier carefully reconstructed a horrible event that occurred during a period of civil unrest in Paris in 1834. The militia claimed that a shot was fired from a building on

Transnonain Street. Soldiers responded by entering the apartment and killing all the occupants, including many innocent people. Daumier's lithograph of the event was published the following day. The lithograph reflects the artist's feelings, but it also conveys information in the way news photographs and Web sites do today. Rembrandt's influence is evident in the composition of strong light and dark areas that increase the dramatic impact of Daumier's image.

The freedom and directness of lithography made the technique ideal for the spontaneous, witty approach of Henri de Toulouse-Lautrec. In the space of about ten years, this prolific artist created more than three hundred lithographs. Many of them were designed as posters advertising everything from popular nightclub entertainers to bicycles. His posters of cabaret singer and dancer *Jane Avril* made her a star and simultaneously gave Parisians of the 1890s a firsthand look at "modern art" by a leading artist. Toulouse-Lautrec's innovations in lithography, including spatter techniques, large format, and use of vivid color, greatly influenced both lithography and graphic design in the twentieth century.

The popular lithographic poster *Jane Avril* appears to have begun with an awkward photograph and come to life in a dynamic oil sketch. The sketch was then incorporated as the key element in a strong lithograph, drawn with brush and liquid tusche on the litho stone. Compare the angles of the feet and legs in the photograph with those in the sketch. Toulouse-Lautrec used diagonal lines and curves to introduce a sense of motion that is missing from the photograph. In the print he placed Jane Avril in a nightclub setting and balanced her figure with the silhouetted shape of a bass player. A dark line emerging from the bass frames the dancer. Toulouse-Lautrec's strong use of shapes and fluid brush lines retains much of the vigor of the sketch.

Most books that have pictures are today printed with a version of lithography called **offset**. Each page image is burned onto a metal lithographic plate and then inked, but the ink is first transferred, or offset, onto a rubber cylinder before printing on paper. This method, which is suited to rotary presses, gives uniform ink depth across an entire printing. It is used to print this book and many others.

6.15 Henri de Toulouse-Lautrec.
Jane Avril Dansant. c. 1893.
Oil study on cardboard. 38″ × 27″.
Private Collection.

6.14 Henri de Toulouse-Lautrec.
Jane Avril. c. 1893.
Photograph.
Edita S.A.

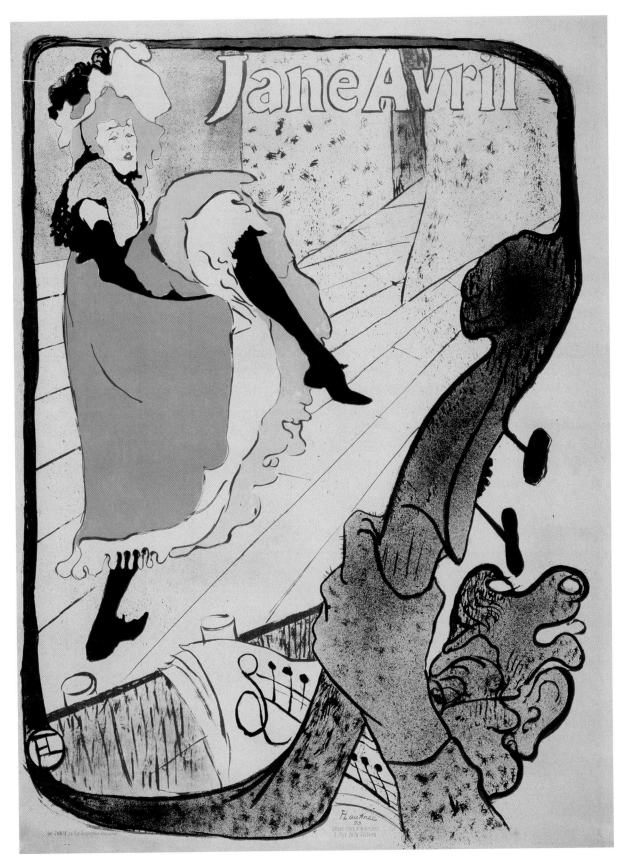

6.16 Henri de Toulouse-Lautrec.
Jane Avril. c. 1893. Poster; lithograph printed in 5 colors. 50⅝" × 37".
Art Resource, N.Y.

STENCIL

In simplest terms, a **stencil** is a sheet with a design cut out of it; painting or spraying over the sheet transfers the design to the picture plane. Stencils are a quick way of making lettering or repeated designs on walls, but here we will consider them as a method for making multiple works of art.

Stencils are a favored method of street artists who communicate political messages, because they permit fast fabrication without the need for re-drawing each time. (One such work, by the well-known street artist Banksy, is pictured in Chapter 25.) A few stencil artists make objects of more subtle design, however. One of these is Kim McCarthy, a Seattle-based artist who also uses the alias Soule. Her *Urban Buddha* shows many repeated patterns in the background that she achieved with stencils using blue and green paint. The black skulls and the dominant Buddha image were also sprayed through stencils. The drawback to using stencils is that shading is not possible, only positive and negative spaces. She overcame this difficulty by adding many colors, brushstrokes, and paint drips. The

6.18 *Screenprinting.*

trails of black and white paint suggest the quick execution of street art.

Screenprinting is a refinement of the technique of stencil printing. Early in the last century, stencil technique was improved by adhering the stencil to a screen made of silk fabric stretched across a frame (synthetic fabric is used today). With a rubber-edged tool (called a squeegee), ink is then pushed through the fabric in the open areas of the stencil to make an image of the stencil on the material being printed. Because silk was the traditional material used for the screen, the process is also known as **silkscreen** or serigraphy (*seri* is Latin for silk). See the *Screenprinting* digram.

Screenprinting is well suited to the production of images with areas of uniform color. Each separate color requires a different screen, but registering and printing are relatively simple. There is no reversal of the image in screenprinting—in contrast to relief, intaglio, and lithographic processes in which the image on the plate is "flopped" in the printing process. The medium also allows the production of large, nearly mass-produced editions without loss of quality.

Silkscreen printing thus lends itself to poster production, and many social movements have allied themselves with silkscreen artists to help spread the word about their causes. For example, Ester Hernández made hundreds of posters that asserted Chicano identity and denounced the working conditions of Mexican-American laborers. Her screenprint *Sun Mad* is both an excellent

6.17 Kim McCarthy.
Urban Buddha. 2009.
Stencils and mixed media on canvas. 36″ × 48″.
Kim McCarthy.

6.19 Ester Hernández.
Sun Mad. 1982.
Silkscreen. 22″ × 17″.
Courtesy of the artist.

example of silkscreen art and a memorable protest against the use of pesticides.

The latest development in screenprinting is the photographic stencil, or **photo screen**, achieved by attaching light-sensitive gelatin to the screen fabric.

Elizabeth Murray's *Exile* takes screenprinting and stenciling to the limit. The base of this work is a piece of irregularly shaped yellow board embossed with a pattern and screenprinted with a design based on newspaper pages. Above this she laid a jagged and perforated blue sheet, which was also silkscreened and lithographed with colors. Finally, she cut a large piece of red paper, screenprinted and lithographed on it, and then set it above the other two layers. All the layers show hand-drawn crayon and pencil marks along with the printed colors. The artist describes *Exile* as a "twenty-three color lithograph and screen-print construction with collage and pastel."

EXPLORE MORE: For a studio video of screenprinting technique, go to **www.myartslab.com**

CURRENT DIRECTIONS

Experimental printmaking in recent years has taken two general directions: new types of printing materials, and digital technology. Each has altered the boundaries of the medium.

African-American artist Ellen Gallagher leafed through stacks of 50-year-old magazines directed at a Black audience, and borrowed advertisements that encouraged people to erase their blackness in various ways. She digitally scanned these ads and then altered them by affixing mold-made plasticine

LEARN MORE: For a Closer Look at *Exile*, go to **www.myartslab.com**

6.20 Elizabeth Murray.
Exile from *Thirty-Eight.* 1993.
Twenty-three color lithograph/screenprint construction with unique pastel application by the artist
30″ × 23″ × 2½″. Thirty-eight unique works.
© 1993 Elizabeth Murray and Gemini G.E.L. LLC.

shapes to their surfaces. *"Mr. Terrific"* is one of sixty panels that make up the larger work *Deluxe*. In this panel we see a man holding a can of hair straightener called Johnson's Ultra-Wave, which the ad says, "will make you *really* proud of your hair." Gallagher satirized this 1950s attempt at self-fashioning by attaching a huge yellow blob that covers both hair and eyes. She said of this work, "I'm creating fiction on top of an existing readability." All sixty panels of *Deluxe* were made in an edition of twenty.

Digital technology has altered printmaking at a basic level by eliminating the tangible plate. A digital matrix is made not by hand but with a keyboard and mouse. Some artists make digital prints using painting and photograph programs, and then erase the matrix files when the "edition" is complete. This technology allows for the creation of prints that are not original in the traditional sense because

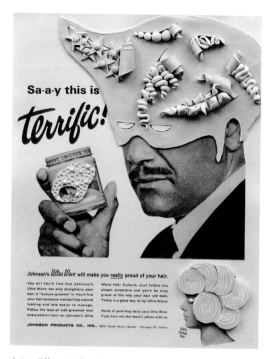

6.21 Ellen Gallagher.
"Mr. Terrific" from *Deluxe*. 2004–2005.
Aquatint, photogravure, and plasticine. 13″ × 10″.
Courtesy Two Palms Press, New York and Gagosian Gallery, New York.

6.22 Alicia Candiani.
La Humanidad. 2004. From Continents series: The Humankind.
Digital print on clear film and waterbased woodcut on Buthan paper. 27″ × 40″.
Courtesy of the artist.

6.23 Nicola López.
Blighted. 2006. Woodblock and lithography on mylar. 20′ × 22′.
Caren Golden Fine Art\Nicola Lopez.

they are infinitely reproducible. Felix González-Torres took advantage of this fact by creating works in infinite editions, such as *Untitled (Death by Gun)*, on page 9.

Other artists have devised novel means of controlling the size of a digital edition. The English duo Gilbert and George (who do not use their last names) in 2007 made a print available for free downloading on the Internet for thirty-six hours. The edition was limited not by the number of downloads, but by the clock.

Argentine artist Alicia Candiani combines digital and traditional technologies in prints that question stereotypical representations of women. In *La Humanidad* (Humanity), she used traditional Japanese woodcut techniques to print a map of the world on paper whose texture and color resemble human skin. Just beneath this grid, she printed a digital image of her own wet body in a pose based on the physical disciplines of yoga. The background includes digitally altered versions of dressmaking patterns. Thus, the artist used ancient and contemporary techniques to map woman onto the surface of the Earth.

Many printmakers today combine printmaking techniques with other kinds of media. One of these is Nicola López, who uses woodcut and lithography to create installations that are specific to each exhibition. In her 2006 work *Blighted*, she printed on mylar, a transparent film. Her images of shattering buildings and tumbling structures are based on her memories of the attacks of Sept. 11, 2001.

PRACTICE MORE: Get flashcards for images and terms and review chapter material with quizzes at **www.myartslab.com**

How and when was photography invented?

What made photography an art form?

How can you make a photograph without a camera?

7.1 Jane and Louise Wilson.
The Silence Is Twice as Fast Backwards I. 2008.
Photograph (c-print). 72″ square.
Courtesy 303 Gallery, New York.

Jane and Louise Wilson's photograph *The Silence Is Twice as Fast Backwards I* captures a magical moment in a lush, green forest. It appears as if the artists went for a morning walk and stumbled upon a wooded glade, flooded with streaking sunlight. The original picture is six feet square, filling our entire field of vision. The image is irresistible: viewers want to dive right into the scene.

The appearance of a happy coincidence is a bit misleading, however, because the work has been carefully composed. Note how the three trees are perfectly positioned in the frame. Note the branch that leads our eye in from the lower left, how it points upward to connect with the foliage of the second tree; note how the branch at the lower right seems to parallel the one at lower left in a rhythmic repetition. These curving branches lie at a roughly ninety-degree angle to the sun's rays that stream in from the upper left. The artists seem to have set the exposure of the shot perfectly as well, so that details are visible even in intense light and darkness. And one more fact completes this photo's contrivances: To create the effect of sunlight, the artists loosed some mist into the scene before shooting it.

A TOOL AND AN ART FORM

Edwin Land, who developed the Polaroid instant camera, emphasized the process of making a photograph when he described how even automatic, "instant" cameras can help us learn to see:

At its best, photography can be an extra sense, or a reservoir for the senses. Even when you don't press the trigger, the exercise of focusing through a camera can

HEAR MORE: Listen to an audio file of your chapter at **www.myartslab.com**

make you better remember thereafter a person or a moment. When we had flowers in this office recently to use as test objects, it was a great experience to take pictures of them. I learned to know each rose. I now know more about roses and leaves, and that enriched my life. Photography can teach people to look, to feel, to remember in a way that they didn't know they could.[1]

The word photography literally means "light-writing," although a more accurate description would be "light-drawing." Like drawing, photography can be either a practical tool or an art form. Beyond its many uses in journalism, science, advertising, and personal record keeping, photography offers artists a powerful means of expression.

The Evolution of Photography

The basic concept of the camera preceded actual photography by more than three hundred years. The desire of Renaissance artists to make accurate depictions of nature was the original impetus behind the eventual invention of photography.

The forerunner of the modern camera was the **camera obscura**, literally "dark room." The concept of photography grew out of the fact that reflected sunlight passing through a small hole in the wall of a darkened room projects onto the opposite wall an inverted image of whatever lies outside. In the fifteenth century, Leonardo da Vinci described the device as an aid to observation and picture making.

As a fixed room, or even as a portable room, the camera obscura was too large and cumbersome to be widely used. In the seventeenth century, when inventors realized that the person tracing the image did not have to be inside, the camera obscura evolved into a portable dark box. During the course of this pre-camera evolution, a lens was placed in the small hole to improve image clarity. Later an angled mirror was added to right the inverted image, enabling anyone, skilled or unskilled, to trace the projected pictures with pen or pencil (see the table model *Camera Obscura*).

The invention of photography had to wait until scientists discovered that certain chemicals were sensitive to light. Thus, it was not until about 1826 that the first vague photographic image was made by Joseph Nicéphore Niépce. He recorded and fixed on a sheet of pewter an image he made by exposing the sensitized metal plate to light for eight hours. During the next decade, the painter Louis Jacques Mande Daguerre further perfected Niépce's process and produced some of the first satisfactory photographs, known as **daguerreotypes**. He made them by exposing iodized silver plates in the presence of mercury vapor; images were fixed on the plate with a mineral salt solution.

7.2 *Evolution of the Camera Obscura.*
  a. Sixteenth-century camera obscura.
  b. Seventeenth-century portable camera obscura.
  c. Seventeenth- to nineteenth-century table model camera obscura.

7.3 Louis Jacques Mande Daguerre.
Le Boulevard du Temple. 1839.
Daguerreotype.
Bayerisches National Museum, Munich (R6312).

At first, because the necessary exposure times were so long, photography could record only stationary objects. In Daguerre's photograph of *Le Boulevard du Temple*, taken in Paris in 1839 (the year his process was made public), the streets appear deserted because moving figures made no lasting light impressions on the plate. However, one man, having his shoes shined, stayed still long enough to become part of the image. He is visible on the corner in the lower left, the first person ever to appear in a photograph. It was a significant moment in human history: At last images of people and things could be made without the hand of a trained artist. Although some painters at the time felt the new medium was unfair competition and spelled the end of their art, the invention of photography actually marked the beginning of a

7.4 Julia Margaret Cameron.
Julia Jackson. March 1886.
Albumen silver print from wet-collodion glass negative.
13¼″ × 11″.
Gernsheim Collection, Harry Ransom Humanities Research Center, The University of Texas at Austin.

period when art would be more accessible to all through photographic reproductions; it also marked not the end but the beginning of new approaches to painting, complemented by the new art of photography.

Before the development of the camera, only the wealthy could afford to have their portraits painted. By the mid-nineteenth century, people of average means were going in great numbers to photography studios to sit unblinking for several minutes in bright sunlight to have their portraits made with the camera.

From the beginning, portrait painting greatly influenced portrait photography. One of the first great portrait photographers was Julia Margaret Cameron. By 1864, she had become an avid photographer, creating expressive portraits. Cameron pioneered the use of close-ups and carefully controlled lighting to enhance the images of her subjects, who were often family members and famous friends. Her portrait of *Julia Jackson* is an excellent example. Cameron's use of raking light and a soft focus combine with Jackson's intense gaze and slight tilt of the head to suggest thoughtful energy.

Many nineteenth-century photographers looked for ways to duplicate what painters had already done—and thereby failed to find their medium's unique strengths. Painters, meanwhile—now freed by photography from their ancient role as recorders of events—looked for other avenues to explore. Yet some leading painters were greatly influenced by photography. Shorter exposure times, less toxic technology, and printing on paper all helped to popularize photography as the nineteenth century progressed.

Photography as an Art Form

In the beginning, the public was reluctant accept photography as an art because of its reliance on a mechanical device. Today, however, most people agree that the camera can be a vehicle for personal expression and symbolic communication. An early crusader in the art photography movement was the American Alfred Stieglitz, who opened a photography gallery in New York City in 1905. He also founded an influential magazine, *Camera Work*, which published photography along with essays about modern art and culture.

Stieglitz's own photography was almost always "straight"—that is, produced with no technical manipulation of the negative. In his 1903 photograph *The Flatiron Building*, Stieglitz arranged visual fields so that they echo each other. The basic shape of the foreground tree is answered in the stand of trees in the middle

7.5 Alfred Stieglitz.
The Flatiron Building from *Camera Work*, (Vol. IV). October 1903. Gravure on vellum. 12⅞″ ×6 ⅝″.
Digital Image © The Museum of Modern Art/Licensed by SCALA / Art Resource, NY. © 2010 Georgia O'Keeffe Museum / Artists Rights Society (ARS), New York.

French photographer Henri Cartier-Bresson captured a subtle moment of drama in *Place de l'Europe Behind the Gare St. Lazare, Paris*. Here he released the shutter at exactly the right moment to capture a man leaping over a puddle. The man's shape is echoed in both his own reflection and that of the dancer in the poster behind, just as semicircular ripples find a parallel in the round shapes close by in the water. For Cartier-Bresson, good photography is a matter of capturing the decisive moment:

To me, photography is the simultaneous recognition, in a fraction of a second, of the significance of an event as well as of a precise organization of forms which give that event its proper expression.[2]

Other photographers went beyond the camera itself to achieve more inventive effects. Man Ray made innovative photographs, which he called

7.6 Henri Cartier-Bresson.
Place de l'Europe Behind the Gare St. Lazare, Paris. 1932.
Photograph.
© H. Cartier-Bresson/Magnum Photos.

7.7 Man Ray.
Rayograph. 1927.
Gelatin silver print, 29.1 × 23.2 cm.
Courtesy George Eastman House. © 2010 Man Ray Trust/Artists Rights Society (ARS), NY/ADAGP, Paris.

ground, but the fork of its branches also suggests the angle of the building (the "Flatiron" of the title). Like the foreground tree, this building seems to emerge from the ground, an impression supported by the row of seats in the snowy park. The recession of the ground from front to back of the picture is contradicted above the horizon, where the Flatiron and the black tree branches seem to touch. In early photographs such as this one, Stieglitz showed the poetry he found in quiet urban scenes.

7.8 Jacob Riis.
   Five Cents a Spot. Unauthorized lodging
   in Bayard Street Tenement. c. 1890.
   Gelatin silver print. 6³⁄₁₆″ × 4¾″.
   Museum of the City of New York, The Jacob A.
   Riis Collection (#155) (90.13.4.158).

Rayographs, by placing objects on light-sensitive paper and exposing them to sunlight. The rayographs are not really photographs, because they are not "pictures" of anything and no cameras or lenses are used. Rather, they are visual inventions recorded on film. Sometimes, as in the work pictured here, it is not clear what the original subject was.

Photography and Social Change

Each generation produces its own memorable photographs. Such photographs move us not only because of the way their subjects are presented, but also because we know the photographer was there. We join the photographer as witnesses. The significance of such images lies not simply in their ability to inform us, but in their power to stir our emotions.

Only a few decades after the invention of the medium, photographers began to bring public attention to suffering caused by war, poverty, hunger, and neglect. The new tool made visual statements believable in ways that no other medium could. Of all the arts, photography is uniquely suited not only to documenting events and social problems, but to bringing about empathetic awareness that can lead to reform.

An early leader in the use of photography for social change was the Danish-born American Jacob Riis. In the late nineteenth century, he photographed squalid living and working conditions in poor areas of New York and published them for the world to see. Photographs such as *Five Cents a Spot* drew public attention that led directly to stricter housing codes and improved work safety laws. The vividness of this photo was made possible by the recent invention of flash photography, which took the camera into unforeseen places. His most famous book, *How the Other Half Lives*, was a landmark in the social impact of photography.

For most of the twentieth century, photography enjoyed an unquestioned reputation as a vehicle of truth, giving rise to the saying, "The camera never lies." During the 1930s, Margaret Bourke-White introduced the concept of the photographic essay—an approach that was soon adopted by other photographers. A photo essay is a collection of photographs on a single subject, arranged to tell a story or convey a mood in a way not possible with a single photograph. She documented construction projects, industrial plants, foreign customs, and

7.9 Margaret Bourke-White.
Louisville Flood Victims. 1938.
Photograph.
Margaret Bourke-White/*Life* Magazine © TimePix.

Depression-era poverty in many such works. On assignment to document the effects of a flood in 1937, she created *Louisville Flood Victims*, one of the iconic images of the Depression in the United States.

In addition to focusing on social problems, photography has aided the efforts of environmentalists. Ansel Adams very often used his photographs to increase public awareness of the need for conservation of the natural environment.

His *Clearing Winter Storm, Yosemite National Park* reflects the symphonic grandeur of nature's design. It renders the cathedral-like Yosemite Valley as an orchestration in black and white where stark rock mingles with soft mist.

Adams viewed aspects of nature as symbols of spiritual life, capable of transcending the conflicts of society. In his majestic black-and-white photographs, nature becomes a timeless metaphor for spiritual harmony.

7.10 Ansel Adams.
Clearing Winter Storm, Yosemite National Park, California. 1944.
Photograph.
Ansel Adams Publishing Rights Trust.

Today's environmental photographers are more likely to focus on climate change or environmental degradation. Gary Braasch, for example, has been photographing the diminishing habitat of polar bears since 2000. His photo of a *Polar Bear Outside Barrow, Alaska* gives vivid evidence of warmer temperatures in the Arctic regions and testifies to the power of a picture to wake us up to a new social issue. See also *The View North toward Burj Dubai* for a contemporary document on recent economic problems (page 3).

7.11 Gary Braasch.
Polar Bear Outside Barrow, Alaska. 2008.
© 2008 Gary Braasch.

MARGARET BOURKE-WHITE

"A Photographer at My Very Core"

FEW PHOTOGRAPHERS HAVE had a greater impact on the American public than Margaret Bourke-White. A pioneer in photojournalism, she made memorable images of most of the world's major events for nearly thirty years.

Her early family environment encouraged her to expand the boundaries of a woman's traditional role: "Learning to do things fearlessly was considered important by both my parents," she said.[3] She began to use a camera seriously when she took a group of landscape photographs in upstate New York that she sold to help pay her tuition at Cornell University. By 1927, she had her own studio in Cleveland, where she specialized in photographing industrial buildings such as steel mills.

Her life changed radically in the spring of 1929, when she became chief photographer for *Fortune* magazine. In this new venture, "Pictures and words would be conscious partners ... The camera would act as interpreter, recording what modern industrial civilization is, how it looks, how it meshes." She recalled:

This was the very role I believed photography should play . . . I could see that this whole concept would give photography greater opportunities than it had ever had before.

Thus began one of the most important careers in American journalism. She climbed on buildings, stood in swamps, and suspended herself in midair, as we can see in *Margaret Bourke-White Atop the Chrysler Building. Fortune* sent her to Russia to record the process of industrialization under Stalin's five-year plan.

When the Depression took hold in the United States, Bourke-White collaborated on a book documenting its effects. With writer Erskine Caldwell, she made *You Have Seen Their Faces,* a record of individual suffering and endurance in the face of the economic crisis. In 1936, when Henry Luce founded *Life* magazine, Bourke-White became its lead photographer.

Her work with *Life* anchored the rest of her career. She recalled, "I loved the swift pace of *Life* assignments, the exhilaration of stepping over the threshold into a new land. Everything could be conquered. Nothing was too difficult. And if you had a stiff deadline to meet, all the better. You said yes to the challenge." The Air Force sent her as a war correspondent to most of the battlefronts of Europe in World War II.

Her pace hardly slackened when the war ended. Besides regular assignments within the U.S. borders, she

7.12 *Margaret Bourke-White Atop the Chrysler Building.* 1934.
Photo by Oscar Grauber. Courtesy Margaret Bourke-White Estate, *Life* Magazine © TimePix.

witnessed and photographed the decolonization of India, the Korean War, and struggles of South African gold miners. She was negotiating to be the first photographer sent to the moon when Parkinson's disease forced her retirement.

She said that she never recalled consciously choosing between marriage and a career, but as she grew older she realized that hers was "a life into which marriage doesn't fit very well. If I had had children, I would have charted a widely different life. . . . Perhaps I would have worked on children's books instead of going to wars. . . . One life is not better than the other; it is just a different life." What settled the matter for her was probably this feeling: "There is nothing else like the exhilaration of a new story boiling up. To me this was food and drink."

Color Photography

Photography began as a black-and-white (sometimes brown-and-white) process. For the first one hundred years, black and white was the only practical option for photographers. Through much of the twentieth century, technical problems with color persisted: film and printing papers were expensive, and color prints faded over time. Even when fairly accurate color became practical, many photographers felt that color lacked the abstract power of the black-and-white image.

The development of color photography began in 1907 with the invention of positive color transparencies. In 1932, the Eastman Kodak Company began making color film. Then, in 1936, the invention of Kodachrome substantially improved the versatility and accuracy of color film. Later progress improved the relative permanence of color prints.

Through the 1960s, most art photographers disdained color film, first because the negatives were unstable, later because color was associated with family snapshots and tourist photographs. But when William Eggleston exhibited his color work at the Museum of Modern Art in 1976, the world took notice and a new branch of art photography was born.

Eggleston's pictures from the *Los Alamos Portfolio* are elegant compositions of everyday things. In the *Untitled* photo shown here (*Nehi Bottle on Car Hood*), two cars block out an abstract composition of off-balance diagonals against a paved background darkened by wedges of shadow. The soda bottle seems perfectly positioned to both anchor the composition and capture the sunlight. Besides the skillful arrangement, the photo rivets our attention because it immediately evokes a world: a casual social setting in some American rural area on a warm afternoon. To prove the validity of Eggleston's commitment to color photography, all we have to do is imagine this work in black and white.

7.13 William Eggleston.
Untitled (Nehi Bottle on Car Hood).
From *Los Alamos Portfolio.* 1965–1974.
Color photograph.
© 2009 Eggleston Artistic Trust, courtesy Cheim & Read, New York. Used with permission. All rights reserved.

PUSHING THE LIMITS

Artists have explored a variety of techniques to go beyond photography's assumed limits. In the middle 1960s, Los Angeles artist Wallace Berman used an early version of the photocopy machine as a camera to make *Untitled (B-3 Masterlock)* (on the following page). He held a transistor radio in his hand and laid it on the glass bed of a Verifax machine. The resulting print gave him the base for embedding other images where the radio speaker was, so that instead of hearing different stations, we see different images. The addition of Hebrew letters to some frames adds a mysterious note.

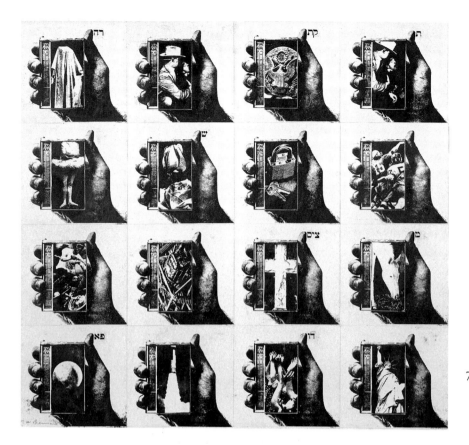

7.14 Wallace Berman.
Untitled (B-3 Masterlock). 1965.
Verifax collage. 24″ × 25″.
Hirshhorn Museum and Sculpture Garden, Smithsonian
Institution, Joseph H. Hirshhorn Purchase Fund, 1990.

Vietnamese-born artist Binh Danh invented his own method of recording photographs onto plant material. He borrows pictures and attaches them to leaves from his garden. He then places the leaf and photo between layers of glass and exposes them outdoors for up to several weeks on the roof of his house. Soon the sunlight transfers the photographic images to the leaves, in a process he calls chlorophyll printing.

He most often uses images of the victims of war from his native country to create haunting works that memorialize the dead. In the *Iridescence of Life* series, he embedded the printed leaves in resin, and paired them with butterfly specimens. The resulting works seem fragile, precious, and beautiful.

SEE MORE: To see an interview with contemporary photography dealer Stephen Wirtz, go to
www.myartslab.com

7.15 Binh Danh.
Iridescence of Life #7. 2008.
Chlorophyll print, butterfly specimen, and resin. 14″ × 11″ × 2″.
Haines Gallery.

AT THE EDGE OF ART

You See I Am Here After All

SOME ARTISTS USE photographs as artifacts, a new method of "taking" a picture. Zoe Leonard gathered over four thousand postcards that depict Niagara Falls and hung them in a large array in a gallery installation that she called *You See I Am Here After All*. Niagara Falls is, of course, one of America's premier tourist destinations, and generally people send postcards to relatives as a way of marking their presence at such famous places. The artist's collection of postcards begins in the early twentieth century, shortly after the postal service first began accepting postcards for mailing. She grouped similar views and spread them out over a 20-foot mural-sized installation. An awe-inspiring natural site thus became a module for seemingly endless repetition.

7.16 Zoe Leonard.
You See I Am Here After All. 2008.
Approximately 4,000 postcards.
Exhibition view at Dia Art Foundation, Beacon, NY.
Galerie Gisela Capitain, Cologne, Germany.

THE DIGITAL REVOLUTION

Near the end of the twentieth century, the chemical photographic negative began to go out of fashion under the imact of the new digital technology. Now most cameras do not use film; rather, the lens focuses information onto an array of sensors that translate the hue and intensity of light into digital files. These files can be manipulated in almost infinite ways, and reproduced endlessly.

The implications of these changes are profound. If a photo can be altered, then its reputation as a vehicle of truth is in danger, and the camera can indeed lie. And the reproducibility of images means that the specialness of a photograph is much reduced. Many contemporary photographers take advantage of these facts.

Andreas Gursky takes pictures of today's public spaces and then seamlessly alters the images to make them seem more real than real. *Stateville, Illinois* is a view of the interior of a prison. Gursky achieved this spotless, tightly focused look with the help of digital editing; he typically removes blemishes, adjusts lighting, adds or removes people, and improves contrast. If this seems artificial, he responds that he makes photographs the same way traditional painters compose a scene. His most common subjects are the public spaces that most of us use: airports, auditoriums, stores. His pictures of these spaces are dazzling in a way that "reality" is not. Although we know that this image is more created than captured, it still looks believable to our media-saturated eyes.

PRACTICE MORE: Get flashcards for images and terms and review chapter material with quizzes at **www.myartslab.com**

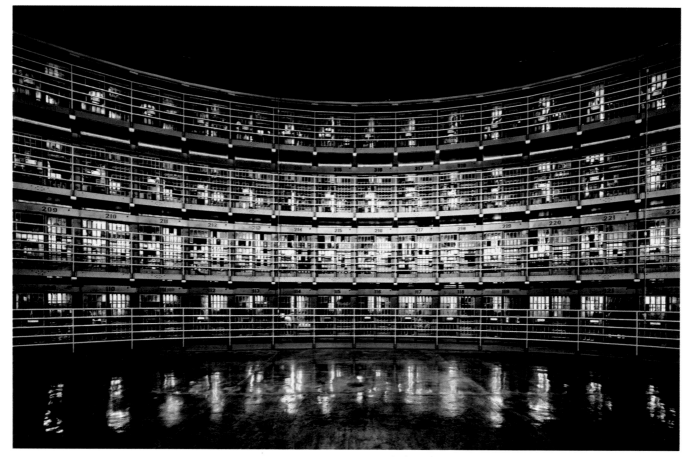

7.17   Andreas Gursky.
Stateville, Illinois. 2002.
C-print mounted on plexiglass on artist's frame. 81″ × 120½″ (206 × 307 cm).
Courtesy Matthew Marks Gallery, New York and Monika Spruth/Philomene Magers, Cologne/Munich. © 2010 Andreas Gursky/Artists Rights Society (ARS), New York/VG Bild-Kunst, Bonn.

MOVING IMAGES: FILM AND DIGITAL ARTS

WHAT ARE THE MAJOR STEPS IN THE EVOLUTION OF FILM?

WHEN WAS THE FIRST COMPUTER ART MADE?

WHAT KIND OF ARTWORKS ARE MADE FOR ONLINE VIEWING?

The first experimental color film ever seen in Germany had to be shown under false pretenses. The year was 1933 and the film was *Circles* by Oskar Fischinger. It was a nonrepresentational film, composed of dancing and interlocking rings and circles that moved and evolved across the screen, accompanied by dramatic orchestral music. Only a few minutes in length, it was screened together with entertaining black-and-white feature films. The public seemed to enjoy Fischinger's experiment in color and form.

However, those were the years in which the Nazi party suppressed all forms of abstract art, which they regarded as "degenerate." In order to avoid such censorship, Fischinger made *Circles* as an advertisement for a public relations company; the last few moments of the film display the name of the company and an advertising slogan. Finding Nazi browbeating intolerable, Fischinger left Germany for Los Angeles in 1936.

HEAR MORE: Listen to an audio file of your chapter at **www.myartslab.com**

8.1 Oskar Fischinger.
Circles. 1933. Still from film.
© Fishinger Trust, courtesy Center for Visual Music.

This story illustrates two important points: First, the cinema is a mass art closely monitored by those in authority; and second, creative people have been making experimental films for generations. In this chapter we will examine films that have broken new creative ground, some in the mass market and others in smaller, more artistic circles.

The digital revolution spun off new art media, and new ways of presenting artworks. In this chapter we will also examine some of these new digital art forms.

FILM: THE MOVING IMAGE

The art of cinema has its roots in 1872, when a man photographed a horse. Leland Stanford (the founder of Stanford University) made a bet that all four of a horse's hooves came off the ground when it ran. To settle the bet, photographer Eadweard Muybridge lined up a series of still cameras close together alongside a California racetrack; each camera shutter was fixed with a string that the horse's front legs tripped as it ran by. The resulting pictures of *The Horse in Motion* proved that all four hooves indeed left the ground. After Muybridge later discovered a way to project his still photographs in rapid succession, he made the first primitive cinema. He called his invention a zöopraxiscope (fortunately for all of us, the name did not survive). Others soon began experimenting with sequences of projected photographs, and cinematography was born, changing forever the way we see movement.

Film and Visual Expression

First and foremost, a movie is a visual experience. The illusion of motion is made possible by the **persistence of vision**, the brief retention of an image by the retina of our eyes after a stimulus is removed. Film's rhythmic, time-based structure makes motion picture photography a very different sort of visual art from painting or from still photography. Whereas a painter or photographer designs a single moment, a filmmaker designs sequences that work together in time.

Each piece of film photographed in a continuous running of the camera is called a **shot**. Film makes possible a dynamic relationship among three kinds of movement: the movement of objects within a shot, the movement of the camera toward and away from the action, and the movement created by the sequence of shots.

Much of the power of film comes from its ability to reconstruct time. Film is not inhibited by the constraints of clock time; it can convincingly present the past, the present, and the future, or it can mix all three in any manner. Film time can affect us more deeply than clock time, because film sequences can be constructed to approximate the way we feel about time. In addition to editing, filmmakers can manipulate time by slowing or accelerating motion. The filmmaker's control over time, sequence, light, camera angle, and distance can create a feeling of total, enveloping experience so believable that it becomes a new kind of reality. Here we will examine a few films from the last hundred years that were either highly innovative or captured some important aspect of the culture of their times.

8.2 Eadweard Muybridge.
The Horse in Motion. 1878.
Photographs.
Courtesy of the Library of Congress.

Creating a New Language of Vision

The recognition of film as a significant art form came slowly. At first, film was simply a novelty. In order to gain public acceptance, early filmmakers tried to make their movies look like filmed theatrical performances. Actors made entrances and exits in front of a camera fixed in place, as though it too were a member of the audience at a stage play. These early films were also silent; the technology for recording sound on film was not perfected until more than thirty years after the first films were made. Total reliance on the visual image forced pioneer filmmakers to develop the visual language of film that continues to be basic to the art form.

Between 1907 and 1916, American director D. W. Griffith helped bring the motion picture from its infancy as an amusement to full stature as a means of artistic expression. Griffith introduced the moving camera by releasing it from its fixed, stagebound position in order to better express narrative content. The camera was placed where it would best reveal the dramatic meaning of each scene. A scene thus came to be composed of several shots taken from different angles, thereby greatly increasing the viewer's feeling of involvement.

Assembling a scene from several shots involves **film editing**, a process in which the editor selects the best shots from raw footage, then reassembles them into meaningful sequences and finally into a total, unified progression.

Later, Griffith used parallel editing to compare events occurring at the same time in different places (person in danger and the approach of would-be rescuer) or in different times, as in his film *Intolerance*, in which he cut back and forth among four stories set in four periods of history.

One of film's most characteristic techniques was discovered when Griffith's camera operator accidentally let the shutter of his camera close slowly, causing the light to gradually darken. Griffith decided that this might be a good way to begin and end love scenes. Fading in or fading out remains a common transition between scenes.

8.3 D. W. Griffith.
Intolerance (The Modern Story). 1916.
Film still ("Belshazzar's Feast").
The Museum of Modern Art/Film Stills Archive.

Griffith was the first to use the close-up and the longshot. Today the close-up is one of the most widely used shots; but when Griffith first wanted to try a close shot, his cameraman balked at the idea of a head without a body! In a longshot the camera photographs from a distance to emphasize large groups of people or a panoramic setting.

When films were silent, movies could be produced in many countries for an international audience, without concern for language barriers. Following the Russian Revolution in 1917, Sergei Eisenstein emerged as a major film artist, honored as much in the West as in Russia. Eisenstein greatly admired Griffith's film techniques; after careful study, he developed them further, becoming one of the first filmmakers to produce epic films of high quality.

One of Eisenstein's major contributions was his skilled use of **montage** to heighten dramatic intensity. Introduced by Griffith in 1916, montage is the editing technique of combining a number of very brief shots, representing distinct but related subject matter, in order to create new relationships, build strong emotion, or indicate the passage of time. With the use of montage, a great deal seems to happen simultaneously, in a short time.

In his film *The Battleship Potemkin*, Eisenstein created one of the most powerful sequences in film history: the terrible climax of a failed revolt. The montage of brief shots, edited into a sequence of no more than a few minutes, effectively portrays the tragedy of the historic event. Rather than shoot the entire scene with a wide-angle lens from a spectator's perspective, Eisenstein intermixed many close-ups to give viewers the sensation of being caught as participants in the middle of the violence. The juxtaposition of close-ups and longshots gives audiences a powerful sense of the fear and tragedy that took place.

A film is like a collective dream, in which a group of people sitting in the dark experience the same vivid story. Surrealist artists Salvador Dalí and Luis Buñuel took advantage of this fact when they made *An Andalusian Dog (Un Chien Andalou)* in 1929.

LEARN MORE: For a Closer Look at *Battleship Potemkin*, go to **www.myartslab.com**

Like our dreams, the film is a sequence of seemingly irrational events: Ants crawl out of a man's palm; two dead donkeys lie bleeding in a pair of grand pianos; a woman's eye is sliced open with a razor. The overall theme of the picture seems to be unrealized sexual desire, and at the end the man and woman are frozen in the soil like a pair of half-buried statues. The manifest illogic of *An Andalusian Dog* influenced the hallucinatory content of music videos decades later.

An Andalusian Dog is silent with a musical accompaniment, but in fact synchronized sound had been introduced two years earlier. Color was introduced in the 1930s; the wide screen and three-dimensional images in the 1950s; 360-degree projection was first seen by the public in the 1960s. Most of these techniques, however, had been conceived of and researched by 1910.

LEARN MORE: To view *An Andalusian Dog*, go to **www.myartslab.com**

8.4 Sergei Eisenstein.
The Battleship Potemkin. 1925.
Selected frames from Odessa Steps sequence. Film stills.
The Museum of Modern Art/Film Stills Archive.

8.5 Salvador Dalí and Luis Buñuel.
An Andalusian Dog. 1929.
Film still.
British Film Institute.

Many film critics rank the 1941 film *Citizen Kane* among the best ever made. Orson Welles coauthored the script, directed, and played the leading role in the thinly disguised biography of the newspaper tycoon William Randolph Hearst. *Citizen Kane* employs an unprecedented array of cinematic devices: dramatic lighting that communicates feeling, distorted lenses, dialog that bridges scenic breaks, innovative camera angles that aid characterizations, and clever editing to show the passage of time. The film is also important for the life that it portrays. Hearst was the prototype of the media mogul who achieves fame and wealth by selling sensational news ("If the headline is big enough, it makes the news big enough," he says). The film's tragic ending, however, is closer to the life of Welles than that of Hearst.

By the 1930s, Hollywood became the film capital of the world. Most Hollywood films simply repeated plot formulas already proven successful at the box office. During that decade, the major studios all adhered voluntarily to the Motion Picture Production Code, which attempted to regulate the moral content of films. The Code forbade profanity in the script, as well as depictions of nudity, sexual activity, drug use, interracial romance, and ridicule of the clergy. It also prohibited the glamorization of crime, so that all gangsters had to be arrested or killed in the end. Studios submitted scripts to the Code authorities prior to shooting, and any film that lacked a Code seal of approval had no chance of wide distribution. At times, Code strictures were relaxed somewhat: Clark Gable's famous farewell to Vivien Leigh in *Gone With the Wind* ("Frankly, my dear, I don't give a damn.") remained in the film, but the producer paid a fine of $5,000 for it. The Code's authority declined in succeeding decades, but remained in effect until 1968, when the Motion Picture Association of America introduced the ratings system that is still in force.

8.6 Orson Welles.
Citizen Kane. 1941.
Film still.
The Museum of Modern Art/Film Stills Archive.

8.7 Walt Disney.
Fantasia. 1940.
Film still. *The Sorcerer's Apprentice.*
© Walt Disney Studios/Photofest.

Walt Disney started out making entertaining cartoons, but in 1940, with *Fantasia*, he tried for something more: a feature-length animated film with stereophonic sound, reserved seating, and an intermission. *Fantasia* is a series of segments that accompany pieces of classical music. Some of these, such as "The Sorcerer's Apprentice," use familiar Disney characters, but others, such as J. S. Bach's "Toccata and Fugue in D minor," are nearly abstract.

Disney evolved his technique with the aid of German émigré Oskar Fischinger. Each frame of film (24 per second) required a new painting, which was laboriously hand-colored and then photographed. A two-hour film naturally required thousands of paintings. Disney recruited Fischinger to work on animating *Fantasia's* "Toccata and Fugue" segment, but because Disney insisted that Fischinger always retain some representational element in his drawings, Fischinger resigned before the film was complete. This would not be the only time a Hollywood studio would recruit an artist. In 1945 Alfred Hitchcock worked more fruitfully with Salvador Dalí to create a dream sequence for *Spellbound*, in which lead character Gregory Peck relates a dream that unlocks his amnesia.

Italian director Federico Fellini's 1961 film *La Dolce Vita* (*The Sweet Life*) foreshadows many of

8.8 Federico Fellini.
La Dolce Vita. 1961.
Film still.
Everette Collection.

8.9 Kenneth Anger.
Scorpio Rising. 1964. Film still.
Anger Management Enterprises.

today's critiques of the mass media. Marcello Mastroianni plays the lead character, a tabloid journalist (also named Marcello) who makes his career reporting on sensations, scandals, and celebrities.

The protagonist follows the lifestyles of the rich and famous, dutifully attending spectacles of all kinds, from the exploits of American movie stars to decadent parties to religious visions. He frolics in a fountain at 4 A.M. with Anita Ekberg. He joins the media circus as thousands throng to a small town where two children say they saw the Virgin Mary. One of these fellow travelers is a photographer friend nicknamed Paparazzo (after the "pop" of the camera flash), and ever since this film's release, intrusive photographers throughout the world have been called *paparazzi*.

Only occasionally, as with Dalí and Hitchcock, did the lives of artists intersect successfully with those of Hollywood directors. By the 1960s, the separation was as complete as it would ever be, as most artists who made films considered their work "underground" and rarely showed it outside galleries and art venues. Sometimes an artist's experimental film influenced the mainstream, as happened with Kenneth Anger's *Scorpio Rising*.

This 1964 film is in effect a documentary about the rituals of a Brooklyn motorcycle gang. They fix their bikes, go to parties, take drugs, and even suffer deadly crashes. Anger filmed it all in highly saturated color above a soundtrack of pop songs of the day. *Scorpio Rising* memorably creates a world, with intercut footage from other films and music that comments on the main action. The film basically created the "biker movie" genre, and Hollywood directors such as Stephen Spielberg and Martin Scorsese said its use of popular music to create a mood influenced them.

The advent of digital technology in the 1980s made animation much easier, and led the way to a special-effects revolution that we are still undergoing. Some of the most elaborate animated films in recent years have been made in Japan, where meaningful characters combine with epic story lines in visually stunning productions. One of the best of these is *Metropolis*, a frightening vision of a future society in which robots have evolved but people remain as greedy and unpredictable as ever. The film is notable for its exploration of human qualities in machines, as well as its impressive urban landscapes.

Another kind of film that shows today's more global society is the international co-production. Companies from several countries may collaborate

8.10 Rintaro.
Metropolis. 2002.
Film still.

8.11 Guillermo del Toro
Pan's Labyrinth. 2006.
Film still.

8.12 James Cameron.
Avatar. Film still. 2009.
Picture Desk, Inc./Kobal Collection.

on these films, which avoid some of the stereotypes of Hollywood. A recent example is *Pan's Labyrinth*, a joint Spanish-American production by Mexican director Guillermo del Toro. The film shows what happens when imagination and reality intersect in the life of an 11-year-old girl in fascist-dominated Spain. Her difficult life under a cruel stepfather leads her to take refuge in a fantasy world populated by tiny flying fairies and trees that move, led by a faun who represents a kingdom beyond this world. He recognizes her as royalty, but she must first prove her status by performing certain tasks that cross the line between her fantasies and "real" existence. The film's principal theme is how imagination can help us cope with adversity, and its many vivid sets and characters are testimony to the director's visual creativity (see pages from his *Sketchbook* on page 79). *Pan's Labyrinth* has moments of both stunning beauty and aching horror; Del Toro refuses to tell us which is real and which imaginary, leaving the final decision to us.

Today, most major Hollywood film studios are owned by large international corporations, and they have discovered that they can draw audience interest around the world with movies that employ luxurious special effects with a fast story line. To aid international receipts, these "blockbusters" generally do not rely on character development or divisive social comment for their success, and they are promoted together with merchandise such as clothing, toys, and video games derived from the film, to enhance their appeal to younger audiences.

The most recent of these pictures is James Cameron's *Avatar*. Humans from the 22nd century invade the small moon Pandora in search of precious minerals. Because the atmosphere is not breathable, the humans must enter in the form of avatars, clones of themselves that share genetic material with the moon's humanoid inhabitants. This film shows the most recent development of **motion capture**, a technique whereby the actions of the actors are scanned and digitized in three-dimensional modeling and used to create alternate versions for the screen. The humanoids in *Avatar* began life as real people; they ended up tall, thin, and blue-skinned, with slightly narrower shoulders and longer heads.

Motion capture has increased in sophistication since its first use in the 1990s, so that now even minute facial movements that show emotion can be scanned. As Cameron said in an interview, "I think we've reached the point where it looks as real as a blue humanoid character can look." However novel *Avatar* may seem, motion capture has been the principal goal of cinema since its beginnings. Muybridge was involved in motion capture of a certain kind; so were Disney animators and Hollywood directors. Motion capture has always been the essence of cinema.

TELEVISION AND VIDEO

Literally "vision from afar," television is the electronic transmission of still or moving images with sound by means of cable or wireless broadcast. Television is primarily a distribution system for advertising, news, and entertainment. Video is the medium for television; it can also be an art form.

Video Art

The Sony corporation set the stage for the beginning of video art in 1965 when it introduced the first portable video recording camera, the Portapak. Although the camera was cumbersome, some artists were drawn to the new medium because of its unique characteristics: The instant feedback of video does away with development times necessary for film. Video works could be stored on inexpensive cassettes, erased and re-recorded. In addition, because a video signal can be sent to more than one monitor, it allows flexibility of presentation.

Early videos by artists were relatively simple, consisting mainly of recordings of the artists themselves performing, or of dramatic scenes staged with only a few actors or props. Because no editing was possible, and the black-and-white image was incompatible with the color resolution of television broadcasts of the time, the medium was most suited to private screenings for small groups. In 1972, the compatibility issue was resolved with the introduction of standardized 3/4-inch tape; this allowed artists to work with television production equipment, and even to broadcast the results of their labors. The 1980s brought vast improvements in video technology in the form of lighter cameras, color, and computerized editing.

In the short history of video art, some artists have consistently tried to expand the limits of the medium's technical capacities. The Korean-born Nam June Paik frequently used the video medium in a slyly humorous fashion to comment on the role of television in our lives. His 1986 work *Video Flag Z*, for example, uses 84 television sets in an array that resembles the American flag. On each

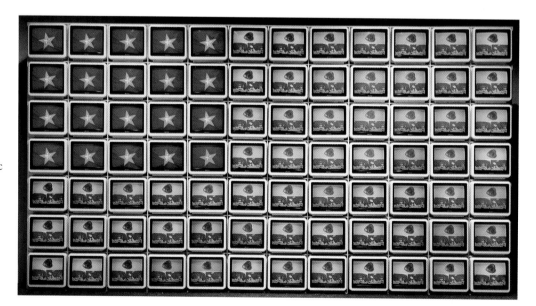

8.13 Nam June Paik. *Video Flag Z*. 1986. Multi-media, television sets, videodiscs, videodisc players, Plexiglas modular cabinet. 74" × 138" × 18½" (187.96 × 350.52 × 46.99 cm). Gift of the Art Museum Council (M.86.156). Digital Image © 2009 Museum Associates/ LACMA/Art Resource, NY. Los Angeles County Museum of Art, Los Angeles, U.S.A.

8.14 Joan Jonas.
Volcano Saga. 1987.
Performance still.
Performing Garage, NY. Pat Hearn Gallery, NYC.

Describing the plot of any of the *Cremaster* movies is difficult, but plot is less important than the symbolic content that each movie has. The portion released on DVD is called "The Order," and it recounts an endurance test that The Apprentice must undergo by passing four ordeals at various levels of the Guggenheim Museum. Allusions to Masonic Orders, Mormon theology, heavy metal music, and famous convicted murderer Gary Gilmore only begin to describe the various layers of this video. The Apprentice passes through each obstacle, and thus gains the right to kill another character called The Architect. The murder takes place at the Chrysler Building, but the building itself takes revenge by killing The Apprentice.

monitor, portions of old Hollywood films flicker endlessly across the screens, as if our very national identity is made up of what we see in movies.

Other video artists have used the medium to create and tell stories using themselves as actors. In *Volcano Saga*, Joan Jonas tells a story of a memorable trip to Iceland. Caught in a fierce windstorm, she is blown off the road and loses consciousness. Awakened by a local woman who offers help, the artist is magically transported back to ancient times in the company of Gundrun, a woman from Icelandic mythology who tells her dreams. The artist sympathizes with Gundrun's struggles in her ancient society, and returns to her New York home feeling kinship with women of the past. In the video, images move back and forth between past and present with the aid of overlays and an evocative musical score.

The cathode ray television tube is disappearing in favor of the flat screen monitor, and videotapes are becoming less common every day; video art will evolve in step. Given the ease of shooting and editing digital video today, the line between video art and filmmaking has blurred. The five films of the *Cremaster Cycle* by Matthew Barney were shot on digital video and are usually projected in art galleries, but part of *Cremaster 3* has been released on DVD as well.

8.15 Matthew Barney.
Cremaster 3. 2002.
Production still.
© 2002 Matthew Barney. Photo: Chris Winget. Courtesy Gladstone Gallery, New York.

8.16 Vera Molnar.
Parcours (Maquette pour un Environment Architectural).
1976.
Courtesy of the artist. © 2010 Artists Rights Society (ARS), New York/ADAGP, Paris.

DIGITAL ART FORMS

The art-making capacity of computer-linked equipment ranges from producing finished art, such as color prints, film, and videos, to generating ideas for works that are ultimately made in another medium. Computers are also used to solve design problems by facilitating the visualization of alternative solutions. The computer's capacity to store images in progress enables the user to save unfinished images while exploring ways of solving problems in the original. Thus, sculptors, photographers, filmmakers, designers, and architects can take advantage of computer software tools.

The multipurpose characteristics of the computer have accelerated the breakdown of boundaries between media specializations. A traditional painter working with a computer can easily employ photo imaging or even add movement and sound to a work. A photographer can retouch, montage, change values, "paint over," or color black-and-white images. Digital technology facilitates the writing, design, and printing of books such as *Artforms.*

The first exhibition of computer-generated digital imagery took place in a private art gallery in 1965; few claimed that it was art. Most of the earliest digital artists used computers to make drawings with a plotter, a small ink-bearing, wheeled device that moves over a piece of paper drawing a line in one color according to programmed instructions. With the help of technicians, Vera Molnar made some of the most visually interesting of these early efforts, such as her 1976 *Parcours*. The computer was programmed to make variations on a basic set of plotter movements, yielding a work that resembles a drawing quickly done by hand. In many of these early types of computer art, the plotter's motions were not entirely predictable, a fact that added to the attractiveness of the images. The expense and complexity of computer technology in those years, however, kept all but a few pioneer artists away from the medium.

The advent of faster computers, color printers, and interactive graphics radically changed the scenario in the middle 1980s; as the computer's capabilities grew, more artists began to take interest.

Camilla Benolirao Griggers used a video-editing application to create her work *Alienations of the Mother Tongue.* She began with a fashion photograph and introduced incremental changes in the subject's face, bit by bit, until by the last frame we have a horrifying image of destruction. She combined all the stages of the frame's evolution into a five-minute video that evolves from something glamorous and desirable into a cry of pain.

This work shows how digital technology has undercut the traditional truth value of photography. If images are so easy to manipulate, then the camera can indeed be made to lie. Seeing is no longer believing, in the traditional sense of the expression. Besides new ways of making art, the digital revolution affords new ways of presenting it.

8.17 Camilla Benolirao Griggers.
Alienations of the Mother Tongue. 1996. Video with digital graphics and animation. 5 minutes.
Courtesy of the artist.

An early creator of sophisticated works for the Internet is Annette Weintraub; her 2001 piece *The Mirror That Changes* joins high-tech execution with social awareness. The title comes from a quote by Leonardo da Vinci: "Water is the mirror that changes with the color of its subject." On opening the work, we see nine adjoined vertical bars, each a portion of a photograph of water. A soundtrack of flowing liquid is a constant background. Clicking on one of the bars enlarges it and presents its related content, which may include video, sound, layered images, voice tracks, or scrolling text. The words that pass and the voices we hear may inform us about past wars fought over water, delight us with poetic quotes from literature about water, or wake us up to current crises that involve water ("We will never have more water on earth than we have right now"). The work's wealth of information, presented in easily accessible layers with elegant presentation, makes it a standout.

If Weintraub's piece raises awareness of our natural environment, Rui Filipe Antunes made a digital video work in 2006 that creates its own unreal world. He describes *XTNZ* (on the following page) as a garden, made of slowly evolving shapes that resemble life-forms, but they are in fact computer-drawn modules driven by software. They grow and

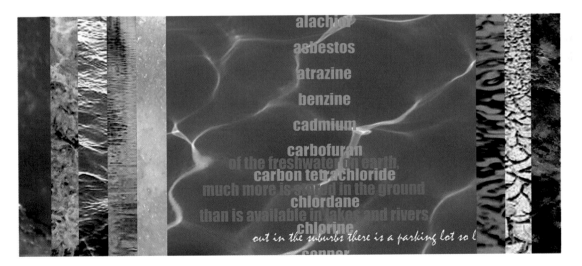

8.18 Annette Weintraub.
The Mirror That Changes: Aquifer 2. 2003.
Screenshot. Interactive World Wide Web work.
Courtesy of the artist.

8.19 Rui Filipe Antunes.
Still from *XTNZ*. 2006.
Digital video.

interact, accompanied by both natural and manufactured sounds. The artist created these various "lifeforms," divided them into families, and turned them loose in a digital environment to see what would happen. The title is based on David Cronenberg's feature film *eXistenZ*, which deals with the question of real and virtual reality, and indeed the shapes of *XTNZ* could be real if not for the dreamy, fluorescent colors. The work is available for viewing at any time because the artist created a YouTube channel for it.

As we all know, almost anything can be found on the Internet, and Natalie Bookchin took advantage

of this abundance in creating the digital video *Location Secured* in 2006. She surfed the Internet to gather random examples of surveillance camera footage from about a dozen locations around the world, and then strung them together into a 12-minute film. For a soundtrack she used the recorded telephone conversations of President Lyndon Johnson from 1963 to 1965, alternating with telephone calls placed to Dr. Ruth Westheimer's radio advice program *Sexually Speaking* (yes, both are freely available for listening on the Internet). Sometimes the video footage is poor, as when rain distorts the camera lens, or vegetation blocks the view, or the equipment is of low quality. But as we look at a Japanese garden, for example, we hear President Johnson's staff discussing where to find him in the White House. Over footage of janitors sweeping a gymnasium somewhere, a woman complains because her boyfriend started asking out her twin sister. These odd juxtapositions are common in today's cyber-driven world, but when the artist puts them together for display in an art gallery, the jarring effect is magnified. And because all of the material that she gathered deals with private realities, *Location Secured* highlights the issue of what is public and what is private, an urgent concern in a time when surveillance cameras in public places are on the rise.

Lynn Hershman Leeson directly confronted the issue of digital simulation when she created the video cyborg *DiNA* in 2004. (The name comes from the phrase "digital DNA.") *DiNA* appears on a video installation in which viewers walk up to a

8.20 Natalie Bookchin.
Still from *Location Secured*. 2007. Digital video, 12 minutes.
Courtesy of the artist.

8.21 Lynn Hershman Leeson.
DiNA. 2004.
Artificially intelligent agent, network connection, custom software, video, and microphone.
Dimensions variable.
Courtesy Bitforms Gallery.

microphone and interact with the virtual woman on the screen before them. *DiNA* is running for the imaginary office of Telepresident, and in her slightly disembodied cybervoice she invites viewers to use the microphone to raise questions and concerns. *DiNA*'s responses sound surprisingly intelligent for a machine, but she is linked to the Internet and searches in real time for text to use in response to viewer input. After interacting with *DiNA* for a few minutes, viewers learn that she takes moderately liberal positions on abortion and capital punishment, for example. Most viewers conclude either that *DiNA* could indeed run for office, or that she seems more thoughtful than most politicians. Her campaign slogan is "Artificial intelligence is better than no intelligence." In an age when telling the real from the pre-packaged is difficult, *DiNA* complicates the issue in a memorable way. The artist created a campaign Web site in time for the 2004 presidential elections and stocked it with "live footage," just to ensure that *DiNA*'s positions on the issues would be available to voters.

PRACTICE MORE: Get flashcards for images and terms and review chapter material with quizzes at **www.myartslab.com**

AT THE EDGE OF ART

RMB City

A CONTEMPORARY QUESTION underlying all moving-image art is this: How real can the virtual become? In the case of *RMB City* by Chinese artist Cao Fei, the answer is, "surprisingly so." She made a virtual city on the Web site Second Life (SL) that is like a check-up on today's China. *RMB City* can be viewed only by members of that virtual community, and viewers have the same privileges as in other SL regions: to collect objects, meet people, have relationships, and build things. But *RMB City* is also a thoughtful microcosm of today's China. New skyscrapers go up all the time; the ancient and the contemporary mix in compelling ways; China's communist past lurks in the background. The *RMB* of the title is an abbreviation for the name of the Chinese currency. At the official opening, which took place in cyberspace in early 2009, visitors saw the new mayor, heard a speech by the artist, and rubbed elbows with SLebrities.

Digital art has evolved as quickly as computers themselves. Many artists today include digital technology in their works in one way or another. The need for a separate category called "digital art" is subject to further debate. Whether it remains a medium with its own properties, or becomes integrated into others, is yet to be decided.

8.22 Cao Fei.
RMB City. 2007–2009.
Still from Second Life project.
Lombard-Freid Projects.

GRAPHIC DESIGN

WHAT ARE THE MAJOR BRANCHES OF GRAPHIC DESIGN?

WHAT CAUSES PEOPLE TRAINED IN THE ARTS TO GO INTO DESIGN?

HOW HAS THE COMPUTER INFLUENCED DESIGN PRACTICES?

Every manufactured object, printed image, and constructed space has been designed by someone. From clothing to airplanes, from homes to public buildings, from billboards to toys, good design can make the difference between success and failure.

DESIGN DISCIPLINES

As consumers, we discover that some things are well designed and some are not. When the form and function of an object do not complement each other, the object is poorly designed. Good design solves problems; bad design creates problems.

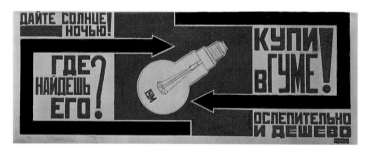

9.1 Aleksandr Rodchenko and Vladimir Maiakovskii.
Give Me Sun at Night. 1923.
Design for Poster.
Gouache, ink, pencil, gelatin silver print. 4⅜″ × 18″.
Collection Merrill C. Berman. Photograph by Jim Frank. © Estate of
Aleksandr Rodchenko/RAO, Moscow/Licensed by VAGA, New York, NY.

Design disciplines include, graphic design, interactive design, motion graphics, product design, textile design, clothing design, interior design, architecture, and environmental design. In this chapter, we will focus on graphic design, interactive design, motion graphics, and product design.

Of all art forms, we encounter graphic design most frequently in our daily life. We interact with graphic design on an almost constant basis; most designers have chosen it as their profession because they relish that close interaction with people in all situations. Our encounters with graphic design are usually casual and unintended; we do not seek out graphic design the way we might seek other art forms in a gallery or museum. This fact gives designers an unequalled opportunity to attract, inform, persuade, delight, bore, offend, or repel us.

Text dominates Russian designer Aleksandr Rodchenko's sketch for a 1923 sign. *Give Me Sun at Night!* exclaims the text in the upper left. "Where do we find this?" reads the inscription just below. "Buy it at GUM," is the answer, referring to Moscow's largest department store. In the lower right, a slogan hammers the point home: "Blinding

HEAR MORE: Listen to an audio file of your chapter at
www.myartslab.com

and cheap." In the center, surrounded by arrows, is the lightbulb that will illuminate everyone at night. Not many people in Russia used light bulbs at the time, so the tone is emphatic.

Graphic design often has the goal of getting us to do something. The French designer Cassandre designed the poster *l'Atlantique* in 1932 to promote travel by ship. The text of the poster merely informs viewers that the ship weighs forty thousand tons, and frequently goes to South America under the auspices of the Sud-Atlantique Steamship Company. The designer lets the image do most of the persuading in this poster, and it dominates the composition. The angle of view is from below, as if we were bobbing on the ocean surface as the ship looms majestically above. The implication is that if we travel by ship, we participate in something larger than life.

GRAPHIC DESIGN

The term *graphic design* refers to the process of working with words and pictures to enhance visual communication. Much of graphic design involves designing materials to be printed, including books, magazines, brochures, packages, posters, and imagery for electronic media. Such design ranges in scale and complexity from postage stamps and trademarks to billboards, film, video, and Web pages.

Graphic design is a creative process employing art and technology to communicate ideas. With control of symbols, type, color, and illustration, the graphic designer produces visual compositions meant to attract, inform, and persuade a given audience. A good graphic designer can memorably arrange image and text for the benefit of both.

Corporate Logos

In our age, when image seems to be everything, companies spend large sums on graphic design to present the best "identity package." A **logo** is an identifying mark, or trademark, based on letterforms

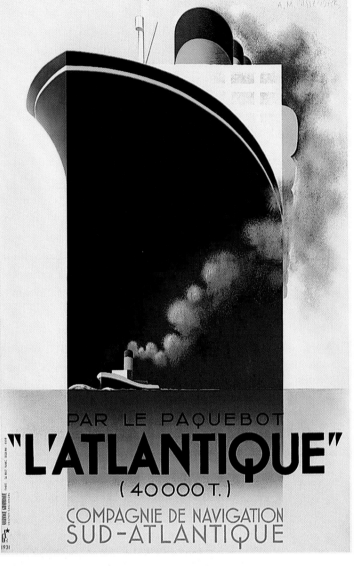

9.2 Cassandre (Adolpe Jean-Marie Noreau).
l'Atlantique. 1932.
Lithograph. 39½″ × 24½″.
Collection Merrill C. Berman. Photograph by Jim Frank.

combined with pictorial elements. Corporations finely calibrate logos to present a distinctive and memorable appearance.

An organization's logo may even change over time, reflecting a different cultural climate, a different set of goals, or new management. When the National Aeronautics and Space Administration (NASA) was founded in the late

a. 1959. Logo designer James Modarelli.

b. 1974. Designers Danne & Blackburn, New York.

c. 1992. Logo designer James Modarelli.

9.3 *NASA Letterhead.*
Cooper-Hewitt, National Design Museum, Smithsonian Institution. Gift of the National Aeronautics and Space Administration, 1996-36-1, 1996-36-3, 1996-36-5.

1950s, the first *NASA Letterhead* used a celestial globe with the Earth, the Moon, and a stylized arrow symbolizing space flight (a). In 1973, with space travel more commonplace, the logo was changed to the stylized initials in red (b). The letters "A" symbolize rocket nose cones in this second NASA logo.

In the early 1990s, in the aftermath of federal budget cuts and in a demoralized environment caused by the explosion of the space shuttle *Challenger*, the logo was redesigned again. NASA decided to return to a version of its previous logo, which administrators thought better exemplified an optimistic and exploratory mood (c). This time they used the color blue to symbolize the heavens.

In today's media-saturated world, where excessive familiarity can be deadening, keeping a corporate identity package both contemporary and recognizable is a big challenge. One of the most original solutions to this problem is the *Saks Fifth Avenue Logo* by Michael Bierut of Pentagram. Most people have been familiar with the Saks brand for years; for most of its history it used logos based on elegant cursive script to decorate its shopping bags. Bierut cut the old logo into 64 equal squares and reassembled them randomly, making the new logo both recognizable and utterly new. Moreover, the logo can be continuously varied by shifting the squares or adjusting their scale. Thus, said Bierut, the new logo "creates consistency without sameness," a worthwhile motto.

Typography

Letterforms are art forms. **Typography** is the art and technique of composing printed material from letterforms (typefaces or **fonts**). Designers, hired to meet clients' communication needs, frequently

9.4 Michael Bierut.
Saks Fifth Avenue Logo. 2007.
Design Firm: Pentagram. Courtesy of Saks Fifth Avenue.

create designs that relate nonverbal images and printed words in complementary ways.

Just a few decades ago, when people committed words to paper, their efforts were handwritten or typewritten—and nearly all typewriters had the same typeface, the name of which was unknown to most users. Now anyone who uses a computer can select fonts and create documents that look professional, producing desktop publications such as newsletters, brochures, and Web pages. But computer programs, like pencils, paintbrushes, and cameras, are simply tools: They can facilitate artistic aims if their operator has artistic sensibilities.

Since the Chinese invention of printing in the eleventh century, thousands of typefaces have been created—helped recently by digital technology. For the text of *Artforms*, Adobe Garamond was selected for its elegance and readability.

Many European-style typefaces are based on the capital letters carved in stone by early Romans. **Roman** letters are made with thick and thin strokes, ending in **serifs**—short lines with pointed ends, at an angle to the main strokes. In typesetting, the term "roman" is used to mean "not italic." **Sans serif** (without serifs) typefaces have a modern look due to their association with modernist designs. They are actually ancient in origin. 𝔅𝔩𝔞𝔠𝔨 𝔩𝔢𝔱𝔱𝔢𝔯 typefaces are based on Northern medieval manuscripts and are rarely used today. Typographer Tobias Frere-Jones approaches his work the way an artist does. When an interviewer asked him about the importance of the art of typography, he said, "A designer choosing typefaces is like a casting director," meaning that the fonts function like actors saying the lines. Just as different actors interpret a role differently, each typeface has its own style for interpreting any given text. We see him in action with *Three Typefaces*: *Nobel* is a redesign of a Swiss modern font invented in 1929; he developed the *Armada* font to refer to the arches of nineteenth-century urban warehouses; *Garage Gothic* recalls the printing on parking garage tickets.

Heidi Cody took a more ironic stance with her 2000 work *American Alphabet*. She found all twenty-six letters in the initials of corporate logos. She said, "I try to get viewers to consciously acknowledge how indoctrinated, or 'branded' they are."[1]

Posters and Other Graphics

A poster is a concise visual announcement that provides information through the integrated design of typographic and pictorial imagery. In a flash, an effective poster attracts attention and conveys its message. The creativity of a poster designer is directed toward a specific purpose, which may be to advertise or to persuade.

The concept of the modern poster is more than a hundred years old. In the nineteenth centry, most

Nobel
Armada
Garage Gothic

9.5 Tobias Frere-Jones.
Three Typefaces: Nobel™, *Armada*™, *Garage Gothic*™. 1992–1994.
The Font Bureau, Boston.

posters were lithographs, and many artists made extra income by designing them. Henri de Toulouse-Lautrec was the most important of these, as we saw on page 115. Early lithographic posters were all hand-drawn; designers added color to their work by printing the same sheet with multiple stones, one for each color. In the 1920s and 1930s, advances in printing methods made high-quality mass production possible, including the printing of photographs at large scale with text. Since the 1950s, radio, television, and print advertising have

LEARN MORE: To see an interview with Heidi Cody about *American Alphabet* and other works, go to
www.myartslab.com

9.6 Heidi Cody.
American Alphabet. 2000.
A set of 26 light boxes which feature the isolated first letters of American grocery products. Lambda Duratrans print in an aluminum light box, each box: 28″ × 28″ × 7″.
American Alphabet © 2000 Heidi Cody, www.heidicody.com.

9.7 Chaz Maviyane-Davies.
*Article 15: Everyone Has the Right to
Nationality and to Change It.* 1996.
Poster.
Courtesy of the artist.

overshadowed posters. Although they now play a lesser role than they once did, well-designed posters can still fulfill needs for instant communication.

Many social causes find vivid expression in posters. The Black Panther Party, an African-American activist organization, made many creative (and militant) posters in the 1960s and 1970s. At the same time, the Chicano movement commissioned many artists to make silkscreens promoting the causes of Mexican Americans. An example of the latter is the poster by Ester Hernández on page 117.

Some posters remind us of our rights rather than urge us to change our behavior. Chaz Maviyane-Davies in 1996 based a set of posters on the United Nations Universal Declaration of Human Rights. His poster *Article 15* includes text that guarantees the right to a nationality. He used the face of a Black man who watches hopefully between the stripes of a flag, because a great many images of Africans that we see in the media are associated with disaster or famine. Maviyane-Davies has also made more urgent graphic appeals, as the essay on the next page shows. As long ago as 1997, he was warning us about the effects of global climate change. See his poster for a United Nations Convention, pictured on page 10.

CHAZ MAVIYANE-DAVIES   Design Between the Eyes

CHAZ MAVIYANE-DAVIES grew up in Zimbabwe when it was still a British colony. His first jobs were low-paying drafting tasks for a telecommunications company. He recalled, "discrimination was the order of the day so very few opportunities existed for me to pursue anything outside of the life that a racist government had planned for me."[2] He went to London and earned an M.A. degree at the Central School of Art and Design. While he was away, Zimbabwe became independent under the leadership of the Patriotic Front party headed by Robert Mugabe. He established a graphic design firm called the Maviyane Project in the capital, Harare. Most of his clients were charities, public service agencies, and nongovernmental organizations.

As years passed, the Mugabe regime became more and more suspicious and repressive of alternative viewpoints. Maviyane-Davies tried to remain apart from the growing fray but found it difficult. He recalled, "Designers can choose to be active or passive in what they do, regardless of their ideology—but if they think they are neutral they should be careful whose interests they really serve." By trying to remain neutral, he grew to believe that he was only giving support to the regime.

His work took a step toward militancy when the Mugabe government began restricting participation in the 2000 legislative elections. Suddenly opposition parties had trouble getting candidates on the ballot, and voters were prevented from registering in many areas. Maviyane-Davies created dozens of posters for free distribution encouraging people to keep democracy alive.

The Mugabe regime began using many of the same procedures during the 2002 presidential campaigns, even imprisoning the leading candidate for treason. Maviyane-Davies again swung into action, making posters for free distribution on paper and over the Internet. One of these is *Absolute Power*, a simple design based on a popular drink advertisement in which the designer changed the original beverage into blood.

This graphic agitation must have been effective: The government forced Maviyane-Davies to leave the country in 2003. He now teaches graphic design and continues his public service work. One of his best-known projects was a set based on the United Nations Universal Declaration of Human Rights. He said the series "grew out of the indignation I have always felt in the way that Africans are constantly portrayed. Hence, the series gives prominence to Black persons."

His advice for aspiring designers: "I'd just say believe in yourself, really believe in yourself; research, work as hard as you can at the process and not the ends, strive to realize your vision, listen with your eyes and ears and use your soul."

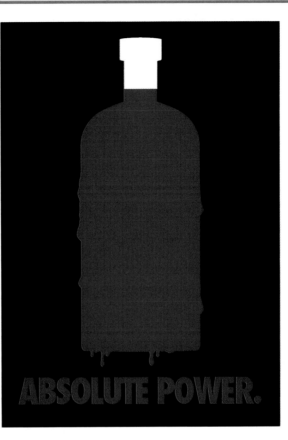

9.8 Chaz Maviyane-Davies.
Absolute Power. 2000.
Poster, Graphic Commentary 6.
Courtesy of the artist.

9.9 Chaz Maviyane-Davies.
Courtesy of Chaz Maviyane-Davies.

Humor has great appeal in design. Maira Kalman's *New Yorker Cover* gently mocks the boisterous subcultures of Manhattan and environs with exotic-sounding names. Some of these are Botoxia, Hiphopabad, Trumpistan, and al-Zeimers. Published in December 2001, the design allowed New Yorkers to laugh at themselves again after the tragedy of September 11.

English designer Jonathan Barnbrook mocked the media overload that seems to accompany every

9.11 Jonathan Barnbrook.
Olympuke ("Drowning in Advertising"). 2009.
iPhone wallpaper, 320 × 480 pixels.
Barnbrook Design.

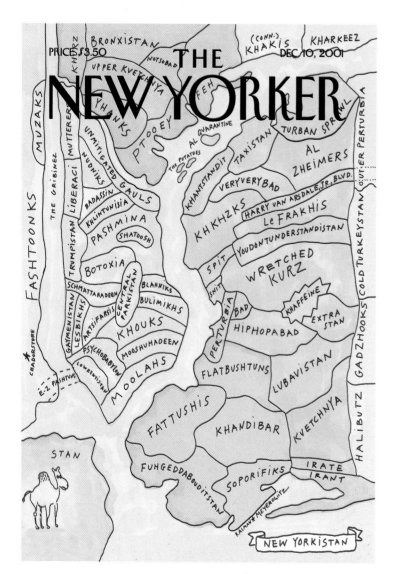

9.10 Maira Kalman and Rick Meyerowitz.
Newyorkistan.
New Yorker cover. December 10, 2001.
Kalman and Meyerowitz/The New Yorker/Conde Nast Archive.
Copyright © Conde Nast.

renewal of the Olympic Games. For the 2010 Winter Games, he created a logo called the *Olympuke* for a new sport, Drowning in Advertising. In a sea of deep red and wavy lines borrowed from the logo of a famous brand of soft drink, we see the head and arm of a submerged consumer calling for help. He designed this *Olympuke* as desktop wallpaper for an iPhone and made it available as a free download.

Advertising design goes far beyond posters, album covers, and books, as creative designers today think of other ways to transcend two-dimensional media and help spread the message. An example of cheeky design creativity in three dimensions was the campaign for *Avenue Q: The Musical* when it opened in Las Vegas in 2006. *Avenue Q* is a humorous

9.12 Vinny Sainato and Spot Co.
Avenue Q: The Musical. Advertising Campaign. 2006.
Fur-covered taxicab, metal sign.
Courtesy of the designer.

homage to the famous children's TV program *Sesame Street*, but the characters are adults with adult problems. To attract attention in the gambling-mad city of Las Vegas, Vinny Sainato covered 20 taxicabs in synthetic orange fur, leaving a bold white *Q* on the doors. A sign atop each cab urged the public to "see what the fuzz is all about." He told an interviewer, "I hope I can create work that's even a little unexpected or at least fun."

The subculture of punk music developed its own design style, which does not look designed at all. The Sex Pistols released their first single, *God Save the Queen*, to coincide with the Silver Jubilee celebrations of the twenty-fifth year of the reign of Queen Elizabeth. The song was so controversial that it was banned from the airways, yet it still became the number one selling song. Twenty-five years later, the book *100 Best Record Covers of All Time* judged Jamie Reid's cover the best record cover ever produced.

9.13 Jamie Reid.
God Save the Queen. 1977.
Album cover.
Michael Ochs Archives\Getty Images Inc. – Michael Ochs Archives.

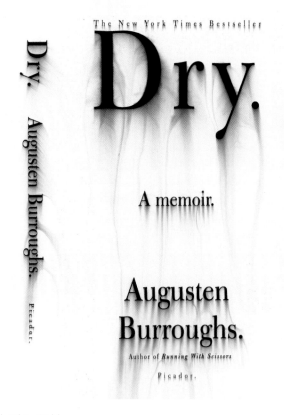

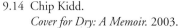

9.14 Chip Kidd.
Cover for Dry: A Memoir. 2003.
Book by Augusten Burroughs.
Geoff Spear Photography.

INTERACTIVE DESIGN

As more and more of our media become interactive, designers work to organize the information presented and keep the layouts attractive. This is a relatively new area of design, but already there have been a few standout projects.

For New York's Clo Wine Bar, Potion Design created an *Interactive Table* that ran the length of the venue's 24-foot bar. By merely touching the projection on the table top, patrons can select wines and then pull up information about their sources, characteristics, and prices. They can also search for wines by color, type, or region. Because each taster's search for information is carried out in real time and in public, the design facilitates interaction with other patrons standing nearby. The business owners can also easily re-program the display to change the products on offer.

Before Sugar Labs went to work, using a computer required literacy, as users read menus, commands, and applications. But for the educational project One Laptop Per Child (OLPC), it designed an interface called *Sugar* that consists entirely of icons. This new laptop system can be used in any country by anyone, regardless of their literacy level. The *Sugar Interface* also did away with the old "desktop" metaphor by placing the user at the center of the array of applications. Choosing an application means simply going

Book covers function like corporate logos, uniting image and text to extend the message of a book and condense it into a single memorable image that shoppers will see in bookstores. Chip Kidd is a leader in this field, as evidenced by his work on the *Cover for Dry: A Memoir.* This book tells the story of an advertising executive's fast-paced life fueled by excessive drinking, and his eventual recovery from alcoholism. Kidd's cover resembles a dry landscape where water once flowed around the title letters, just as liquor once flowed through the author's life. The designer counted his work a success when a bookstore customer once asked the sales clerk for a copy that had not suffered water damage.

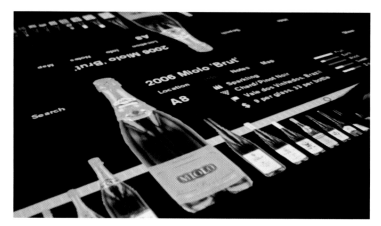

9.15 Potion Design.
Interactive Table. 2008.
Lucy Schaeffer\Potion.

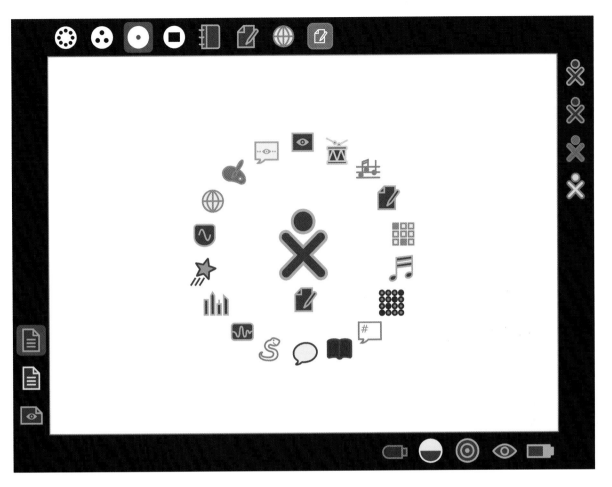

9.16 Sugar Labs.
Sugar Interface. 2007.
Activity Management 11. Home view. Computer Screenshot.

toward the icon of an activity, which comes under one of four headings: Home, Friends, Neighborhood, and Activity. The OLPC computers are intended for local networking (which facilitates teaching), and because they cost only $100 each, they are gaining popularity in school systems around the world. The best place to see the *Sugar Interface* in action is in Uruguay, where every child has been given one.

MOTION GRAPHICS

The cutting edge of design right now is in the field of motion graphics, in which a designer uses visual effects, live action, and animation to create a two-dimensional project that moves. Designers combine these techniques in various ways for time-based sequences in Web sites, television commercials, and music videos.

Motion graphics as a discipline began in the 1950s with title sequences for Hollywood movies. Most title sequences were merely slow scrolls of names until the arrival of Saul Bass, and his collaboration with Alfred Hitchcock. Bass said in an interview that an opening title sequence for a film can "create a climate for the story that is to follow," because "the audience involvement with a film should really begin with the first frame."

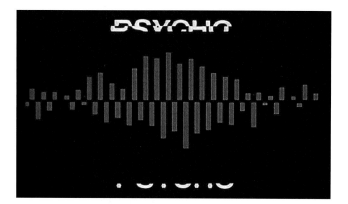

9.17 Saul Bass.
Title Sequence for Psycho. 1960.
Film directed by Alfred Hitchcock.
Universal Studios.

Thus, for the 1960 film *Psycho*, he split the name of the movie into three horizontal sections that grind against each other before flying apart, pushed by an array of moving vertical bars. The fast motion of the sequence captures the restless energy and surging passions of the film, just as the title's fragmentation parallels the psychic breakdown of the film's main character, a murderer. Bass created the *Psycho* title sequence by moving actual bars and letters on tracks and photographing them, an extremely tedious process.

The arrival of advanced digital editing in the 1990s ensured the takeoff of motion graphics. The new computer applications enable designers to create each frame of a sequence with all the freedom that photo editing allows. Thus, motion graphics designers are increasingly directors of short but intense projects that combine input from many sources.

The most original use of the new technologies came with Kyle Cooper's work on the *Title Sequence for Se7en*, which like *Psycho* is a dramatic crime story. The title sequence has a plot of its own, as a man with bandaged fingers assembles and stitches together a booklet about murder and sexual deviance. Layered images, film clips, and spoiled type nervously twitch across the screen along with the hand-lettered credits, over a sound-track by the Nine Inch Nails. Most important, this haunting close-up sequence has a function in the script: It introduces the audience to the mind of the killer, who does not appear until 40 minutes into the film. Cooper said that his aptitude for vivid graphics came in part from his earlier study at Yale with Paul Rand, one of America's legendary designers.

Cooper's tense style was widely imitated in credits for other thriller and sci-fi films, but the motion graphics medium is capable of almost any mood. When Stardust Studios made a television commercial for *Hugo Boss* in 2006, they staged actor Jonathan Rhys Meyers walking through an

SEE MORE: For a Closer Look at *Title Sequence for Se7en*, go to **www.myartslab.com**

9.18 Kyle Cooper.
Title Sequence for Se7en.
1995.
Film directed by David Fincher.
New Line Cinema/
A Time Warner Company.

9.19 Stardust Studios.
Hugo Boss Commercial. 2006.
Still from digital video.
Televison spot directed by Jake Banks, Stardust Studios,
live-action cinematography and motion graphics.

exuberantly animated urban environment that surges and sways like kelp on the seabed. Buildings spring up and turn on their sides, passersby morph into bouncing balls, sidewalks fold like Japanese screens, and a lamppost lies down to become the tone arm of a turntable before the entire scene swirls and rushes back into the fragrance bottle. Only a few years ago, these effects were impossible.

PRODUCT DESIGN

We all handle designed products every day, and industrial designers work to make these products more beautiful and useful. We close this chapter by examining four objects that have made history by integrating utility, technology, and cutting-edge design.

The Sony Corporation of Japan started the personal audio revolution with the *TR-610 Transistor Radio* in 1957. This new radio fit in the hand, and consumers could select the color of its elegant exterior. It also had a wire loop that swung out to allow placement on a table. The model sold nearly a half million units during its two years of shelf life. The name Sony was itself invented near the time of the release of the *TR-610*, in order to facilitate global sales. The name is a combination of the Latin *sonus* ("sound") and the endearing nickname Sonny. This corporate brand name is not obviously tied to any nationality and is far easier to pronounce than the company's previous name, Tokyo Tsushin Kogyo.

Sony introduced the FM band into its transistor radios the next year, thus beginning a long chain of innovations in personal audio that lasted for decades. In the 1970s, the company united miniature headphones with the new cassette technology and invented the Walkman. When compact disc recordings became feasible in the 1980s, Sony developed a portable player that soon became known as the "boom box." The advent of computer-based digital audio as the century turned led to a proliferation of personal mp3 players.

9.20 Sony Corporation.
TR-610 Transistor Radio. 1957.
Still from digital video.
Enrico Tedeschi.

9.21 Frogdesign/Harmut Esslinger.
Apple Macintosh. 1984.
Personal computer.
Will Mosgrove\Apple Computer, Inc.

New technology and sleek design came together in the *Apple Macintosh* computer in 1984. With its curvy, off-white exterior and new mouse-driven user interface, this model set off the Silicon Valley boom. Designed with an eye for "the rest of us" rather than button-down business types or techno-savvy geeks, the Macintosh was promoted as a vehicle of personal creativity. Its graphical user interface made most tasks much easier than the old command-line interface, and it had a small footprint on the personal desktop. It was also one of the first new products to be introduced to the public in a television advertisement during the Super Bowl football championship.

The *Macintosh* came out just as desktop computers were making great leaps in processing power. The machine's ease of use and faster speeds contributed to a radical decentralization of the design industry in the 1990s; one person at a workstation could now do the work of an entire team.

The *Oral-B Cross-Action Toothbrush* came directly out of the Silicon Valley environment. Consumer research determined that people generally hold toothbrushes in one of five ways. The Oral-B company commissioned Lunar Design

to create a new brush to more comfortably accommodate all of them while delivering the bristles at a more effective angle than traditional rectangular brushes. The designers used ergonomics, three-dimensional computer modeling, and advanced resin materials to create the new brush in 1999. It became an industry leader and set a new aesthetically pleasing and effective norm for what had been a very common object.

Many product designers today are finding ways to make their projects greener; a notable event in this evolution occurred in 2009 when some English designers applied themselves to making a new kind of wind turbine for generating electricity. Most wind turbines resemble huge aircraft propellers: they are large, noisy, and need fairly strong breezes, making them suitable only for rural areas (where they often damage birds). But the

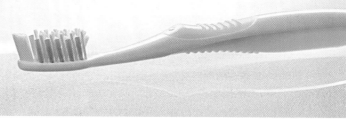

9.22 Lunar Design.
Oral-B Cross-Action Toothbrush. 1999.
Industrial Design by Lunar Design. Photo by Sandbox Studio.

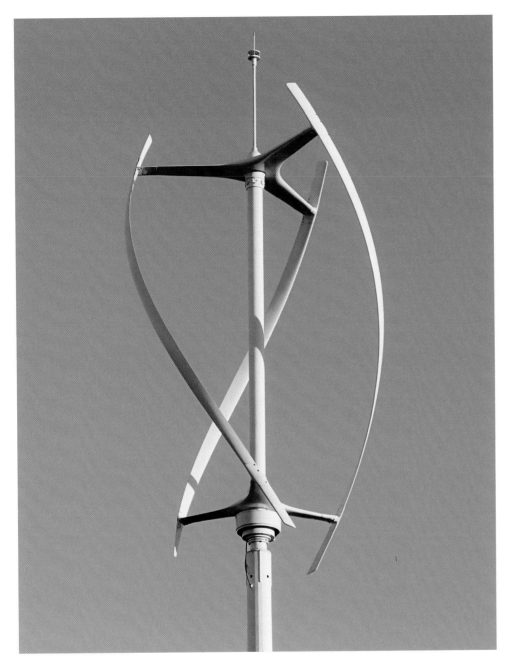

9.23 Quietrevolution Ltd.
QR5 Wind Turbine. 2009.
Carbon fiber and epoxy resin. Height of unit: 16′5″.
Quietrevolution, Ltd.

QR5 Wind Turbine solved all of those problems with a new design in a graceful-looking frame. This new turbine is almost perfectly silent, runs on lighter breezes, is small enough to place atop a house, and has not injured a single bird. The *QR* in the turbine's name stands for both the company name and its main selling point: quiet revolution.

From shopping bags to toothbrushes to wind machines, good design can make the difference between a successful product and a failure.

PRACTICE MORE: Get flashcards for images and terms and review chapter material with quizzes at **www.myartslab.com**

HOW DO MODELING, CASTING, CARVING, AND ASSEMBLING DIFFER?

WHICH MEDIA ARE MORE SUITABLE FOR ADDITIVE METHODS, AND WHICH FOR SUBTRACTIVE?

HOW ARE MOST PUBLIC MONUMENTS MADE?

When an artist creates a work in three dimensions, we call the result sculpture. It exists in space, as we do. The total experience of a sculpture is the sum of its surfaces and profiles.

FREESTANDING AND RELIEF SCULPTURE

Sculpture meant to be seen from all sides is called in-the-round, or **freestanding**. As we move around it, our experience of a sculpture is the sum of its surfaces and profiles. No one had to suggest moving around Calder's *Obus* to the little girl in our photograph. A single photograph shows only one view of a sculpture under one kind of light; thus, we receive only a limited impression of a sculpture unless we can see many photographs or, better yet, a video, or best of all, view the piece ourselves.

A sculpture that is not freestanding but projects from a background surface is in **relief**. In **low-relief** (sometimes called *bas-relief*) sculpture, the projection from the surrounding surface is slight. As a result, shadows are minimal. Coins, for example, are works of low-relief sculpture stamped from molds. A high point in the art of coin design was reached on the island of Sicily during the classical period of ancient Greece. The *Apollo* coin, shown here slightly larger than actual size, has a strong presence in spite of being in low relief and very small.

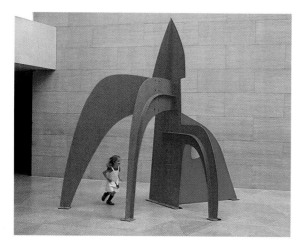

10.1 Alexander Calder.
Obus. 1972.
Painted sheet metal. 3.618 × 3.859 × 2.276 cm
(142½″ × 152″ × 89⅝″).
Collection of Mr. and Mrs. Paul Mellon, Photograph © 2001 Board of Trustees, National Gallery of Art, Washington. 1983.1.49.(A-1859)/SC. © 2010 Calder Foundation, New York/Artists Rights Society (ARS), New York.

10.2 *Apollo.* c. 415 B.C.E.
Greek silver coin. Diameter 1⅛″.
Photograph: Hirmer Fotoarchiv, Munich Germany.

HEAR MORE: Listen to an audio file of your chapter at **www.myartslab.com**

10.3 *Army on the March.*
Relief from Angkor Wat, The Great Temple of the
Khmers, Cambodia, 1100–1150. Sandstone.
Eliot Elisofon, *Life* Magazine © TimePix.

Some of the world's best and most varied low-relief sculptures are found at the temple of Angkor Wat in Cambodia. This vast temple complex was the center of the Khmer empire in the twelfth century. Here Khmer kings sponsored an extensive program of sculpture and architecture. Within the chambers of the complex, carvings are in such delicate low relief that they seem more like paintings than sculpture. One scene depicting an *Army on the March* is a king's army commanded by a prince. The rhythmic pattern of the spear-carrying soldiers contrasts with the curving patterns of the jungle foliage in the background. The soldiers and background provide a setting for the prince, who stands with bow and arrow poised in his carriage on the elephant's back. Intricate detail covers entire surfaces of the stone walls.

In **high-relief** sculpture, more than half of the natural circumference of the modeled form projects from the surrounding surface, and figures are often substantially undercut.

This is the case with Robert Longo's *Corporate Wars: Wall of Influence*, where male and female figures convulse in painful conflict. Much of the composition is high relief; in only a few areas are limbs and garments barely raised above the background surface. Dynamic gestures and the diagonal placement of torsos and limbs make the sculpture very active. The emotional charge of the piece suggests that Longo is horrified by the intense competition of corporate life.

METHODS AND MATERIALS

Traditionally, sculpture has been made by modeling, casting, carving, constructing, and assembling, or a combination of these processes.

Modeling

Modeling is usually an **additive process**. Pliable material such as clay, wax, or plaster is built up, removed, and pushed into a final form.

10.4 Robert Longo.
Corporate Wars: Wall of Influence. 1982.
Middle portion. Cast aluminum. 7′ × 9′.
Metro Pictures.

10.5 *Ballplayer with Three-Part Yoke and Bird Headdress.*
Maya Classic Period. A.D. 600–800. Ballplayer
figurine. Ceramic with traces of blue pigment.
Pre-Columbian Pottery. 34.2 × 17.8 cm.
Princeton University Art Museum. Museum purchase, Fowler
McCormick, Class of 1921, Fund, in honor of Gillett G. Griffin
on his 70th birthday. 1998–36. Photo by Bruce M. White.

Tool marks and fingerprint impressions are visible on the surface as evidence of the modeling technique employed to make *Ballplayer with Three-Part Yoke and Bird Headdress.* Body volume, natural gesture, and costume detail are clearly defined. The ancient Maya, who lived in what are now parts of Mexico, Guatemala, and Honduras, used clay to create fine ceramic vessels and lively naturalistic sculptures like this one.

The working consistencies of wax, clay, and plaster are soft. To prevent sagging, sculptors usually start all but very small pieces with a rigid inner support called an **armature**. When clay is modeled to form large sculptures, the total piece can be built in relatively small, separately fired, structurally self-sufficient sections, thereby eliminating the need for an armature.

10.6 Robert Arneson.
California Artist. 1982.
Stoneware with glazes. 68¼″ × 27½″ × 20¼″
(173.4 × 69.9 × 51.4 cm).
San Francisco Museum of Modern Art, Gift of the Art Council.
© Estate of Robert Arneson/Licensed by VAGA, New York, NY.

Robert Arneson used an armature while building his clay work *California Artist*. Arneson considered all art self-portraiture. He made this piece in response to an attack on his work by a New York critic, who said that, because of California's spiritual and cultural impoverishment, Arneson's work could have no serious depth or meaning.

Arneson created a life-sized ceramic figure with empty holes in place of eyes, revealing an empty head, depicted himself as a combination biker and aging hippie—complete with the appropriate visual clichés on and around the base. Those who think that clay is only for making bricks and dinnerware were acknowledged by Arneson, who put his name on the bricks, as any other brick maker would. The artist stated his point of view:

I like art that has humor, with irony and playfulness. I want to make "high" art that is outrageous, while revealing the human condition which is not always high.[1]

Artworks made through modeling need not be representational, as Ken Price's *Vink* shows. He modeled this work out of clay, fired it, painted it with multiple layers of acrylic paint, and then sanded the surface to expose spots of the paint layers below. Though the title refers to a small European songbird, any resemblance is coincidental. Rather, this piece suggests body parts, undersea organisms yet undiscovered, or some kind of knobby plant life. The iridescent color adds to the mysteriousness of the shape.

Casting

Casting processes make it possible to execute a work in an easily handled medium (such as clay) and then to reproduce the results in a more permanent material (such as bronze). Because most **casting** involves the substitution of one material for another, casting is also called a substitution process. The process of bronze casting was highly developed in ancient China, Greece, Rome, and parts of Africa. It has been used extensively in the West from the Renaissance to modern times.

Casting requires several steps. First, a **mold** is taken from the original work. The process of making the mold varies, depending on the material of the original and the material used in the casting. In any

10.7 Ken Price.
Vink. 2009.
Acrylic on fired ceramic. 9″ × 20″ × 11″.
L.A. Louver.

case, the mold completely surrounds the original, leaving no gaps. Materials that will harden can be used to make molds: clay diluted with water, molten metal, concrete, or liquid plastic. Second, the original sculpture is removed from the mold; this may require disassembly of either the original or the mold. Next, the casting liquid is poured into the resulting hollow cavity of the mold. Finally, when the casting liquid has hardened, the mold is removed.

Some casting processes use molds or flexible materials that allow many casts to be made from the same mold; with other processes, such as the **lost wax** process, the mold is destroyed to remove the hardened cast, thus permitting only a single cast to be made.

Castings can be solid or hollow, depending on the casting method. The cost and the weight of the material often help determine which casting method will be used for a specific work.

The process of casting a large object like Giacometti's *Man Pointing* (page 26) is extremely complicated. Except for small pieces that can be cast solid, most artists turn their originals over to foundry experts, who make the molds and do the casting. Most of our monuments in public parks were cast in bronze from artists' clay or wax models.

EXPLORE MORE: To see a studio video about lost wax casting, go to **www.myartslab.com**

10.8 Charles Ray.
Self-Portrait. 1990.
Mixed media. 75″ × 26″ × 20″.
Copyright © Charles Ray/Courtesy Matthew Marks Gallery, New York.

Robert Longo's *Corporate Wars: Wall of Influence* (earlier in this chapter) is made from cast aluminum.

In recent years, many sculptors have turned to modern synthetic media such as plastics, which can be cast and painted to look like a variety of other materials. Cast polyvinyl resin can be made to resemble human flesh, and some artists have exploited this property to create sculptures of unbelievable realism by adding clothing. Charles Ray's *Self-Portrait* is a very witty creation in this vein. He made the statue taller than he actually is—wouldn't we all like to be taller—and put a mannequin stand at the bottom.

Kaz Oshiro used paint, canvas, and bondo to create the strikingly realistic *Tailgate (Ota)*. This eye-popping work duplicates the size, shape, and worn look of a real pickup truck tailgate. He completed the illusion with bondo, a compound used in auto body repair shops. Viewers who peer around behind the work are rewarded with a glimpse of the wooden armature that holds it together. Both works play an elaborate game between image and reality.

Sculptors who attempt to fool our eyes with works that resemble real things are working in an ancient Western tradition that values realism as evidence of artistic skill. According to myth, the classical Greek artist Zeuxis once painted a man holding a bowl of grapes so realistically that a bird flew down and tried to eat the fruit. Zeuxis was unsatisfied with the work, however, because, he reasoned, if he had painted the man with equal skill, the bird would have been frightened off by the painted figure. Unfortunately, none of his works survive. The belief that the greatest artists are the best at capturing a likeness still holds much sway in our society,

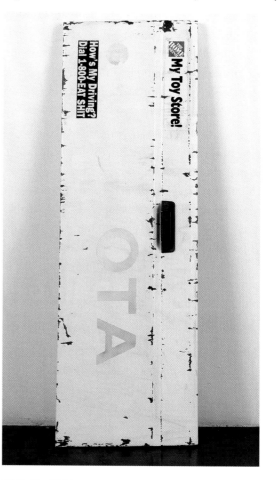

10.9 Kaz Oshiro.
Tailgate (OTA). 2006.
Acrylic and bondo on canvas. 53″ × 17⅞″ × 1¾″.
Bottom edge 12″ from wall.
Collection of Barry Sloane, Los Angeles. Courtesy of Rosamund Felsen Gallery, Santa Monica.

SEE MORE: To see a video interview with Kaz Oshiro, go to **www.myartslab.com**

10.10 Rachel Whiteread.
       Public Art Fund Watertower Project. 1997.
       12′ high, 9′ diameter.
       Courtesy of the artist and Luhring Augustine and
       Environmental Justice Foundation (EFT).

and artists such as Ray and Oshiro make charming allusion to it in their works.

Sculpture made with materials such as polyvinyl or epoxy resin is often formed in separate pieces in plaster molds, then assembled and unified with the addition of more layers of plastic. Although molds are used, the initial pouring process differs from conventional casting because forms are built up in layers inside mold sections rather than being made out of material poured into a single mold all at once.

English artist Rachel Whiteread uses these new materials in fascinating cast pieces that turn empty spaces into solid volumes. She made her 1997 *Public Art Fund Watertower Project* by pouring nine thousand pounds of clear urethane into a mold made from an actual water tank. The piece looks as though the wooden container vanished, leaving only the water.

10.11 Michelangelo Buonarroti.
       Awakening Slave. 1530–1534. Marble. Height 9′.
       Nimatallah/Art Resource, N.Y.

Carving

Carving away unwanted material to form a sculpture is a **subtractive** process. Michelangelo preferred this method. Close observation of his chisel marks on the surfaces of the unfinished *Awakening Slave* reveals the steps he took toward increasingly refined cutting—even before he had roughed out the figure from all sides. Because Michelangelo left this piece in an unfinished state, it seems as though we are looking over his shoulder midway through the carving process. For him, making sculpture was a process of releasing the form from within the block of stone. This is one of four figures, later called *Slaves*, that Michelangelo abandoned in various stages of completion.

EXPLORE MORE: To see a studio video about carving, go to **www.myartslab.com**

10.12 *Massive Stone Head.*
　　　12th–10th centuries B.C.E. Olmec.
　　　Basalt. Height 65″.
　　　Werner Forman/Anthropology Museum, Mexico/Art Resource, N.Y.

Carving is the most challenging of the three basic sculptural methods because it is a one-way technique that provides little or no opportunity to correct errors. Before beginning to cut, the sculptor must visualize the finished form from every angle within the original block of material. Another example of Michelangelo's carving is his *Pietà* on page 73.

The various types of stone with their different characteristics greatly influence the type of carving that can be done with them. The marble that Michelangelo and many sculptors in the European tradition prefer is typically soft and workable enough that it can be cut with a chisel. Final polishing with a light abrasive yields a smooth and creamy surface not unlike human skin. Marble has been a preferred material in the West for outdoor sculpture for centuries, but modern air pollution and acid rain harm the stone, making it far less desirable today. Granite avoids these pitfalls, and thus is often used for outdoor

monuments such as tombstones, but granite is so hard that carving in detail is difficult. Sandstone and limestone are sedimentary materials that have also found wide use in many parts of the world. The Cambodian creators of *Army on the March*, for example (see page 163), took advantage of the qualities of sandstone. Sedimentary stones are relatively soft, allowing much detail, and can be polished to a high gloss, though weather reduces this over time.

The ancient Egyptians used schist, a dense stone similar to slate. The jade that the Chinese favored is so hard and brittle that it can only be ground down by abrasion or filing; hence, it is suitable only for small pieces. The Olmecs of ancient Mexico used basalt, common in their area of the Gulf Coast. We can see its coarse-grained character in the *Massive Stone Head*. Even though the sculptor achieved an intense facial expression, there is little detail. The relative hardness of the stone forced the sculptors to keep most of its original boulder-like shape. The coarseness of basalt is even more obvious when we consider that this piece is nearly five and a half feet tall and weighs several tons.

In wood carving, many sculptors prefer walnut and cypress because of their strength and ease of working. The gesture of the mother in Elizabeth Catlett's carved *Mother and Child* suggests anguish, perhaps over the struggles all mothers know each child will face. Both figures have been abstracted in a composition of bold sweeping curves and essential shapes. Solidity of the mass is relieved by the open space between the uplifted chin and raised elbow and by the convex and concave surfaces. An engraved line indicating the mother's right hand accents the surface of the form. The highly polished smooth wood invites the viewer to touch.

Carving from a single block of wood is risky because the outside of a piece of wood dries much more readily than the inside, and the resulting difference in rates of shrinkage causes splits and cracks. The Chinese, who have traditionally excelled at wood carving, solved this problem many centuries ago by developing the technique called joined-block construction. Here, different parts of a sculpture are carved separately and fitted together.

The whole piece is then hollowed out. If the work is done well, as it is in *Guanyin of the Southern Sea*, the joints between the pieces of wood are not noticeable except to experts. This work was finished with paint.

Constructing and Assembling

For most of recorded history, the major sculpting techniques in the Western world were modeling, carving, and casting. Early in the twentieth century, assembling methods became popular. Such works are called **assembled sculpture** or constructions.

In the late 1920s, Spaniard Julio González pioneered the use of the welding torch for cutting and welding metal sculpture. The invention of oxyacetylene welding in 1895 had provided the necessary tool for welded metal sculpture, but it

10.14 *Guanyin of the Southern Sea (Nanhai Guanyin).*
Chinese, 11th–12th century, Liao Dynasty (907–1125).
Wood with multiple layers of paint, 95″ × 65″ (241.3 × 165.1 cm).
The Nelson Atkins Museum of Art, Kansas City, Missouri. Purchase: William Rockhill Nelson Trust 34-10. Photograph: Jamison Miller.

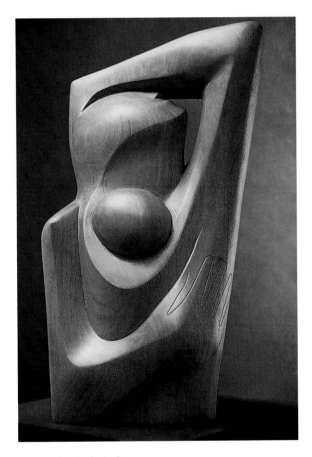

10.13 Elizabeth Catlett.
Mother and Child #2. 1971.
Walnut. Height 38″.
Photograph by Samella Lewis. © Elizabeth Catlett/ Licensed by VAGA, New York.

took three decades for artists to utilize the new tool's potential. González had learned welding while working briefly in an automobile factory. After several decades—and limited success—as a painter, González began assisting Picasso with the construction of metal sculpture. Subsequently, González committed himself to sculpture and began to create his strongest, most original work. In 1932 he wrote:

The Age of Iron began many centuries ago by producing very beautiful objects, unfortunately mostly weapons. Today it makes possible bridges and railroads as well. It is time that this material cease to be a murderer and the simple instrument of an overly

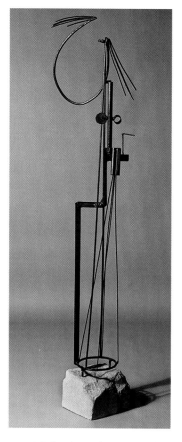

10.15 Julio González.
Maternity. 1934.
Welded iron. Height 49⅞″.
Copyright Tate Gallery, London/Art
Resource, NY. © 2010 Artists Rights
Society (ARS), New York/ADAGP,
Paris.

10.16 Julio González.
The Montserrat. 1936–1937.
Sheet iron. 163 × 60.5 ×
45.5 cm.
Stedelijk Museum, Amsterdam.
© 2010 Artists Rights Society (ARS),
New York/ADAGP, Paris.

presence. The artist intends her sculpture to *feel* like horses rather than simply look like them. The old car bodies she has used for many of her welded and wired metal horses add a note of irony: the scrapped autos take on a new life as a horse.

Some sculptors assemble found objects in ways that radically change the way we see familiar things. Yet we see enough of the objects' original characteristics that we can participate in their transformation. Such work requires metaphorical visual thinking by both artists and viewers. This type of constructed sculpture is called **assemblage**.

Picasso found a wealth of ready-made ingredients from salvaged fragments of daily life. For his assemblage *Bull's Head*, he cut the creative process to a single leap of awareness. Describing how it happened, Picasso said:

One day I found in a pile of jumble an old bicycle saddle next to some rusted handle bars . . . In a flash they

10.17 Deborah Butterfield.
Conure. 2007.
Found steel, welded. 92½″ × 119″ × 30″
(235 × 302.3 × 76.2 cm).
Courtesy L.A. Louver, Venice. © Deborah Butterfield/Licensed
by VAGA, New York, NY.

mechanical science. The door is wide open, at last! for this material to be forged and hammered by the peaceful hands of artists.[2]

González welded iron rods to construct his linear abstraction *Maternity*. It is airy and playful. In contrast, *The Montserrat*, created a few years later, is a representational figure. The figure, named for Catalonia's holy mountain, is a symbol of Spanish will and resistance to Nazi aggression.

Since the 1970s, Deborah Butterfield has created figures of horses from found materials such as sticks and scrap metal. She spends much of her time on ranches in Montana and Hawaii where she trains and rides horses and makes sculpture. Painted, crumpled, rusted pieces of metal certainly seem an unlikely choice for expressing a light-footed animal, yet Butterfield's *Conure* has a surprisingly lifelike

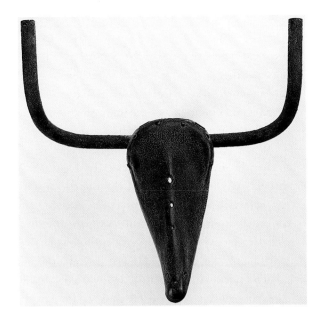

10.18 Pablo Picasso.
Bull's Head. 1943.
Bronze. Seat and handles of a bicycle. Height 16⅛".
Photo by Bernice Hatala. Musee Picasso, Paris, France. Copyright Reunion des Musees Nationaux/Art Resource, NY. © 2010 Estate of Pablo Picasso/Artists Rights Society (ARS), New York.

were associated in my mind . . . The idea of this Bull's Head came without my thinking of it . . . I had only to solder them together . . . [3]

Some assemblages gather meaning from the juxtaposition of real objects. Marc André Robinson shops in thrift stores for pieces of old used furniture and assembles new objects from them. The *Throne for the Greatest Rapper of All Time* is one such work. We see at the lower center that the piece is based on found chairs, but he added a higher back and wings to the sides. If the purpose of a throne is to dignify whoever sits in it, this assemblage accomplishes that. This throne is a higher form of chair, made mostly from chairs.

KINETIC SCULPTURE

Alexander Calder was among the first to explore the possibilities of **kinetic sculpture**, or sculpture that moves. Sculptors' traditional focus on mass is replaced in Calder's work by a focus on shape, space, and movement (see page 38). Works such as his huge *Untitled* sculpture at the National Gallery of Art in Washington, D.C., are often called **mobiles** because the suspended parts move in response to small air currents.

10.19 Marc André Robinson.
Throne for the Greatest Rapper of All Time. 2005.
Wood. 76" × 69" × 48".
Salmatina Gallery.

If Calder's mobiles are massive and exuberant, far more delicate are the mobiles of Jesús Rafael Soto, such as *Hurtado Writing.* Against a background of painted, thin vertical stripes, suspended curves of wire slowly sway. These wire pieces resemble the strokes of handwriting; hence the title. Their motion makes the background seem to vibrate.

10.20 Jesús Rafael Soto.
Hurtado Writing (Escritura Hurtado). 1975.
Paint, wire, nylon cord, wood. 40" × 68" × 18".
Collection: OAS Art Museum of the Americas, Washington, D.C.

10.21 Cai Guo-Qiang.
Inopportune, Stage One. 2004.
Nine cars and sequenced
multichannel light tubes.
Dimensions variable.
Collection of Seattle Art Museum, Gift of Robert
M. Arnold, in honor of the 75th Anniversary of
the Seattle Art Museum, 2006.

hell. This tense, lurking figure seems to exude the nervous energy of an adolescent combined with the quick eye of a bird. But it stands six feet tall, like a gangling teenager, and the work's title may remind us of a brooding, trenchcoat-clad youth. There is an additional feminist message to most of Schnitger's work as well, because she is doing a sort of "dressmaking," a traditional woman's art form. Rather than creating beautiful adornments, though, she fashions curious quasi-human beings.

MIXED MEDIA

Today's artists frequently use a variety of media in a single work. Such works may be labeled with a long list of materials, or they may be identified only as **mixed media**. The media may be two-dimensional, three-dimensional, or a mixture of the two. Often, the choice of media expresses some cultural or symbolic meaning.

The contemporary Chinese artist Cai Guo-Qiang created a huge and symbolic mixed media piece in 2004 with *Inopportune, Stage One*, now in the Seattle Art Museum. The work consists of nine automobiles with light tubes perforating them. The cars are arrayed as if we see one car flipping through the air in momentary glimpses, as it explodes. Cai intended this work to refer to both contemporary action movies (where cars often explode and fly through the air) and to car bombings by terrorists. The work challenges us to consider if this is a thrilling scene, as in a movie, or a horrendous one, as in real life.

When Lara Schnitger drapes and stretches fabric over wooden armatures, she creates both a sculpture and a hollow interior space. The work of this Los Angeles-based artist straddles the boundary between sculpture and fashion design, just as the figures she creates hover nervously between human and some other living thing. In *Grim Boy*, for example, she used various dark-colored fabrics together with beads and fur to suggest a mannequin from

10.22 Lara Schnitger.
Grim Boy. 2005.
Wood, fabric, and mixed media. 71″ × 59″ × 20″.
Anton Kern Gallery, New York.

Matthew Monahan cobbles together various media to make works that seem like museum exhibits gone wrong. He carved the two principal figures in *The Seller and the Sold* out of floral foam. The upper figure is tensely posed in a manner similar to one of Michelangelo's *Awakening Slaves*. The larger figure in the box is tipped head downward, like a toppled statue of a dictator. The artist painted the face of this figure in deep earth tones and gave it a faraway expression, like some mummified king. Seeing this work in a gallery is like finding the ruins of a dead civilization, encased in a museum exhibit. But its title leads us to think of the business world; perhaps the figure above is the seller and the upended figure is the sold.

INSTALLATIONS AND SITE-SPECIFIC ART

Many artists now use the three-dimensional medium of **installation** to tell a story visually. An installation artist transforms a space by bringing into it items of symbolic significance. This medium is most similar to constructed sculpture, but the artist treats the entire space as an artwork and transforms it.

Many art critics regard Cady Noland as a pioneering American installation artist. In the middle

10.23 Matthew Monahan.
The Seller and the Sold. 2006.
Mixed media. 67″ × 25″ × 25″.
Modern Art.

1980s, she began arranging rooms with symbolic items that seemed to comment on contemporary culture. Typical is a 1989 work called *This Piece Doesn't Have a Title Yet.* Here we see row upon row

10.24 Cady Noland.
This Piece Doesn't Have a Title Yet. 1989.
Installation, dimensions variable.
Cady Noland.

of beer cans, held in place by aluminum frames. Once we notice the American flag, we immediately see that the beer cans use the same colors. We might also reflect on how some beer commercials encourage us to associate their product with nationalism or with America. After all, "consumption" is an American thing to do. The aluminum scaffolding resembles the structure of bleachers commonly assembled for sports events. The artist left some tools lying about, to suggest that this is a special occasion that required larger audience seating. Beer, sports, and nationalism: three elements of American culture that Noland brought together in her installation. We might not notice this constellation much in everyday life, but seeing it in an art gallery raises our awareness of how often they go together.

Cady Noland's piece could theoretically be relocated and installed in another spot, but some installations are intended only for particular locations. Such works are called **site-specific**.

The best-known work of site-specific art in the United States became famous because of a lawsuit that tested the limits of the artist's power. In 1981, the government installed Richard Serra's work *Tilted Arc* in the plaza adjoining a federal office building; it was a tilting, curving, blade of steel twelve feet high. Soon the office workers began to complain about it: it blocked the view; it forced them to walk a detour around it; it became a homeless shelter; it collected graffiti. When the government announced plans to relocate the work, the artist filed a lawsuit, claiming that *Tilted Arc* was meant for that spot, and to relocate it would be to destroy it. The artist lost his case, but the matter did not turn on any legal requirement of site-specificity; rather, the court held that the government as owner of the work could dispose of it. After four years of court cases, *Tilted Arc* was removed in 1989.

When the Tate Modern took over an old power plant in London in 2000, the museum inherited a uniquely large indoor space for site-specific art: a huge atrium nearly five hundred feet long that it now uses for large-scale temporary installations. One of the most striking of these installations so far has been *The Weather Project* by Danish artist Olafur Eliasson. He installed a huge semicircular sun of bright lamps and then covered the ceiling in mirrors, so that the yellow orb seems whole. The lights that illuminated it were single-frequency bulbs, which created an intense yellow glow throughout the hall. A few strategically placed fans blew mist from melting dry ice, creating clouds that lazily gathered and dispersed.

Museum officials estimated that *The Weather Project* drew two million visitors over its five-month run during the bleak London winter of 2003–2004. Viewers basked in the seeming warmth of a huge yellow sun that never set; they watched the passing indoor weather; they lay on the floor and looked at their reflections on the ceiling 115 feet above. The installation generally served as a space of communal meditation.

10.25 Richard Serra.
Tilted Arc. 1981.
Steel. Height 12′.
AP Photo/Mario Cabrera.

10.26 Olafur Eliasson.
The Weather Project (The Unilever Series). 2003.
Installation in Turbine Hall, Tate Modern, London. Monofrequency lights, projection foil, haze
machines, mirror foil, aluminium, and scaffolding. 26.7 m × 22.3 m × 155.4 m.
Photo: Jens Ziehe. Courtesy the artist; neugerriemschneider. Berlin: and Tanya Bonakdar Gallery, New York © Olafur Eliasson 2003.

FLIRTING WITH FUNCTION

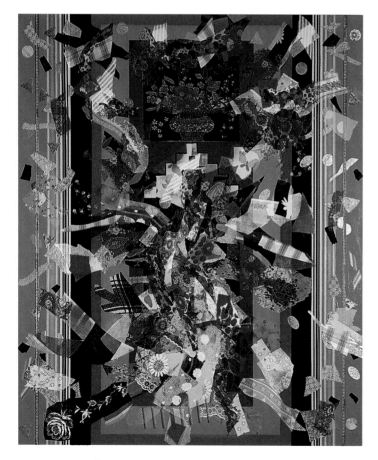

11.1 Miriam Schapiro
Personal Appearance #3. 1973.
Acrylic and fabric on canvas. 60" × 50".
Collection Marilyn Stokstad, Lawrence, Kansas. Courtesy of Bernice Steinbaum Gallery,
Miami, FL. Photo: Robert Hickerson.

Miriam Schapiro's work *Personal Appearance #3* is large enough to cover a small bed. Its composition includes a large orange rectangle at its center that describes a bedlike shape, and the black square near the top is placed like a pillow. The work is exuberant and vibrant, and made partly from cloth scraps like a quilt. This was certainly part of the artist's intent: to pay homage to quilt makers past and present, by making a work that resembles a quilt in many ways but is not one. The work thus hovers on the brink of usefulness; it takes on the appearance of a useful object without exactly being one.

Many artists throughout history have found stimulation in working along the boundary between art and useful objects. They create works that challenge our notion of function, either by making artworks that resemble useful things, as Miriam Schapiro did, or by creating useful objects of such beauty that to actually use them would seem a crime. In fact, most of the world's cultures have always regarded an excellent piece of pottery as highly as a painting, and a book

HEAR MORE: Listen to an audio file of your chapter at
www.myartslab.com

illustration as equal in merit to a piece of sculpture; in this chapter we will consider such works. They are made from various media, including clay, glass, metal, wood, and fiber; and most are three-dimensional.

In a previous era, we might have regarded the works in this chapter as "craft works." But in this day and age (and in this book!) they are all art forms.

CLAY

Clay comes from soil with a heavily volcanic makeup, mixed with water. Since humans began to live in settled communities, clay has been a valuable art material. It is extremely flexible in the artist's hands, yet it hardens into a permanent shape when exposed to heat.

The art and science of making objects from clay is called **ceramics**. A person who works with clay is a **ceramist**; one who specializes in making dishes is a **potter**. A wide range of objects, including tableware, dishes, sculpture, bricks, and many kinds of tiles, are made from clay. Most of the basic ceramic materials were discovered, and processes developed, thousands of years ago. All clays are flexible until baked in a dedicated high-temperature oven called a **kiln**, a process known as **firing**.

Clays are generally categorized in one of three broad types. **Earthenware** is typically fired at a relatively low temperature (approximately 700°C to 1,200°C) and is porous after firing. It may vary in color from red to brown to tan. Earthenware is the most common of the three types, and a great many of the world's pots have been made from it. **Stoneware** is heavier, is fired at a higher temperature (1,200°C to 1,350°C), and is not porous. It is usually grayish or brown. Combining strength with easy workability, stoneware is the preferred medium of most of today's ceramists and potters. **Porcelain** is the rarest and most expensive of the three types. Made

from deposits of decomposed granite, it becomes white and nonporous after firing at a typically high temperature (1,250°C to 1,450°C). It is translucent and rings when struck, both signs of its unique quality. Porcelain was first perfected in China, and even today in England and America the finest white dishes are called "china," no matter where they are made.

With any type of clay, the ceramic process is relatively simple. Ceramists create functional pots or purely sculptural forms from soft, damp clay using hand-building methods such as modeling, or by **throwing**—that is, by shaping clay on a rapidly revolving wheel. Invented in Mesopotamia about six thousand years ago, the potter's wheel allows potters to produce circular forms with great speed and uniformity. In the hands of a skilled worker, the process looks effortless, even magical, but it takes time and practice to perfect the technique. After shaping, a piece is air dried before firing in a kiln.

Two kinds of liquids are commonly used to decorate ceramics, though rarely on the same piece. A **slip** is a mixture of clay and water about the consistency of cream, sometimes colored with earthen powders. With this relatively simple technique, only a limited range of colors is possible, but many ancient cultures made a specialty of this type of pottery decoration.

A **glaze** is a liquid paint with a silica base, specially formulated for clay. During firing, the glaze vitrifies (turns to a glasslike substance) and fuses with the clay body, creating a nonporous surface. Glazes can be colored or clear, translucent or opaque, glossy or dull, depending on their chemical composition. Firing changes the color of most glazes so radically that the liquid that the potter applies to the vessel comes out of the kiln an entirely different color.

EXPLORE MORE: To see a studio video on Ceramics, go to **www.myartslab.com**

Recent works by two of today's leading ceramists will help to show the possibilities of this medium; both are vessels with handles, but they show widely divergent styles. Betty Woodman's *Divided Vases (Christmas)* have an exuberant, freeform look that preserves the expressiveness of spontaneous glaze application. The handles are actually flat perforated panels that still show traces of the working process. She used earthenware, a relatively coarse clay that is conducive to natural shapes like the bamboo segments that the vase bodies suggest. She threw each in three pieces on the wheel, and then joined them before adding the handles. The *Divided Vases* have a fresh look, as if they just came out of the firing kiln.

11.2 Betty Woodman.
Divided Vases (Christmas): View B. 2004.
Glazed earthenware, epoxy resin, lacquer, and paint.
34½″ × 39″ × 7″.
Frank Lloyd Gallery, Santa Monica.
Image courtesy of the artist and Max Protetch Gallery, New York.

11.3 Adrian Saxe.
Les Rois du Monde Futur (Rulers of the Future World). 2004.
Porcelain, stoneware, overglaze enamel, lusters,
mixed media. 26¼″ × 13¼″ × 10″.
Frank Lloyd Gallery, Santa Monica.
Photo: Anthony Cunha.

Adrian Saxe's *Les Rois du Monde Futur (Rulers of the Future World)* seems precious and exquisite by comparison. He used porcelain for the main body, working it into a gourdlike shape before tipping it slightly off-axis. The overly elegant handles recall antique picture frames, while the rough base quotes the style of traditional Chinese pottery. The work's title shows the artist's sarcastic mind-set: The *Rulers of the Future World* are insects, two of which crawl up the cap.

The acceptance of clay as an art medium (rather than something to shape into dishes) owes a great deal to the California sculptor Peter Voulkos. He was trained as a potter and had a studio that sold dishes in upscale stores until the middle 1950s. Then he began to explore abstract art, and he found ways to incorporate some of its techniques into his ceramic work. At first he took a fresh approach to plates: He flexed them out of shape and scratched their surface as if they were paintings, thereby rendering them useless in the traditional sense. We see the results of this treatment in his *Untitled Plate CR952.* His first exhibition of these works in 1959 caused a great deal of controversy because most people did not

SEE MORE: To see an interview with Adrian Saxe, go to **www.myartslab.com**

think of stoneware as an art medium. Yet none could deny the boldness of his inventions.

Both Peter Voulkos and Toshiko Takaezu were influenced by the earthiness and spontaneity of some traditional Japanese ceramics, as well as by Expressionist painting, yet they have taken very different directions. Voulkos's pieces are rough and aggressively dynamic, but Takaezu's *Makaha Blue II* offers subtle, restrained strength. By closing the top of container forms, she turns vessels into sculptures, thus providing surfaces for rich paintings of glaze and oxide. She reflected on her love of the clay medium:

When working with clay I take pleasure from the process as well as from the finished piece. Every once in a while I am in tune with the clay, and I hear music, and it's like poetry. Those are the moments that make pottery truly beautiful for me.[1]

Ceramic processes evolved very slowly until the mid-twentieth century, when new formulations and even synthetic clays became available. Other changes have included more accurate methods of firing and less toxic techniques and equipment.

11.5 Toshiko Takaezu.
Makaha Blue II. 2002.
Stoneware. 48″ × 18½″.
Courtesy of Toshiko Takaezu and Charles Cowles Gallery, NY.

11.4 Peter Voulkos.
Untitled Plate CR952. 1989.
Wood-fired stoneware. 20½″ × 4½″.
Sherry Leedy Contemporary Art.

GLASS

Glass has been used for at least four thousand years as a material for practical containers of all shapes and sizes. Stained glass has been a favorite in churches and cathedrals since the Middle Ages. Elaborate, blown-glass pieces have been made in Venice since the Renaissance. Glass is also a fine medium for decorative inlays in a variety of objects, including jewelry.

Glass is an exotic and enticing art medium. One art critic wrote, "Among sculptural materials, nothing equals the sheer eloquence of glass. It can assume any form, take many textures, dance with color, bask in clear crystallinity, make lyrics of light."[2]

Chemically, glass is closely related to ceramic glaze. As a medium, however, it offers a wide range of unique possibilities. Hot or molten glass

11.7 Dale Chihuly.
Mauve Seaform Set with Black Lip Wraps from the
"Seaforms" Series. 1985. Blown glass.
Courtesy of Dale Chihuly. Photography by Dick Busher.

is a sensitive, amorphous material that is shaped by blowing, casting, or pressing into molds. As it cools, glass solidifies from its molten state without crystallizing. After it is blown or cast, glass may be cut, etched, fused, laminated, layered, leaded, painted, polished, sandblasted, or slumped (softened for a controlled sag). The fluid

nature of glass produces qualities of mass flowing into line, as well as translucent volumes of airy thinness.

The character of any material determines the character of the expression; this statement is particularly true of glass. Molten glass requires considerable speed and skill in handling. The glassblower combines the centering skills of a potter, the agility and stamina of an athlete, and the grace of a dancer to bring qualities of breath and movement into crystalline form.

The fluid and translucent qualities of glass are used to the fullest in Dale Chihuly's *Seaforms Series.* He produces such pieces with a team of glass artists working under his direction. In this series, he arranged groups of pieces and carefully directed the lighting to suggest delicate undersea environments.

Chihuly is one of many artists today who treat glass as a sculptural medium, but Mona Hatoum returns us to the contemplation of usefulness with her provocative work *Still Life with Hand Grenades.* She researched the design of various sorts of small explosive devices that the world's armies use, and re-created them in color-

AT THE EDGE OF ART

Boolean Valley

MANY PEOPLE MIGHT think that ceramic arts, with all of their earthiness, would be incompatible with computer mathematics, but a 2009 exhibition proved them wrong. The potter Adam Silverman collaborated with architect Nader Tehrani on an installation called *Boolean Valley* that used mathematical logic to create an abstract landscape of pots in a gallery. The potter made 195 tall cones and then split each of them in two, creating 195 cylinders and 195 cones of varying heights—or domes and hoops, as the artists called them. The architect then applied Boolean mathematics to arrange these parts in waves along the gallery floor. Boolean logic tracks the geometry of intersecting forms, and is used in computer searches. It yielded a mysterious-looking array that suggested organic growth, as if pots were rising and falling through the surface of the floor.

11.6 *Boolean Valley.* 2009.
Installation by Adam Silverman and Nader Tehrani.
390 glazed ceramic pieces. Maximum height 24″.
Installation view of Boolean Valley at MOCA Pacific Design Center,
March 22–July 5, 2009, photo by Brian Forest.

11.8 Mona Hatoum.
*Still Life with Hand Grenades
(Nature Morte aux Grenades).*
2006–2007.
Crystal, steel, rubber.
38″ × 82″ × 27″.
Marc Domage\Alexander and Bonin.

ful pieces of solid crystal. She placed these precious-looking objects on a gurney as if they were specimens of some kind, which they are: specimens of humanity's tendency to violence. She used the beauty of glass to represent "useful" objects of a lethal sort.

METAL

Metal's primary characteristics are strength and formability. The various types of metal most often used for crafts and sculpture can be hammered, cut, drawn out, welded, joined with rivets, or cast. Early metalsmiths created tools, vessels, armor, and weapons.

In Muslim regions of the Middle East in the thirteenth and fourteenth centuries, artists practiced shaping and inlaying with unparalleled sophistication. The *d'Arenberg Basin*, named after a French collector who owned it for many years, was made for the last ruler of the Ayyubid dynasty in Syria in the mid-thirteenth century. The body of the basin was first cast

in brass; its extremely intricate design included lowered areas into which precisely cut pieces of silver were placed. Although most of the silver pieces are only a fraction of an inch in size, they enliven a carefully patterned design that occupies several finely proportioned horizontal bands. The lowest band is a decorative pattern based on repeated plant shapes. Above is a row of real and imaginary animals that decorates a relatively narrow band. The next band depicts a scene of princely pleasure, as well-attired people play polo. The uppermost contains more plant shapes between the uprights of highly stylized Arabic script that expresses good wishes to the owner of the piece. A central panel in this upper row depicts a scene from the life of Christ, who is regarded as an important teacher in Islam.

Cal Lane combines some of the intricate metalwork of Middle Eastern pieces with ideas ripped from today's

11.9 *d'Arenberg Basin.*
Probably Damascus, Syria. 1247–1249.
Brass inlaid with silver inlay. 22.5 × 50.0 cm.
Freer Gallery of Art, Smithsonian Institution, Washington, DC.
F1955.10.

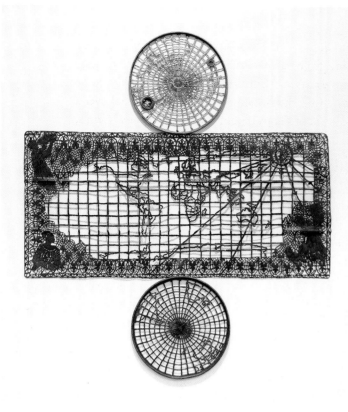

11.10 Cal Lane.
Untitled (Map 3). 2007. Plasma cut steel. 78½″ × 71¾″.
Samuel Freeman.

headlines, in works such as *Untitled (Map 3)*. She worked for years as a welder, a woman in a traditionally male occupation, and she used those skills on a 55-gallon oil drum to create this work. First she flattened it, and then she cut it to show a map of the world, with the lid and base of the drum forming the poles. The oil drum has tremendous symbolic significance as a source of much of the world's energy, wealth, conflicts, and pollution. This work, with its

sun-shaped form at the upper right, suggests the global dominance of oil in our economy and our energy. It also creatively transforms a useful object into an artwork that comments on its own significance.

WOOD

The living spirit of wood is given a second life in handmade objects. Growth characteristics of individual trees remain visible in the grain of wood long after trees are cut, giving wood a vitality not found in other materials. Its abundance, versatility, and warm tactile qualities have made wood a favored material for human use and for art pieces. Like many natural products, wood can be harvested in a sustainable manner or a wasteful one. Many woodworkers today have moved toward sustainability by using wood that is already down or harvested in certified forests.

Henry Gilpin generally makes furniture on commission, but when he heard about a huge elm tree near his studio that had died because of encroaching construction, he secured a piece of it. He found that the crowded conditions caused the wood grains in the tree to cross and twist, so that when he dried the piece it emerged contorted. He decided to make this casualty of progress into a table by mounting the warped plank atop a frame. The surface is so uneven that this work titled *Curiously Red* is barely usable. To honor the tree's sacrifice of its life, he poured red stain over it, and left the drips to show at the bottom of the legs to resemble bloodstains. What might at first glance appear to be a warped side table thus becomes a meditation on life and death.

The Nature Conservancy in 2009 commissioned Maya Lin to create a piece of furniture from a forest that is certified by the Forest Stewardship Council, and she responded with the *Terra Table*. It is actually a bench built of red maple. She made it by piecing together lateral slices of the wood, and leaving their tops mostly uneven to remind users that they are sitting on a tree. The grain of the wood

11.11 Henry Gilpin.
Curiously Red. 2006.
Stained elm, pigment, magnets. 36″ × 74″ × 16″.
Courtesy the artist and Gallery NAGA.

11.12 Maya Lin.
Terra Table. 2009. Red Maple.
Dan Whipps\The Nature Conservancy.

is visible at the ends, and she used a transparent stain to further show the richness of the maple planks.

FIBER

Fiber arts include such processes as weaving, stitching, basketmaking, surface design (dyed and printed textiles), wearable art, and handmade papermaking. These fiber processes use natural and synthetic fibers in both traditional and innovative ways. Artists working with fiber (like artists working in any medium) draw on the heritage of traditional practices and also explore new avenues of expression. Fiber arts divide into two general classes: Work made with a loom, and work made without one.

All weaving is based on the interlacing of fibers. Weavers generally begin with long fibers in place, called the **warp** fibers, which determine the length of the piece they will create. Often the warp fibers are installed on a **loom**, a device that holds them in place and may pull them apart for weaving. They cross the warp fibers at right angles with **weft** fibers (from which we get the word *weave*). Weavers create patterns by changing the numbers and placements of interwoven threads, and they can choose from a variety of looms and techniques. Simple hand looms can produce very sophisticated, complex weaves. A large tapestry loom, capable of weaving hundreds of colors into intricate forms, may require several days of preparation before work begins.

Some of the world's most spectacular carpets came from Islamic Persia during the Safavid dynasty in the sixteenth century. Here, weavers employed by royal workshops knotted carefully dyed wool over a network of silk warps and wefts. *The Ardabil Carpet,*

11.13 *The Ardabil Carpet.* Tabriz. 1540.
Wool pile on silk warps and wefts. 34′ × 17′6″.
V & A Images/Victoria and Albert Museum, London.

long recognized as one of the greatest Persian carpets, contains about three hundred such knots, over fine silk threads, per square inch. Thus, this carpet required approximately 25 million knots!

The design of the carpet is centered on a sunburst surrounded by sixteen oval shapes. Two mosque lamps of unequal size share space with an intricate pattern of flowers. At the corners of the main field, quarters of the central design are repeated. A small panel at the right gives the date and the name of an artist, who must have been the designer. Another inscription is a couplet by Hafiz, the best known lyrical poet in Iran: "I have no refuge in this world other than thy threshold. My head has no resting-place other than this doorway." The carpet originally covered the floor of a prayer chapel.

Fiber can be worked in infinite ways, and Chicago-based Nick Cave has likely used them all at one time or another to create his ongoing series of Soundsuits. These extravagant costumes are all wearable, and over the years they have included such offbeat materials as human hair, twigs, toys, garbage, buttons, dryer felt, stuffed animals, fake fur, feathers, and flowers, besides sequins and beads of all kinds.

In the *Soundsuit* shown here, a cloud of ceramic birds surrounds a body suit of crocheted yarn pieces. Cave (who is not related to the Australian musician of the same name) grew up in a large family where he personalized the hand-me-down clothing he often wore. However, the Soundsuits do the opposite: most of them completely hide the wearer, thus conferring an alternate identity. The roots of these pieces are in New Orleans Mardi Gras costumes and African ceremonial garments, but in Cave's hands they become both exuberant and mysterious.

11.14 Nick Cave.
Soundsuit. 2009.
Mixed media. Height 7′.
Photo: James Prinz Courtesy of the artist and Jack Shainman Gallery, NY.

11.15 Jessie Pettway.
Bars and String-Piece Columns.
1950s.
Cotton quilt. 95" × 76".
Photo: Steve Pitking/Pitking Studios.
Copyright 2003. Provided by
Tinwood Alliance Collection, Atlanta
(www.tinwoodmedia.com).

In some African-American communities, women have carried on a traditional of quilt making for generations. One of the most active groups has been meeting in Gees Bend, Alabama for over a hundred years, where the quilters gather to share fabric, discuss neighborhood news, and encourage creativity. Jessie Pettway made *Bars and String-Piece Columns* from leftover pieces of cloth. This quilt, like many produced at Gees Bend, resembles some kinds of African textiles (see Chapter 19). Many Gees Bend quilters create their work with only a minimum of advance planning, and this lends their work a look of spontaneity and exuberance. The coincidental resemblance to modern art also attracts the attention of collectors.

Faith Ringgold uses the quiltmaking tradition to speak eloquently of her life and ideas. Memories of her childhood in Harlem in the 1930s provide much of her subject matter. Commitments to women, the family, and cross-cultural consciousness are at the heart of Ringgold's work. With playful exuberance and insight, she draws on history and recent events to tie her own history to wider struggles about gender, race, and class. Her sophisticated use of naiveté gives her work the appeal of the best folk art, but her work has also dealt with more urgent themes such as unemployment and discrimination. In the biographical essay on the following page, we consider one of her most famous quilts, *Tar Beach.*

LEARN MORE: For a Closer Look at *Tar Beach,* go to
www.myartslab.com

11.16 Faith Ringgold.
Tar Beach. 1988.
Acrylic pieced and printed fabric. 74″ × 69″.
Collection: Solomon R. Guggenheim Museum © 1988 Faith Ringgold Inc.

FAITH RINGGOLD

A PROLIFIC CREATOR of many art forms, from paintings to quilts to children's books, Faith Ringgold has taken the reality of racial discrimination and made from it uplifting stories about finding sustenance and overcoming adversity.

Born in Harlem to working-class parents, she was encouraged as a child to succeed by their example. Acknowledging the double disadvantage of being an African-American woman, her parents taught her that "you have to be twice as good to go half as far."[3] Her mother was a seamstress and fashion designer, her father a sanitation truck driver. After receiving bachelor's and master's degrees in art from City College of New York, she taught in New York City public schools from 1955 to 1972. She later recalled that the experience of teaching children encouraged her own creativity: "They showed me what it is to be free, to be able to express yourself directly."

During the early years of her teaching career, she painted landscapes. But the civil rights movement of the 1960s encouraged her to address directly in her art the issues of inequality that seemed then to be present everywhere. She sought advice from the elder African-American artist Romare

Bearden (see page 8), who included her work in a group show in Harlem in 1966. She also took part in several protest actions at New York museums, urging greater inclusion of African-American artists and more outreach to ethnic minority neighborhoods.

Leaving her teaching position in 1972, she began to devote full time to art. She also began a ten-year collaboration with her mother in the creation of works on cloth. Quilt making had been a family tradition as far back as her great-great-grandmother, who had made them as a slave in Florida. Now the mother–daughter team collaborated on a new type of textile art that included images and stories on the sewn fragments. In addition to continuing ancient African textile art traditions, these cloth works were also portable.

Her themes are highly varied. Some are personal and autobiographical, such as *Change: Faith Ringgold's Over 100 Pound Weight Loss Performance Story Quilt*. Others expose injustice, such as *The Slave Rape Series*, which dealt with the mistreatment of African women in the slave trade. Some are about important African-American cultural figures, such as *Sonny's Quilt*, which depicts the jazz

saxophonist Sonny Rollins, performing as he soars over the Brooklyn Bridge.

A standout among the artist's "story quilts" is *Tar Beach*, which tells the story of the fictional Cassie, an eight-year-old character who is based on Ringgold's own childhood memories. She would go up to the asphalt roof of her apartment building ("Tar Beach") with her family on hot nights, because there was no air-conditioning in the home. Cassie describes Tar Beach as a magical place, with a 360-degree view of tall buildings and the George Washington Bridge in the distance. She dreams that she can fly, that she can do anything she imagines, as she lies on a blanket with her little brother. She dreams that she can give her father the union card that he has been denied because of his race. She dreams that she can let her mother sleep late, and eat ice cream every day for dessert. She even dreams that she can buy the building her father works in, and that her mother won't cry when her father can't find work. The quilt depicts the two children on the blanket, and her parents playing cards with the neighbors next to a table set with snacks and drinks. *Tar Beach* was later made into a children's book, one of

11.17 Faith Ringgold. With detail of *The Purple Quilt*. 1986.
C'Love\Faith Ringgold, Inc.

four that Ringgold has written.

The combination of fantasy and hard reality in this work, with imagination the key to overcoming obstacles, is typical of Ringgold's work as well as her life. Near the end of her memoir, she said, "I don't want the story of my life to be about racism, though that has played a major role. I want my story to be about attainment, love of family, art, helping others, courage, values, dreams coming true."

Most fiber art is divided between works made on a loom, such as the *Ardabil Carpet*, and **off-loom** pieces such as quilts. Over the last generation or so, fiber arts have gone very far off the loom, as Nick Cave's *Soundsuits* show. Note also *Her Secret Is Patience*, the large piece illustrated at the beginning of Chapter 1.

Polly Apfelbaum dyes off-loom fabrics to create installations that show the influence of both modern abstract art and feminism. She said that she wanted to do a contemporary version of the traditional crazy quilt, in which random fragments of leftover cloth are stitched together in dazzling patterns. In this way she claims descent from the women who have traditionally woven and sewn most textiles. In *Blossom*, she used bright colors to stain oval-shaped pieces of velvet. She attached them together to heighten the resemblance to quilts, and then installed them on the floor of a gallery. The resulting work resembles a quilt, a carpet, and a luxurious bed of flower petals. She applied fabric dye to each part with a squeeze bottle. For this piece, she prevented the dye from reaching the edge of each oval, leaving a white border that sets each color apart. Her dyeing process resembles painting, but the works she creates are closer to sculpture and textile art. She sometimes calls her works "fallen paintings," because placing the work on the floor allows viewers to interact with the work from more angles.

PRACTICE MORE: Get flashcards for images and terms and review chapter material with quizzes at **www.myartslab.com**

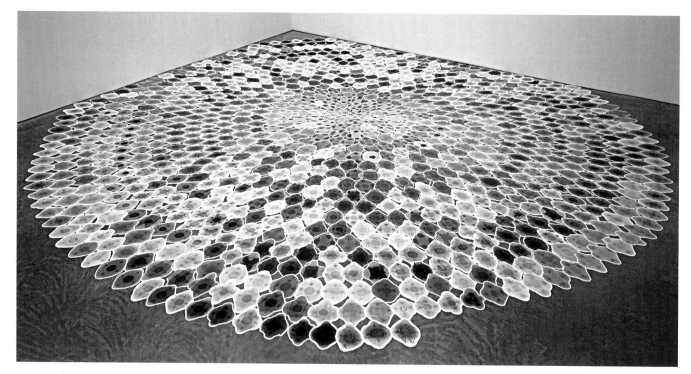

11.18 Polly Apfelbaum.
Blossom. 2000.
Installation at D'Amelio Terras Gallery, New York. Velvet and dye. Diameter 18′.
Photo: Adam Reich. Courtesy of the artist and D'Amelio Terras Gallery, New York. Collection of The Museum of Modern Art, New York: gift of Donald S. Bryant, Jr., Bobbie Foshay-Miller, Ricki Conway, Susan Jacoby, Steven M. Bernstein, Jo Carole Lauder, and Brook Berlind.

ARCHITECTURE

DOES IT MAKE A DIFFERENCE IF AN ARCH IS ROUND OR POINTED?

WHAT WAS THE BIGGEST PROBLEM WITH EARLY CAST-IRON BUILDINGS?

WHAT MAJOR INNOVATIONS IN WORLD ARCHITECTURE BEGAN IN THE UNITED STATES?

All students at Frank Lloyd Wright's architecture school had the same first assignment: He handed them some canvas and some poles and told them to go out into the Arizona desert and build themselves shelters. He forced them to face one of the most basic human needs with simple tools (they were allowed to include surrounding rocks and dirt). This exercise is useful because it shows precisely where architecture begins.

The oldest surviving human structures, such as the *Dolmen* in northwest France, are as primitive as the pole-and-canvas models that the students made: some uprights and a roof create a space. In this chapter we will examine the art and craft of architecture, from primitive structures to today's high-tech creations. We will see that beyond the necessity for shelter, architecture can make important expressive statements that record and communicate a society's values.

AN ART AND A SCIENCE

No matter what sort of structure they are building, architects address and integrate three key issues: function (how a building is used); form (how it looks); and structure (how it stands up). As an art, architecture both creates interior spaces and wraps them in an expressive shape.

12.1 *Dolmen.*
Crocuno, north of Carnac, France.
James Lynch/The Ancient Art & Architecture Collection Ltd.

As a science, architecture is a physics problem: How does a structure hold up its own weight and the loads placed on it? Architecture must be designed to withstand the forces of compression, or pushing (→←); tension, or stretching (←→); and bending, or curving (↘↙); and any combination of these physical forces.

HEAR MORE: Listen to an audio file of your chapter at **www.myartslab.com**

Like the human body, architecture has three essential components. These are a supporting skeleton; an outer skin; and operating equipment, similar to the body's vital organs and systems. The equipment includes plumbing; electrical wiring; appliances; and systems for cooling, heating, and circulating air as needed. In earlier centuries, structures of wood, earth, brick, or stone had no such equipment, and the skeleton and skin were often one.

STYLES, MATERIALS, AND METHODS

The evolution of architectural techniques and styles has been determined by the materials available and by the changing needs and values of societies. In ancient times, when nomadic hunter-gatherers became farmers and village dwellers, housing evolved from caves, huts, and tents to more substantial structures.

Because early building designers (as well as those in nonindustrialized countries today) made structures only out of the materials at hand, regional styles developed that blended with their sites and climates. Modern transportation and the spread of advanced technologies now make it possible to build almost anything anywhere.

Since the beginning of history, most structures have been made of wood, stone, earth, or brick. Each of these natural materials has its own strengths and weaknesses. For example, wood, which is light, can be used for roof beams. Stone, which is heavy, can be used for load-bearing walls but is less effective as a beam. Much of the world's major architecture has been constructed of stone because of its permanence, availability, and beauty. In the past, entire cities were slowly built by cutting and placing stone upon stone.

Dry Masonry

Probably the simplest building technique is to pile stones atop one another, as we saw with the *Dolmen* above. The process has been used to make such rudimentary structures as markers, piles, and cairns throughout the world. When such massing is done with a consistent pattern, the result is called **masonry**. In dry masonry, where no mortar is used, the weight of the stones themselves holds the structure up. If the stones are cut or shaped before use, they are **dressed**.

The *Great Zimbabwe* ("Great Stone House") in East Africa is an elliptical structure that gave its name to the country in which it is located. Built sometime in the twelfth century, it was used for

12.2 *Great Zimbabwe.*
　　Zimbabwe. Before 1450.
　　Height of wall 30′.
　　Casement Creative Services Inc.

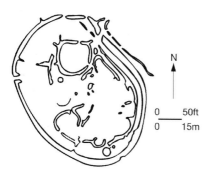

a. Plan.

b. Interior.

about three hundred years. *Great Zimbabwe* is nearly round, with several conical structures inside whose original function is still unknown. Its walls, made of dressed local stone, are approximately thirty feet high. For added stability, the walls were built up to fifteen feet thick at the base, tapering slightly toward the top. Roofing was probably grass or thatch held together with sticks. The structure is the largest of a group of ancient stone dwellings that formed a trading city of perhaps twenty thousand people at its height. Though the outer walls of *Great Zimbabwe* have openings in selected locations for entry and exit, there are no windows; because these tend to weaken masonry walls, only structures that are considerably smaller can use them without external support.

Great Zimbabwe is the largest ancient stone structure in Africa south of the great pyramids of Egypt, which are also built of dry masonry. Other notable examples of such buildings are Machu Picchu in Peru and the ancient pueblos of the American Southwest, such as Mesa Verde.

Post and Beam

Prior to the twentieth century, two dominant structural types were in common use: **post-and-beam** (also called post-and-lintel) and **arch** systems, including the **vault**. Most of the world's architecture, including modern steel structures, has been built with *Post-and-Beam Construction*. Vertical posts or columns support horizontal beams and carry the weight of the entire structure to the ground.

The form of post-and-beam buildings is determined by the strengths and weaknesses of the materials used. Stone beam lengths must be short, and posts relatively thick to compensate for stone's brittleness. Wood beams may be longer, and posts thinner, because wood is lighter and more flexible. The strength-to-weight ratio of modern steel makes it possible to build with far longer beams and thus to create much larger interior spaces.

Bundled reeds provided the model for the monumental post-and-beam Egyptian temples at Luxor. A row of columns spanned or connected by beams is called a **colonnade**, as seen in the *Colonnade and*

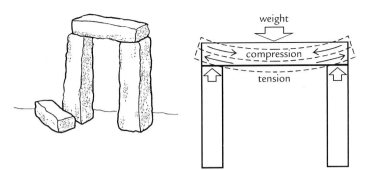

12.3 *Post-and-Beam Construction.*

12.4 *Colonnade and Court of Amenhotep III.*
Temple of Amun-Mut-Khonsu. View of the great court with double row of papyrus-clustered columns. 18th dynasty. Luxor, Thebes, Egypt. c. 1390 B.C.E.
Alistar Duncan © Dorling Kindersley.

Court of Amenhotep III. Most ancient Egyptian temples were symmetrical, with aisles for processions that connected adjacent pavilions. Their arrangement was also generally hierarchical, with the more remote precincts accessible only to the higher-ranking priests.

Following the lead of the Egyptians, the Greeks further refined stone post-and-beam construction. For more than two thousand years, the magnificence of the Parthenon and other classical Greek architecture (see Chapter 15) has influenced the designers of a great many later buildings.

Round Arch, Vault, and Dome

Both Egyptian and Greek builders had to place their columns relatively close together because stone is weak under the load-bearing stresses inherent in a beam. The invention of the semicircular *Round Arch* allowed builders to transcend this limitation and create new architectural forms. An arch may be supported by either a column or a **pier**, a more massive version of a column. When extended in depth, the *Round Arch* creates a tunnel-like structure called a *Barrel Vault*. Roman builders perfected the round arch and developed the *Groin Vault*, formed by the intersection of two barrel vaults.

A vault is a curving ceiling or roof structure, traditionally made of bricks or blocks of stone tightly fitted to form a unified shell. In recent times, vaults have been constructed of materials such as cast reinforced concrete.

Early civilizations of western Asia and the Mediterranean area built arches and vaults of brick, chiefly for underground drains and tomb chambers. But it was the Romans who first used the arch extensively in above-ground structures. They learned the technique of stone arch and vault construction from the Etruscans, who occupied central Italy between 750 and 200 B.C.E.

A round stone arch can span a longer distance and support a heavier load than a stone beam because the arch transfers the load more efficiently. The Roman arch is a semicircle made from wedge-shaped stones fitted together with joints at right angles to the curve. During construction, temporary wooden supports carry the weight of the stones. The final stone that is set in place at the top is called the **keystone**. When the keystone is placed, a continuous arch with load-bearing capacity is created and the wood support is removed. A series of such arches supported by columns forms an *Arcade*.

Roman builders used the arch and arcade to create structures of many types throughout their vast empire in most of Europe, the Near East, and North Africa. The aqueduct called *Pont du Gard*, near Nîmes, France, is one of the finest remaining examples of the functional beauty of Roman engineering. The combined height of the three levels of arches is 161 feet. Dry masonry blocks, weighing up to two tons each, make up the large arches of the two lower tiers. Water was once carried in a conduit at the top, with the first level serving as a bridge for traffic. Its persistence after two thousand years attests to the excellence of its design and construction.

keystone

12.5 *Round Arch.*

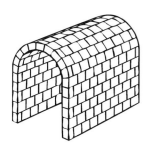

12.6 *Barrel Vault.*

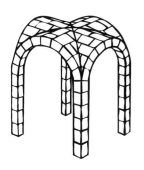

12.7 *Groin Vault.*

12.8 *Arcade.*

12.9 *Pont du Gard.*
Nîmes, France. 15 C.E. Limestone. Height 161′, length 902′.
Photograph: Duane Preble.

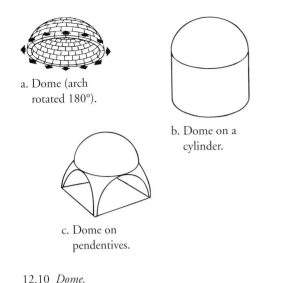

a. Dome (arch rotated 180°).

b. Dome on a cylinder.

c. Dome on pendentives.

12.10 *Dome.*

a. Exterior.

b. Interior.

12.11 *Hagia Sophia.* 532–535.
Istanbul, Turkey.
Copyright Erich Lessing/Art Resource, NY.

Roman architects borrowed Greek column design and combined it with the arch, enabling them to greatly increase the variety and size of their architectural spaces. The Romans also introduced liquid **concrete** as a material for architecture. Concrete is a mixture of water, sand, gravel, and a binder such as lime or gypsum. Cheap, stonelike, versatile, and strong, concrete allowed the Romans to cut costs, speed construction, and build on a massive scale.

An arch rotated 180° on its vertical axis creates a **Dome**. Domes may be hemispherical, semihemispherical, or pointed. In general usage the word *dome* refers to a hemispherical vault built up from a circular or polygonal base. The weight of a dome pushes downward and outward all around its circumference. Therefore, the simplest support is a cylinder with walls thick enough to resist the downward and outward thrust.

One of the most magnificent domes in the world was designed for the Byzantine cathedral of *Hagia Sophia* (Holy Wisdom) in Istanbul, Turkey. It was built in the sixth century as the central sanctuary of the Eastern Orthodox Christian Church. After the Islamic conquest of 1453, **minarets** (towers) were added and it was used as a mosque. It is now a museum. The dome of *Hagia Sophia* rests on curving triangular sections called **pendentives** over a square base.

Hagia Sophia's distinctive dome appears to float on a halo of light—an effect produced by the row of windows encircling its base. The huge dome is supported on what appears to be a larger dome with its top and sides removed. Pendentives carry the enormous weight from the circular base of the upper dome downward to a square formed by supporting walls.

Pointed Arch and Vault

After the round arch, the pointed arch was the next great structural advance in the Western world. This new shape seems a small change, but its effect on the building of cathedrals was spectacular. Vaults based on the pointed arch made it possible to build wider aisles and higher ceilings. We see the results of this new technology in the awesome height of the central aisle at *Notre Dame de Chartres*.

Although a pointed arch (or *Gothic Arch*) is steeper and therefore sends its weight more directly

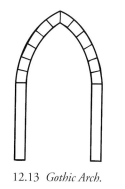

12.13 *Gothic Arch.*

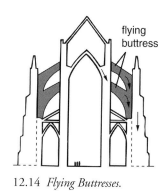

flying buttress

12.14 *Flying Buttresses.*

downward, a substantial sideways thrust must still be countered. Gothic builders accomplished this by constructing elaborate supports called **buttresses** at right angles to the outer walls. In the most developed Gothic cathedrals, the outward force of the arched vault is carried to large buttresses by stone half-arches called *Flying Buttresses*.

By placing part of the structural skeleton on the outside, Gothic builders were able to make their cathedrals higher and lighter in appearance. Because the added external support of the buttresses relieved the cathedral walls of much of their structural function, large parts of the wall could be replaced by enormous stained-glass windows, allowing more light (a symbol of God's presence) to enter the sanctuary. From the floor of the sanctuary to the highest part of the interior above the main altar, the windows increase in size. Stones carved and assembled to form thin ribs and pillars make up the elongated columns along the nave walls, which emphasize verticality and give the cathedral its apparent upward thrust. (We will consider the stylistic features of Gothic architecture in more detail in Chapter 15.)

After the Gothic pointed arch and vault, no basic structural technique was added to the Western architectural vocabulary until the nineteenth century. Instead, architects designed a variety of structures—at times highly innovative—by combining elements from different periods. Forms and ornamentation from the Classical and Gothic periods were revived again and again and given new life in different contexts.

12.12 *Notre Dame de Chartres.*
Chartres, France. 1145–1513.
Interior, nave. Height 122′, width 53′, length 130′.
Copyright Scala/Art Resource, NY.

Truss and Balloon Frame

Wood has a long history as a building material. Besides the expected post and beam, timbers or logs have been used for centuries in **Trusses**. A truss is a triangular framework used to span or to support. The perfection of mass-produced nails and mechanical saws in the nineteenth century led to advances in wood construction; the most important of these was the **Balloon Frame**. In balloon framing, heavy timbers are replaced with thin studs held together only with nails, leading to vastly reduced construction time and wood consumption. (Old-timers who were unwilling to use the new method called it balloon framing because they thought it was as fragile as a balloon.) The method helped to make possible the rapid settlement of America's western frontier and is still used in suburban new construction today.

Cast Iron

Iron has much greater strength than stone or wood and can span much larger distances. After

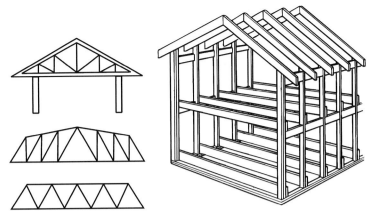

12.15 *Trusses.*   12.16 *Balloon Frame.*

the technology for uniform smelting was perfected in the nineteenth century, cast and wrought iron became important building materials. Iron supports made possible lighter exterior walls and more flexible interior spaces because walls no longer had to bear structural weight. Architects first used this new material in factories, bridges, and railway stations.

The *Crystal Palace* was a spectacular demonstration of what cast iron could do. It was built for the

12.17 Joseph Paxton.
Crystal Palace.
London. 1850–1851. Cast iron and glass.
Stock Montage, Inc. © The Newberry Library.

Great Exhibition of the Works of Industry of All Nations, the first international exposition, held in London in 1851. Designed to show off the latest mechanical inventions, the *Crystal Palace* was built in six months and covered nineteen acres of park land! This was the first time new industrial methods and materials were used on such a scale.

Paxton used relatively lightweight, factory-made modules (standard-size structural units) of cast iron and glass. Using modular construction and a cast-iron skeleton, Paxton created a whole new architectural vocabulary. The light, decorative quality of the glass and cast-iron units was created not by applied ornamentation, but by the structure itself. Paxton, inspired by leaf structures, said, "Nature gave me the idea." The modular units provided enough flexibility for the entire structure to be assembled on the site, right over existing trees, and later disassembled and moved across town.

Unfortunately, the building also showed the great defect of early cast-iron buildings: The unprotected metal struts tend to buckle on exposure to heat, making such buildings very susceptible to destruction by fire. The *Crystal Palace* indeed burned in 1936 after a fire broke out in its interior.

Steel and Reinforced Concrete

The next breakthrough in construction methods for large structures came between 1890 and 1910 with the development of high-strength structural steel, used by itself and as the reinforcing material in reinforced concrete. The extensive use of cast-iron skeletons in the mid-nineteenth century had prepared the way for multistory steel-frame construction in the late 1880s.

Steel frames and elevators, together with rising urban land values, impelled a fresh approach to structure and form. The movement began to take shape in commercial architecture, symbolized by early skyscrapers, and found one of its first opportunities in Chicago, where the big fire of 1871 had cleared the way for a building boom.

Leading the Chicago school was Louis Sullivan, regarded as the first great modern architect. Sullivan rejected references to past buildings and sought to

12.18 Louis Sullivan.
Wainwright Building.
St. Louis, Missouri. 1890–1891.
© Art on File/CORBIS. All Rights Reserved.

meet the needs of his time by using new methods and materials. Sullivan had a major influence on the early development of what became America's and the twentieth century's most original contribution to architecture: the "skyscraper."

Among the first of these skyscrapers was Sullivan's *Wainwright Building* in St. Louis, Missouri, which was made possible by the invention of the elevator and by the development of steel for the structural skeleton. The building boldly breaks with nineteenth-century tradition. Its exterior design reflects the internal steel frame and emphasizes the height of the structure by underplaying horizontal elements in favor of tall

LEARN MORE: To read Louis Sullivan's innovative thoughts on designing tall buildings, go to **www.myartslab.com**

vertical shafts. Sullivan demonstrated his sensitivity and adherence to the harmony of traditional architecture by dividing the building's façade into three distinct zones, reminiscent of the base, shaft, and capital of Greek columns. These areas also reveal the various functions of the building, with shops at the base, offices in the central section, and utility rooms at the top. The heavily ornamented band at the top stops the vertical thrust of the piers located between the office windows.

Thus, the exterior form of the building shows its interior functions; this was a novel concept. Sullivan's observation that "form ever follows function" eventually helped architects to break with their reliance on past styles and to rethink architecture from the inside out.[1]

In this spirit, modern architecture arose in Europe between 1910 and 1930. Younger architects rejected decorative ornamentation and references to the past, as well as traditional stone and wood construction, and they began to think of a building as a useful arrangement of spaces rather than as a mass. The resulting **International Style** expressed the function of each building, its underlying structure, and a logical (usually asymmetrical) plan that used only modern materials such as concrete, glass, and steel.

The French architect and planner Le Corbusier demonstrated the basic components of steel-column and reinforced-concrete-slab construction in a system that he called the *Domino Construction System*. (The six steel supports are placed in concrete slabs at the same approximate locations as the spots on a domino game piece.) Le Corbusier's idea of supporting floors and roof on interior load-bearing columns instead of load-bearing walls made it possible to vary the placement of interior walls according to how the various rooms were used. He called one of his homes a "machine for living in," but in fact its flexible spaces made it very comfortable. And because walls no longer bore any weight, they could become windows and let in a great deal of natural light.

Walter Gropius used the principles of the International Style in his new building for the *Bauhaus* when the school moved to Dessau, Germany. The workshop wing, built between 1925 and 1926, follows the basic concept illustrated in Le Corbusier's drawing. Because the reinforced-concrete floors and roof were supported by steel columns set back from the outer edge of the building, exterior walls did not have to carry any weight: they could be **curtain walls** made of glass. Even interior walls were non-load-bearing and could be placed anywhere they were needed.

Le Corbusier's idea for alleviating urban crowding by using tall, narrow buildings surrounded by open space, and Sullivan's concept for

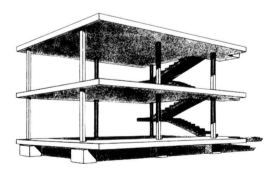

12.19 Le Corbusier.
Domino Construction System. Perspective drawing for Domino Housing Project. 1914.
© 2010 Artists Rights Society (ARS), New York/ADAGP, Paris/F.L.C.

12.20 Walter Gropius.
Bauhaus. Exterior. 1926–1927.
Bauhaus, Dessau, Germany. Vanni/Art Resource, NY. Walter Gropius © 2010 Artists Rights Society (ARS), New York/VG Bild-Kunst, Bonn.

12.22 Ludwig Mies van der Rohe and Philip Johnson.
Seagram Building.
New York. 1956–1958.
Photograph: Ezra Stoller © Esto.

high-rise buildings that express the grid of their supporting *Steel-Frame Construction*, came together in the *Seagram Building*, designed by Ludwig Mies van der Rohe and Philip Johnson. Non-load-bearing glass walls had been a major feature of

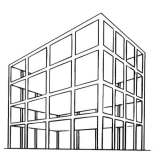

12.21 *Steel-Frame Construction.*

Mies's plans for skyscrapers conceived as early as 1919, but it was not until the 1950s that he had the chance to build such structures. In the *Seagram Building*, interior floor space gained by the height of the building allowed the architects to leave a large, open public area at the base. The vertical lines emphasize the height and provide a strong pattern that is capped by a top section designed to give a sense of completion. The austere design embodies Mies's famous statement "Less is more."

By the mid-twentieth century, modern architecture had become synonymous with the International Style. The uniformity of glass-covered rectilinear grid structures was considered the appropriate formal dressing for the bland anonymity of the modern corporation.

Recent Innovations

In the late twentieth century, improved construction techniques and materials, new theories regarding structural physics, and computer analyses of the strengths and weaknesses in complex structures led to the further development of fresh architectural forms such as the *Suspension Structure* and the *Shell Structure.*

Eero Saarinen's 1962 *TWA Terminal* was for many years the epitome of the excitement of flight. A boldly shaped *Shell Structure* at JFK International Airport, the terminal's soaring

EXPLORE MORE: Contemporary with the International Style was a more exuberant style called Art Deco; to see an audio slide show about Art Deco, go to **www.myartslab.com**

wings symbolized the glamour and speed of air travel. Increasing security needs and the bankruptcy of the airline forced its closure in 2001. A budget carrier has recently taken it over, and soon the *TWA Terminal* will serve as a gateway to a larger structure more accommodating to contemporary air travel. Although the original structure will not have the same function as before, it will remain intact.

The most dramatic recent use of the *Suspension Structure* in a major public building was in the *Jeppesen Terminal Building* at Denver International Airport. Its roof is a giant tent composed of fifteen acres of woven fiberglass, making it the largest suspension building on Earth. This white roofing material lets in large amounts of natural light without conducting heat, and it is coated with Teflon for water resistance and easy cleaning. Its exterior

12.25 *Jeppesen Terminal Building.*
Denver International Airport. 1994. Fentress-Bradburn Architects.
Photograph provided courtesy of the Denver International Airport.

design was inspired by the snow-capped Rocky Mountains, which are visible from inside.

Architecture's first technical innovation of the twenty-first century is carbon fiber, and it may have an important impact on how we build in the future. Scientists found that heating carbon atoms in an oxygen-free environment fuses them together into some of the lightest and strongest materials yet discovered. Certain aircraft parts, racing car bodies, and bicycle frames already use carbon fiber. Shaping this fiber carefully and coating it with polyester or nylon yields a new material that can be literally woven to create a building.

The architectural firm of Testa and Weiser has explored the possibilities of carbon fiber, writing computer programs that make possible a completely new approach to structure. For example,

12.23 *Suspension Structure.*

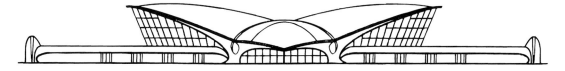

12.24 Eero Saarinen.
Shell Structure (TWA Terminal).
Kennedy Airport, New York. 1956–1962.

12.26 Testa and Weiser.
Carbon Tower. 2005.
Model of proposed 40-story skyscraper.

their *Carbon Tower* is a plan for a 40-story sky-scraper supported by one-inch-thick filaments woven into a helix-shaped web. The tower will have no columns and no central core, and its exterior walls can be paper-thin and translucent. The expense of the *Carbon Tower* makes its realization today very difficult, but the future potential is enormous.

In recent years, art museums have become showplaces for cutting-edge architecture. Zaha Hadid designed the *Contemporary Arts Center* in Cincinnati to reflect the most up-to-date ideas about museums. Frank Gehry's *Guggenheim Museum Bilbao* is more like a piece of functional sculpture. The design—he calls it a "metallic flower"—is a dramatic limestone and titanium–clad cluster of soaring, all-but-dancing volumes climaxing in a gigantic, glass-enclosed atrium. Museum director Thomas Krens envisioned a museum that would celebrate the ever-evolving, at times large-scale inventions of leading contemporary artists while also featuring the art of the architecture—a great world-class museum for world-class art. Two other examples in this book are the Museum of Contemporary Art, Denver, later in this chapter, and the new Modern Wing of the Chicago Art Institute at the end of Chapter 25.

DESIGNING WITH NATURE

Most of the stylistic revolutions of the twentieth century did not consider a building in relation to its environment. An early exception to this trend was the work of American Frank Lloyd Wright, one of the most important (and iconoclastic) architects of the era. Wright was among the first to use open planning in houses, even before the International Style took hold (see his *Robie House* in Chapter 21). Wright eliminated walls between rooms, enlarged windows, and discovered that one of the best ways to open a closed-in room was to place windows in corners. With these devices, he created flowing spaces that opened to the outdoors, welcomed natural light, and related houses to their sites and climates. Sliding glass doors were influenced by the sliding paper-covered doors in traditional Japanese architecture.

Wright also made extensive use of the **cantilever** to unite indoor and outdoor spaces.

12.27 Frank O. Gehry.
Guggenheim Museum Bilbao.
Bilbao, Spain. 1997.

ZAHA HADID

Deconstructing a Building

ONE OF THE most creative and controversial architects now at work is Zaha Hadid. Indeed, many of her buildings have remained in the planning stages because they are too radical to be built. But her realized projects are adventurous designs that radically alter the viewer's experience of space.

Born in Baghdad, as a young girl she worked weaving carpets. She has said that their intricate and dazzling designs later influenced her building ideas. She studied architecture at London's Architectural Association, where she was constantly challenged to reinvent modern architecture. This private academy was an incubator of new ideas where the teachers often threw practicality to the winds. Hadid's graduation project was to redesign a busy bridge over the Thames River so that people could live on it. The fact that few would want to live on a heavily trafficked bridge bothered neither her nor her teachers, who pronounced it excellent.

Most people's experience of built space comes from rectangular, orderly, self-contained, often symmetrical rooms. Her plans often give such a break from these kinds of spaces that she was soon termed a Deconstructive architect. That is, she makes buildings in such a way that they look flexed, twisted,

crushed, or shattered: constructed and not constructed at the same time. She uses digital animation programs to help her visualize and develop her ideas.

We see her skills to good advantage at the *Contemporary Arts Center* in Cincinnati. The trustees wanted the building to reflect the unpredictable nature of contemporary art. The building has a translucent skin on the outside, so that passersby on the street will see some of the art displayed within. The entry lobby is an inviting space, with galleries visible above as if suspended from the ceiling. A ramp with switchbacks gives access to the exhibition spaces while providing periodic glimpses of the

lobby and the city outside. Each of these galleries is radically different in shape and structure, so that viewers cannot predict what sort of space lies ahead. Thus, viewers proceed along a ramp toward yet-unseen works whose very unpredictability can be exciting and stimulating.

Hadid is concerned about modern urban life, which is getting more crowded in many parts of the world. Referring to Tokyo, she said, "In such a dense city, light and air are valuable commodities. We must release these spaces from their constricted sites and breathe light and air into the urban

condition."[2] She sees her loose and open spaces helping to contribute to the liberation of people from surroundings that are at times oppressive.

Hadid's practice has ranged widely. She has made an archaeological museum in Vienna, a music video pavilion in Holland, a sports complex in Abu Dhabi, the Irish Prime Minister's residence, and a ski jump in Austria. For these and other projects she was awarded the Pritzker Prize in 2004.

12.28 Zaha Hadid.
Photograph: Michael Wilson, 1998. Courtesy The Contemporary Arts Center, Cincinnati, Ohio.

12.29 Zaha Hadid.
Contemporary Arts Center. Cincinnati, Ohio. 2003.
The Lois and Richard Rosenthal Center for Contemporary Art.
Photograph: Roland Halbe.

When a beam or slab is extended a substantial distance beyond a supporting column or wall, the overhanging portion is called a cantilever. Before the use of steel and reinforced concrete, cantilevers were not used to a significant degree because the available materials could not extend far enough to make the concept viable.

One of the boldest and most elegant uses of the principle occurs in Wright's *Kaufmann Residence* (also known as *Fallingwater*) at Bear Run, Pennsylvania. Horizontal masses cantilevered from supporting piers echo the rock ledges on the site and seem almost to float above the waterfall. Vertical accents were influenced by surrounding tall, straight trees. The intrusion of a building on such a beautiful location seems justified by the harmony Wright achieved between the natural site and his equally inspiring architecture.

Green Building

More and more architects in recent years are thinking of ways to reduce the impact of building on the environment and to make the interiors more healthful. In the United States, the Green Building Council gives annual awards for leadership in environmentally sensitive design. Architects can submit their plans to the Council for rating, and the Council assigns points for such factors as harmony with prevailing wind or sunshine patterns, indoor energy efficiency, use of recycled water, and reduction of transportation costs for materials. The Council then makes annual awards for Leadership in Energy and Environmental Design, presenting Silver, Gold, and Platinum certificates each year to projects that reach designated point levels.

12.30 Frank Lloyd Wright.
Fallingwater (Edgar Kaufmann Residence).
Bear Run, Pennsylvania. 1936.
Scott Frances\Esto Photographics, Inc.

FRANK LLOYD WRIGHT

Radical Innovator

FRANK LLOYD WRIGHT, the most influential twentieth-century American architect, was born in Wisconsin, the son of a Baptist minister.

At age eighteen, Wright took a job with a local builder while studying civil engineering part-time at the University of Wisconsin. In 1887, he went to Chicago, where he worked as an apprentice in the newly formed architectural firm of Adler & Sullivan. When Louis Sullivan was designing the *Wainwright Building* (page 196), Wright was his chief draftsman. Eager to do his own work, Wright began designing houses on his own at night. Sullivan took offense at this practice, and Wright left the firm. Wright, however, was strongly influenced by Sullivan and continued throughout his life to refer to him as Lieber Meister (beloved master).

By 1893, Wright had opened his own office in the rapidly growing community of Oak Park, Illinois, where he designed a series of houses with low horizontal lines that echoed the flat prairie landscape. This distinctive approach became known as his Prairie Style.

That same year, at the Columbian Exposition in Chicago, Wright saw a Japanese tea house. The encounter led to a deep interest in Japanese architecture and long stays in Japan. He found the asymmetrical balance, large extended eaves, and flexible open plan (with sliding doors and walls) of traditional Japanese houses

more sensitive to nature and to human life than the often static symmetry of traditional American homes.

Wright brought his own poetic sense of nature into harmony with the new materials and the engineering technology of the machine age. In terms of both structure and aesthetics, Wright was a radical innovator. He used poured reinforced concrete and steel cantilevers in houses at a time when such construction was usually confined to commercial structures. His *Kaufmann Residence* is dramatically cantilevered over a waterfall, and two of his major buildings were designed with flowing interior spaces and spiral ramps. Among his many notable buildings was the structurally innovative Imperial Hotel in Tokyo, built between 1916 and 1922. His use of the cantilever in this hotel was criticized as a violation of sound construction—until the devastating quake of 1923, when it remained one of the few undamaged buildings in the city.

In his later years, Wright continued his large practice and devoted considerable time to writing and to teaching apprentices in his workshop-homes. Throughout his career Wright was guided by his awareness that buildings have a profound, life-shaping influence on the people who inhabit them.

Among Wright's many unrealized projects was a plan for a mile-high skyscraper. His last major work was the controversial

12.31 Frank Lloyd Wright. 1936.
Photo by Edmund Teske. Courtesy The Frank Lloyd Wright Archives, Scottsdale, AZ/ © 2010 Frank Lloyd Wright Foundation, Scottsdale, AZ/ Artists Rights Society (ARS), NY.

Solomon R. Guggenheim Museum, built in the late 1950s. Its immense spiraling ramp enables viewers to see exhibitions in a clearly defined continuous path, but the sloping, eye-filling space tends to overpower the presentation of other works of art.

Wright's guiding philosophy is most apparent in his houses, where his concern for simplicity and his sensitivity to the character of space and materials express what he defined as an organic ideal for architecture. According to Wright, the word *organic* goes beyond its strictly biological meaning to refer to the integration of all aspects of a form, the part to the whole and the whole to the part. Thus, in architecture, one should determine the form of a building by designing

in terms of the unique qualities of the site, proceeding from the ground up, and honoring the character of the natural conditions as well as the materials and purposes of the structure. Wright spoke of organic architecture as having a meaning beyond any preconceived style:

Exalting the simple laws of common sense—or of super-sense if you prefer—determining form by way of the nature of materials, the nature of purpose so well understood that a bank will not look like a Greek Temple, a university will not look like a cathedral, nor a fire-engine house resemble a French château. . . . Form follows function? Yes, but more important now [with organic architecture] form and function are one.[3]

12.32 OJK Architecture and Planning.
Gish Family Apartments.
San Jose, California. 2008.
Owner: First Community Housing. Architect:
The Office of Jerome King. Structural Engineer:
Vertech Engineering. Landscape Architect:
Cottong & Taniguchi. Civil Engineer: Charles
Davidson Co. Photo: Bernard André
Photography.

The highest award they have yet given to a public housing project went in 2008 to *Gish Apartments* in San Jose, California. To produce electricity for common areas, this Gold-rated building uses solar collectors atop a reflecting roof. Linoleum and carpeted floors are made from recycled materials. Lumber for the structure was sustainably harvested. All appliances are the most energy efficient available. *Gish Apartments* uses twenty-one percent less energy and thirty-six percent less water than a conventional building of its size.

12.33 David Adjaye.
Museum of Contemporary Art, Denver.
Denver, Colorado. 2007.
Photo by Dean Kaufman, courtesy
Museum of Contemporary Art Denver.

Even some museums have joined the quest to build green. The *Museum of Contemporary Art, Denver* sits atop a cleaned-up hazardous waste site. Heating comes from a radiant floor; cooling is a low-energy evaporative cooler rather than an air conditioner. (But the majority of its exterior wall is a double-skin façade, which reduces the need for both heating and cooling.) The roof is a green garden planted with local native species. Twenty percent of its building materials come from recycled sources. Using thirty-two percent less energy than a comparable conventional structure, this museum is the greenest yet built, and it also earned a Gold rating.

The *mkSolaire Home* by Michelle Kaufmann represents the leading edge in green single-family home design. This prefabricated house can be placed on a wide variety of sites in an orientation to maximize sunlight. It uses the most efficient insulation available, and window placements maximize cross-ventilation. On-demand water heaters, low-flow fixtures, and a green roof also reduce energy demands. The architect certifies that this home, depending on where it is located, will earn either a Gold or a Platinum certification.

In addition to their high efficiency, these buildings all look good too, but not all green buildings appear innovative from the outside. This is because some green designers prefer to redesign existing buildings rather than build new ones.

PRACTICE MORE: Get flashcards for images and terms and review chapter material with quizzes at **www.myartslab.com**

12.34 Michelle Kaufmann.
mkSolaire Home. 2008.
Prefabricated house.
As exhibited at Museum of Science and Industry, Chicago. michelle@michellekaufmann.com. Photo by John Swain Photography, courtesy of Michelle Kaufmann.

EVALUATING ART

HOW DO PROFESSIONALS LOOK AT ART?

WHAT MAKES A WORK OF ART A MASTERPIECE?

WHAT ARE THE PRINCIPAL THEORIES OF ART CRITICISM?

Now that we have considered some ways of making art, it is important to consider how to evaluate it. What makes a work of art worthwhile? Is it visually interesting? Does it move our feelings? Is it skillfully done? Which criteria are even relevant to judging art? Who is qualified to make such judgments? As we consider answers to these questions, we will find that there are many ways of judging the quality of art. Further, we will see that our assessments of quality are usually connected to other values that we also hold about the function of art in society; hence, our preferences about art generally embody other deeply held beliefs.

EVALUATION

Have you ever heard someone say, "I don't know anything about art, but I know what I like"? Each of us expresses likes or dislikes many times a day. When we select one thing over another, or appreciate the specialness of something, we are evaluating.

The creative experience is also a process of selecting and evaluating. For the artist, the creative process involves selecting and evaluating each component before deciding to include it in the final form. After the work is complete, the viewer's enjoyment comes from recognizing the quality that has been achieved. How do viewers evaluate art to determine whether it has quality?

Quality is relative. How a work of art is evaluated varies from person to person, from culture to culture, and from age to age. In Mexico before the Spanish conquest, the Aztecs judged art to be good if it resembled the style of the Toltecs, an ancient neighboring people that the Aztecs admired. In traditional Chinese art criticism, painters were urged to go beyond mere representation of the outward appearance of their subject matter. A good artist could understand and communicate the inner spirit or "life breath" of a subject. To call an artwork "skillful" was to give it faint praise.

In the European tradition, few famous artists or styles have had unchanging reputations. For example, the Impressionist painters of the late nineteenth century were ridiculed by most critics, museum curators, and the public. Their style differed too radically from those of their predecessors for easy acceptance in their own time. Today, Impressionist paintings have an honored place in museums and are eagerly sought by the public. Likewise, many artists who were celebrated in their times are justifiably forgotten today.

13.1 Dawn Marie Jingagian.
Shy Glance. 1976.
Acrylic on canvas. 18″ × 24″.
The Museum of Bad Art, Dedham, MA.

13.2 Elizabeth Louise Vigee-LeBrun.
Self-Portrait in a Straw Hat. 1782.
Oil on canvas. 97.8 × 70.5 cm
NG1653. © National Gallery, London.

Value judgments about art necessarily involve subjectivity; it is not possible to measure artistic quality objectively. In this regard, let's compare *Shy Glance*, a work generally regarded as "bad," with *Self-Portrait in a Straw Hat* by the well-trained artist Elizabeth Vigee-LeBrun. The painter of *Shy Glance* lacks skill in many areas: color shading (the cheek is blotchy), anatomy (the eyebrow is too narrow and the forehead bulges), composition (it is difficult to tell positive from negative space), and brushwork (the hair and eyelashes!). The feeling it communicates is almost embarrassingly sweet. In contrast, the *Self-Portrait* shows great assuredness in the use of paint to show anatomy. The light seems to fall naturally over the subject's face and shoulder. The eyes and face show a relaxed, confident gaze. The two artists are poles apart in level of traditional skill.

Yet, today's viewers might find *Shy Glance* at least as interesting as the other work. The *Self-Portrait*, for all its skill, looks conventional, even ordinary. In contrast, *Shy Glance* has an obvious sincerity and enthusiasm that may be infectious. The painter of *Shy Glance* showed great boldness in even bringing forth this work after having no training. Hence, the level of traditional skill that an artist shows may be relevant to a judgment of quality, but rarely gives the final answer.

When we look at a work of art and find that we are pleased (or displeased), it is useful to ask why. What we find in a work of art depends on what we are looking for. Would we like art to dazzle our senses? Show great skill? Move our feelings? Inform us about the world? Bare the artist's soul? These are personal value orientations that will lead us to make judgments about works of art.

Each of us applies these assumptions about the function of art each time we look at a work. Some viewers prefer that art entertain us or distract us from life's problems. They may enjoy the posters of Toulouse-Lautrec (page 115) or *He Got Game* by Robin Rhode (page 13). Some would like to see art that builds communication between people; they will want to see works that are as personal as a deep conversation, such as *Border* by Joan Mitchell on page 100. Other viewers may hope that art can lead us to contemplate higher spiritual realms. If so, then *St. Anselm's Altar* on page 5 or Georgia O'Keeffe's *Evening Star VI* (page 368) will likely meet their needs. Still others see art as a vehicle for improving society, and will be drawn to works such as D.W. Griffith's film *Intolerance* on page 135 or *Sun Mad* by Ester Hernández (page 117). These are only a few of the functions that art may fulfill for viewers.

Expressing our taste in art thus involves our personality and our values more than other kinds of judgments. The type of art that we prefer reveals far more about us than does our favorite flavor of ice cream.

Whether you are approaching art for your own enjoyment or for a class assignment, it is most rewarding to begin with an open, receptive mind—to go beyond snap judgments. Give yourself time to get acquainted and to respond.

ART CRITICISM

The term **art criticism** refers to making discriminating judgments, both favorable and unfavorable.

We all do art criticism, but professionals tend to follow one or more of three basic theories:

- Formal theories, which focus attention on the composition of the work and how it may have been influenced by earlier works
- Contextual theories, which consider art as a product and of a culture and value system
- Expressive theories, which pay attention to the artist's expression of a personality or world-view.

These theories emphasize the work, the culture, and the artist, respectively. Let us consider each in turn, as they might be used to analyze three paintings that are pictured in this chapter.

Formal Theories

Critics who use formal theories look carefully at how a work is made: how the parts of the composition come together to create a visual experience that may interest us, or not. They generally believe that the most important influence on a work is other works that the artist has seen or studied. Because the formal organization of the work is the most important factor in evaluating it, the theories are called **formal**. The subject or theme of the work is less important than how the artist presented it. Formalist critics value innovation in style above all; thus, they always want to know when a work was done, so that they can compare it (at least mentally) with its predecessors and contemporaries. They value such stylistic novelty because they believe that art can be an important source of visual refreshment, unconnected to our complicated and strife-torn world.

From a formal perspective, Titian's *Pietà* is very innovative in its brushwork. His immediate predecessors in Italian art were the Renaissance masters Raphael, Michelangelo, and Leonardo, among others. Titian understood the painting methods that they used, but he went beyond them by making his brushwork much bolder and looser, adding a new element of expressiveness to painting that influenced artists for generations to come. The work also uses an innovative composition: the center is an empty niche surrounded by a diagonal row of heads that is balanced by the two figures at the upper right. This emptiness at the center is a bold compositional device for that time.

LEARN MORE: For a Closer Look at Titian's *Pietà*, go to **www.myartslab.com**

13.3 Titian.
Pietà. 1576.
Oil on canvas. 149" × 136".
SCALA\Art Resource, N.Y.

13.4 Sonia Delaunay-Terk.
Simultaneous Contrasts. 1913.
Oil on canvas. 46 × 55 cm.
Museo Thyssen-Bornemisza, Madrid. 518 (1976.81). L & M Services
B. V. Amsterdam.

Sonia Delaunay-Terk was similarly innovative when she painted *Simultaneous Contrasts* in 1913. The work was influenced by Cubism (see Chapter 21), but Delaunay-Terk did not overlap the planes as earlier Cubists did; the elements of this work fit together like a jigsaw puzzle. Yet she used shading to model each zone, as if the zones were curved surfaces. The work is innovative for how it suggests and denies a third dimension at the same time. This painting is also more innovative in its color than most early Cubist works. This painting explores how one bright color can have an impact on our perception of a neighboring one.

Horn Players by Jean-Michel Basquiat is also innovative from a formal standpoint: It uses techniques that the artist learned from making graffiti, something that few artists had done at that time. The parallel arrangement of three vertical panels is also interesting, suggesting a Japanese screen. The composition as a whole barely hangs together, but it does cohere. Note the repeated heads, boxes, and white paint strokes in each panel.

Thus, we can conclude that each of these three paintings is formally interesting, but for different reasons.

Contextual Theories

Critics who use these theories tend to look first at the environmental influences on a work of art: the economic system, the cultural values, and even the politics of the time; because the context matters a great deal, they are termed **contextual theories**. Just as formalist critics will want to know the date of a work, contextual critics are likely to ask, "What else was going on in the culture at that time?" Contextual critics tend to favor works that either cogently embody important cultural values, or memorably express resistance to them. Let us see how they might judge our three paintings.

Titian's *Pietà* is an altarpiece, destined for public viewing in a chapel at a church in Venice; altarpieces generally took up important Christian themes, and this one is no exception. However, Titian painted it during an epidemic of the plague, and its theme of mortality and grief takes on added meaning in that context. The vacant niche probably symbolizes death, and Titian's eloquent depiction of the dead Christ must have given comfort to the many Venetians who lost relatives in the epidemic. The work expresses grief over current events, but Titian has successfully taken it out of its time, so that even today we can still appreciate its mournful aspect.

Simultaneous Contrasts by Sonia Delaunay is less interesting from a contextual perspective, because its subject seems to be a simple sunlit landscape. The work tells us very little about its time (the early twentieth century). The title of the work refers to an optical theory that many artists studied in those days, which dealt with the interaction of colors. Delaunay also did fabric designs, and she used her discoveries in painting to give her ideas for her fashion work. This

13.5 Jean-Michel Basquiat.
Horn Players. 1983.
Acrylic and oil paintstick on three canvas panels.
Overall 8′ × 6′5″ (2.44 × 1.91 m).
Broad Art Foundation, Santa Monica, California. © 2010 The Estate of Jean-Michel Basquiat/ADAGP, Paris/ARS, New York.

painting fueled her innovative clothing designs, which she called "Simultaneous Dresses".

In contrast, *Horn Players* is filled with contextual information. Basquiat admired the leaders of the bebop movement in jazz, and this work is an homage to them. Saxophonist Charlie Parker is at the upper left, red musical notes pouring out of his instrument. The ear that seems about to be cut off may refer to Vincent van Gogh, an artist of similar innovative power who indeed cut off his ear. (Both Parker and van Gogh died young, "cut off" in their prime.) We can make out the name of trumpeter Dizzy Gillespie at the top center and see him pictured at the right.

The word "ornithology" refers to one of Parker's musical compositions that the two of them recorded in a famous track. Together they must have created the "alchemy" (magically transformative mixture) that the artist scrawled at the lower right.

Expressive Theories

All artworks are made by people. The skill level, personal intent, emotional state, mind-set, and gender of the creator must play a role in the creative process. Artist-centered theories are thus termed **expressive theories**. If formalists want to know dates, and contextualists want to know about the background culture, an expressive critic will want to know "Who made it? And who is she or he?" Critics who favor this approach tend to look for powerful personal meanings, deep psychological insight, or profound human concern. Expressive approaches have value because we all wish to be known, and finding artists similar to us in the museum is reassuring. Moreover, art is a means of communication between artist and viewer, and this communication can be done well or poorly. Each of our three paintings is quite expressive.

Titian painted the *Pietà* in the last year of his life; hence, its somber reflection on death expresses the artist's own mortality. Indeed, the figure at the lower right in the red shawl is Titian himself. Anyone who has ever mourned can probably identify with Mary's mournful attitude in this painting. The brushwork here is loose and expressive: Many critics believe that this represents an "old age style" in which the artist cast off the restraint of his younger days.

Sonia Delaunay's ebullient personality comes across in *Simultaneous Contrasts*. No clouds darken its sunlit skies. Her bright and exuberant color palette comes from her memories of brightly colored folk costumes in her native Ukraine, especially wedding costumes that were festooned with ribbons.

Critics of an expressive bent tend to like Jean-Michel Basquiat because his works are full of personal meaning. Most interesting is his use of line: it seems both intent and intense. That intensity contrasts nicely with the seemingly casual arrangement of the figures and script. The painting seems to have come together like a three-verse song. This work also explores the artist's personal history as an African American by upholding examples from the music world. In *Horn Players*, he shares with us some people who are important to him, which is a good way to get a conversation going in almost any context.

WHAT MAKES IT GREAT?

The most obvious answer to this question is, "It's great if you think it is!" And everyone has their own personal list of great artworks. However, with our three theories in hand, we can now say how a work of art comes to be regarded as a "masterpiece," and commands the place of honor in a museum (or appears in a book like this): Some degree of innovation, important cultural meanings, and a recognizable personal statement are key ingredients. Not all three are necessary, but at least one must be strongly present.

Most works hanging in museums have been selected by the specialists on the staff because they embody at least one of the three theories. Your judgments may not agree with theirs, and that is OK.

But to go deeper is rewarding. The three theories of art criticism presented here give us three standards of quality, and three ways of judging artworks. Often we apply one or more of these without thinking, and we say something like, "I like art that I can relate to." Well, why do you relate to it? What are you looking for? A little self-examination should help you to uncover what values are motivating your choices, and can help open an interesting discussion about art with other viewers.

For the non-specialist, formal innovation is the hardest quality to recognize in a work of art. Many artworks hanging in museums are quite innovative (especially modern works), but unless we know something of the history of art, the innovation will likely be lost on us. Thus, the rest of this book is devoted to exploring art history.

PRACTICE MORE: Get flashcards for images and terms and review chapter material with quizzes at **www.myartslab.com**

ART IN THE WORLD

WHAT TO DO IN A MUSEUM

ART MUSEUMS CAN be mind-expanding or sleep-inducing, depending on how you approach them. It is a mistake to enter a museum with the belief that you should like everything you see—or even that you should see everything that is there. Without selective viewing, the visitor to a large museum is likely to come down with a severe case of museum exhaustion.

The English word museum comes from the Greek *mouseion*, "place of the muses." "Muse" indicates the spirit or power believed to be capable of inspiring and watching over poets, musicians, and other artists—or any source of inspiration. A museum is for musing, a place devoted to collecting, caring for, studying, and displaying objects of lasting value and interest.

Unfortunately, museum visitors are often overwhelmed by the many rooms full of art and background information. Some may feel that they should have an extensive knowledge of art history before they even enter a museum. Even the entrance to a museum can be a bit intimidating ("Step this way. Serious art. No smiling.") or it can be inviting and welcoming ("Come on in. Relax. Make yourself comfortable.").

There is a way to enjoy an art museum without experiencing overload. If you were to go to a new restaurant and try to sample everything on the menu, you would probably get sick. In both restaurants and museums, selection is the key to a positive experience.

13.6 Frank Modell.

It makes sense to approach an art museum the way a seasoned traveler approaches a city for a first visit: Find out what there is to see. In the museum, inquire about the schedule of special shows, then see those exhibitions and outstanding works that interest you. Museums are in the process of rethinking their buildings and collections to meet the needs of changing populations and changing values. It is not unusual to find video exhibits, performances of all kinds, and film showings as part of regular museum programming.

If you are visiting without a specific exhibition in mind, follow your interests and instincts. Browsing can be highly rewarding. Zero in on what you feel are the highlights, savoring favorite works and unexpected discoveries.

Don't stay too long in a museum. Take breaks. Perhaps there is a garden or cafe in which you can pause for a rest. Take a friend with you and discuss what you have seen. The quality of your experience is not measured by how many works

you see. The most rewarding experiences can come from finding something that speaks to you, then sitting and enjoying it in leisurely contemplation.

HEAR MORE: To hear an interview with the director of the Monterey Museum of Art about what to do in a museum, go to **www.myartslab.com**

FROM THE EARLIEST ART TO THE BRONZE AGE

HOW OLD IS THE OLDEST CARVED HUMAN FORM?

WHAT ARE THE CHARACTERISTICS OF BRONZE AGE ART?

WHAT ALLOWED EGYPT TO DEVELOP A STABLE CULTURE FOR OVER TWO THOUSAND YEARS?

Art history makes history visible and accessible. It is a record of how the people of the past—our ancestors—lived, felt, and acted in widely separated parts of the world at different periods of time.

Art history differs from other kinds of history because works of art from the past are with us in the present. One-to-one communication still occurs, even when artist and viewer are separated by thousands of years. This communicative power of art makes it possible for us to glimpse some of the experiences of those whose lives preceded ours, to better understand societies other than our own, and to see beyond our own cultural boundaries. Although interesting, old science has little practical use; but old art can be as life-enriching as new art.

There is no "better" or "best" when we compare the art of different societies, or even the art of different times within the same society. Rather, differences in art reflect differences in points of view. Pablo Picasso put the subject of art history in perspective in this way:

To me there is no past or future in art. If a work of art cannot live always in the present it must not be considered at all. The art of the Greeks, the Egyptians, the great painters who lived in other times, is not an art of the past; perhaps it is more alive today than it ever was.[1]

THE PALEOLITHIC PERIOD

Roughly two million years ago, in east-central Africa, early hominids made crude stonecutting tools. The making of these tools enabled our predecessors to extend their skills and thereby gain a measure of control over their surroundings. From such beginnings, human beings developed the abilities to reason and to visualize: to remember the past, to relate it to the present, and to imagine a possible future. As we became form-creating creatures, our ability to conceive mental images set us apart from other animals. Imagination is our special advantage.

About one million years ago in Africa, and more recently in Asia and Europe, people made more refined tools by chipping flakes from opposite sides of stones to create sharp cutting edges. It took another 250,000 years or so for human beings to develop choppers and hand axes that were symmetrical and refined in shape. An awareness of the relationship of form to function, and of form as enjoyable in itself, was the first step in the history of art.

Sprinkled powders and beads accompany many widely dispersed gravesites from about 100,000 years ago. These finds suggest to archaeologists that

HEAR MORE: Listen to an audio file of your chapter at **www.myartslab.com**

TIMELINE

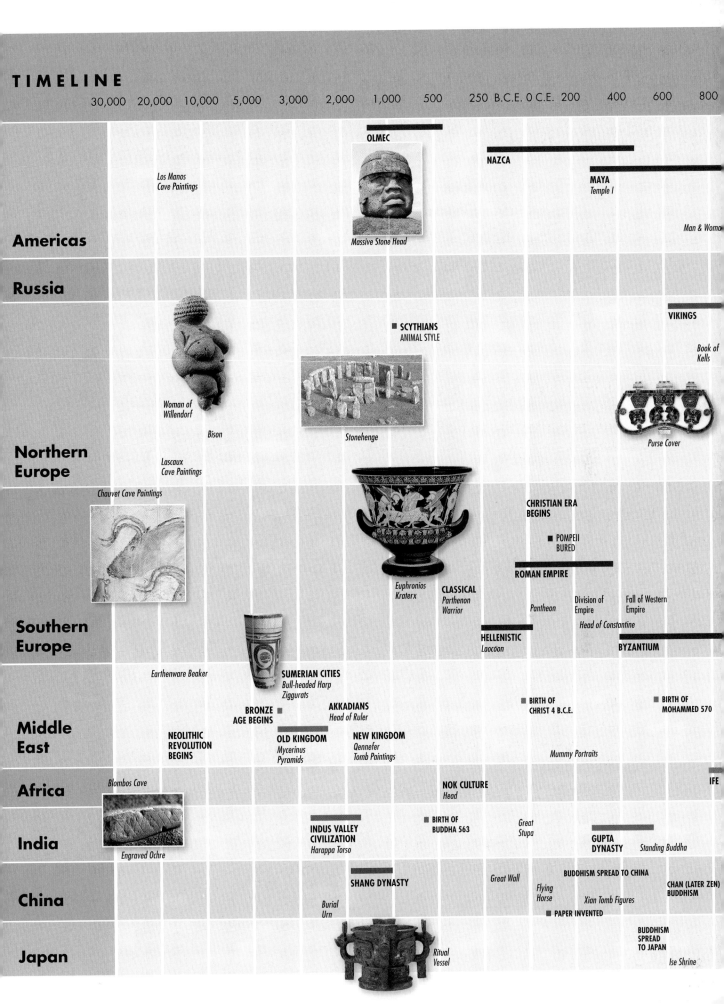

| | 30,000 | 20,000 | 10,000 | 5,000 | 3,000 | 2,000 | 1,000 | 500 | 250 B.C.E. 0 C.E. 200 | 400 | 600 | 800 |

Americas

OLMEC

NAZCA

MAYA
Temple I

Los Manos
Cave Paintings

Massive Stone Head

Man & Woma

Russia

Northern Europe

Woman of
Willendorf

Bison

Lascaux
Cave Paintings

Chauvet Cave Paintings

SCYTHIANS
ANIMAL STYLE

Stonehenge

VIKINGS

Book of
Kells

Purse Cover

Southern Europe

Euphronios
Kraterx

CLASSICAL
Parthenon
Warrior

HELLENISTIC
Laocöon

CHRISTIAN ERA
BEGINS

POMPEII
BURED

ROMAN EMPIRE

Pantheon

Division of
Empire

Head of Constantine

Fall of Western
Empire

BYZANTIUM

Middle East

Earthenware Beaker

NEOLITHIC
REVOLUTION
BEGINS

BRONZE
AGE BEGINS

SUMERIAN CITIES
Bull-headed Harp
Ziggurats

OLD KINGDOM
Mycerinus
Pyramids

AKKADIANS
Head of Ruler

NEW KINGDOM
Qennefer
Tomb Paintings

BIRTH OF
CHRIST 4 B.C.E.

BIRTH OF
MOHAMMED 570

Mummy Portraits

Africa

Blombos Cave

Engraved Ochre

NOK CULTURE
Head

IFE

India

INDUS VALLEY
CIVILIZATION
Harappa Torso

BIRTH OF
BUDDHA 563

Great
Stupa

GUPTA
DYNASTY

Standing Buddha

China

Burial
Urn

SHANG DYNASTY

Great Wall

Flying
Horse

PAPER INVENTED

BUDDHISM SPREAD TO CHINA

Xian Tomb Figures

CHAN (LATER ZEN)
BUDDHISM

Japan

Ritual
Vessel

BUDDHISM
SPREAD
TO JAPAN

Ise Shrine

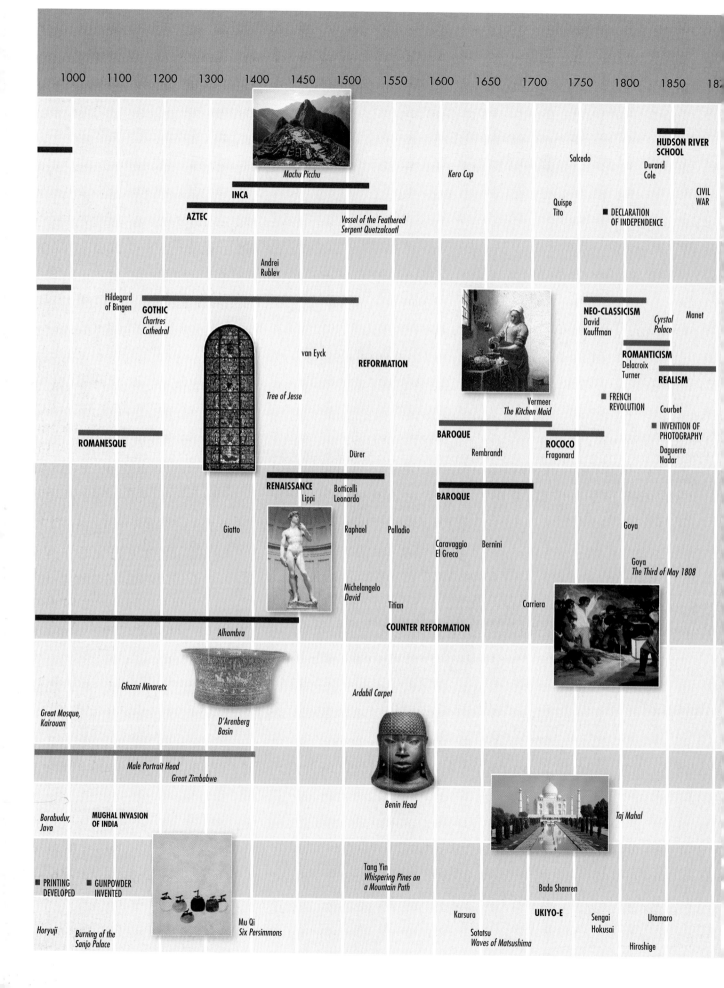

1000 1100 1200 1300 1400 1450 1500 1550 1600 1650 1700 1750 1800 1850 182...

Machu Picchu

INCA

AZTEC

Vessel of the Feathered Serpent Quetzalcoatl

Kero Cup

Salcedo

HUDSON RIVER SCHOOL

Durand
Cole

Quispe
Tito

■ DECLARATION OF INDEPENDENCE

CIVIL WAR

Andrei Rublev

Hildegard of Bingen

GOTHIC
Chartres Cathedral

van Eyck

REFORMATION

NEO-CLASSICISM
David
Kauffman

Cyrstal Palace

Manet

ROMANTICISM
Delacroix
Turner

REALISM

Tree of Jesse

Vermeer
The Kitchen Maid

■ FRENCH REVOLUTION

Courbet

■ INVENTION OF PHOTOGRAPHY

ROMANESQUE

BAROQUE

Dürer

Rembrandt

ROCOCO
Fragonard

Daguerre
Nadar

RENAISSANCE
Lippi

Botticelli
Leonardo

BAROQUE

Giatto

Raphael

Palladio

Caravaggio
El Greco

Bernini

Goya

Michelangelo
David

Titian

Carriera

Goya
The Third of May 1808

COUNTER REFORMATION

Alhambra

Ghazni Minaretx

Ardabil Carpet

Great Mosque, Kairouan

D'Arenberg Basin

Male Portrait Head
Great Zimbabwe

Benin Head

Borabudur, Java

MUGHAL INVASION OF INDIA

Taj Mahal

■ PRINTING DEVELOPED

■ GUNPOWDER INVENTED

Tang Yin
Whispering Pines on a Mountain Path

Bada Shanren

UKIYO-E

Karsura

Sengai
Hokusai

Utamaro

Horyuji

Burning of the Sanjo Palace

Mu Qi
Six Persimmons

Sotatsu
Waves of Matsushima

Hiroshige

| 1880 | 1890 | 1900 | 1910 | 1920 | 1930 | 1940 | 1950 | 1960 | 1970 | 1980 | 1990 | 2000 |

Americas

Cassatt
The Letter

FIRST MOON LANDING

HARLEM RENAISSANCE
Lawrence
Motley
Kahlo
WORLD WAR II

Goldsworthy

ABSTRACT EXPRESSIONISM
Pollack
de Kooning
Frankenthaler
Rauschenberg

CONCEPTUALISM

APPLE COMPUTER

Amaral

REGIONALISM
Benton

POP ART
Rosenquist
Warhol

FEMINISM

Leeson

FIRST TALKING FILM

F.L. Wright

Sherman

Swoon

Nampeyo

O'Keeffe
Oriental Poppies

MINIMALISM
T, Smith
Judd

Rothenberg

POST-MODERNISM

Russia

CONSTRUCTIVISM
Tatlin

SOCIALIST REALISM

Eisenstein

Northern Europe

PRESSIONISM
net
oir
as
in

CUBISM
Braque
Picasso

INTERNATIONAL STYLE

NEO-EXPRESSIONISM
Kiefer

POST-IMPRESSIONISM
Cézanne
Gauguin
van Gogh

BAUHAUS

FAUVISM
Matisse

DE STIJL
Mondrian
Rietveld

Orlan

Gursky

Brancusi

DADA
Duchamp
Höch

PERFORMANCE ART
Beuys

GERMAN EXPRESSIONISM
Kirchner
Nolde

SURREALISM
Magritte

Cézanne
Monte Saint-Victoire

Southern Europe

Miró
Dali

Burri

FUTURISM
Balla
Baccioni

Delauney
Bal Bullier

Middle East

Mukhtar

Raad

Sikander

Neshat

Africa

Congo Power Figure

Sekoto

Okeke

Ibrahim El-Salahi
Funeral and a Crescent

Shonibore

Kota Reliquary Figure

India

Sher-Gil

Husain

Gupta

China

Li Hua

Zhang
Daqian

Cai

CHINESE REVOLUTION

NOTE: *in presenting the Artforms Time Line, it has been necessary to use several different scales to indicate both long and short spans of years on a few pages. If a ten-year scale were used to cover the entire 32,000-year period presented, the time line would be more than a hundred feet long.*

Japan

Takeji

Gutai

Takoezu

GLOSSARY

The following terms are defined according to their use in the visual arts. Words in *italics* are also defined in the glossary.

abstract art Art that is based on natural appearances but departs significantly from them. Forms are modified or changed to varying degrees in order to emphasize certain qualities or content. Recognizable references to original appearances may be very slight. The term is also used to describe art that is *nonrepresentational*.

Abstract Expressionism An art movement, primarily in painting, that originated in the United States in the 1940s and remained strong through the 1950s. Artists working in many different styles emphasized spontaneous personal expression in large paintings that are *abstract* or *nonrepresentational*. One type of Abstract Expressionism is called *action painting*. See also *Expressionism*.

abstract Surrealism See *Surrealism*.

academic art Art governed by rules, especially works sanctioned by an official institution, academy, or school. Originally applied to art that conformed to standards established by the French Academy regarding composition, drawing, and color usage. The term has come to mean conservative and traditional art.

achromatic Having no color (or *hue*); without identifiable hue. Most blacks, whites, grays, and browns are achromatic.

acrylic (acrylic resin) A clear synthetic resin used as a *binder* in acrylic paint and as a casting material in sculpture.

action painting A style of *nonrepresentational* painting that relies on the physical movement of the artist by using such gestural techniques as vigorous brushwork, dripping, and pouring. Dynamism is often created through the interlaced directions of the paint's impact. A subcategory of *Abstract Expressionism*.

additive color mixture The mixture of colored light. When light colors are combined (as with overlapping spotlights), the mixture becomes successively lighter. Light primaries, when combined, create white light. See also *subtractive color mixture*.

additive sculpture Sculptural form produced by adding, combining, or building up material from a core or (in some cases) an *armature*. Modeling in clay and welding steel are additive processes.

aerial perspective See *perspective*.

aesthetics The study and philosophy of the quality and nature of sensory responses related to, but not limited by, the concept of beauty. Within the art context: The philosophy of art focusing on questions regarding what art is, how it is evaluated, the concept of beauty, and the relationship between the idea of beauty and the concept of art.

airbrush A small-scale paint sprayer that allows the artist to control a fine mist of paint.

analogous colors or **analogous hues** Closely related *hues*, especially those in which a common hue can be seen; hues that are neighbors on the color wheel, such as blue, blue-green, and green.

analytical Cubism See *Cubism*.

animal style An art style developed by Eurasian nomads beginning in the late second millennium B.C.E. and lasting into the early Middle Ages in Europe. Based on abstracted forms of animals, often interlacing. Usually appears on personal adornment items, weapons, and horse fittings.

apse A semicircular end to an aisle in a *basilica* or a Christian church. In Christian churches an apse is usually placed at the eastern end of the central aisle.

aquatint An *intaglio* printmaking process in which value areas rather than lines are etched on the printing plate. Powdered resin is sprinkled on the plate, which is then immersed in an acid bath. The acid bites around the resin particles, creating a rough surface that holds ink. Also, a *print* made using this process.

arcade A series of *arches* supported by columns or piers. Also, a covered passageway between two series of arches, or between a series of arches and a wall.

arch A curved structure designed to span an opening, usually made of stone or other

masonry. Roman arches are semicircular; Islamic and Gothic arches come to a point at the top.

armature A rigid framework serving as a supporting inner core for clay or other soft sculpting material.

art criticism The process of using formal analysis, description, and interpretation to evaluate or explain the quality and meanings of art.

artist's proof A trial print, usually made as an artist works on a plate or block, to check the progress of a work.

assemblage Sculpture made by assembling found or cast-off objects that may or may not contribute their original identities to the total content of the work.

assembled sculpture Creating a work of sculpture by putting together pieces that are already formed by the artist.

asymmetrical Without *symmetry*.

asymmetrical balance The various elements of a work are balanced but not symmetrical. This is achieved by balancing visual weights and forces of the parts.

atmospheric perspective See *perspective*.

automatism Action without conscious control, such as pouring, scribbling, or doodling. Employed by *Surrealist* writers and artists to allow unconscious ideas and feelings to be expressed.

avant-garde A term from military theory that was applied to modern art, meaning the advance guard of troops that moves ahead of the main army. Avant-garde artists work ahead of the general public's ability to understand.

balance An arrangement of parts achieving a state of equilibrium between opposing forces or influences. Major types are symmetrical and *asymmetrical*. See *symmetry*.

balloon frame A wooden structural support system developed in the United States in the middle nineteenth century in which standardized, thin studs are held together with nails.

Baroque The seventeenth-century period in Europe characterized in the visual arts by dramatic light and shade, turbulent *composition*, and pronounced emotional expression.

barrel vault See *vault*.

basilica A Roman town hall, with three aisles and an *apse* at one or both ends. Christians appropriated this form for their churches.

bas-relief See *low relief*.

Bauhaus German art school in existence from 1919 to 1933, best known for its influence on design, leadership in art education, and its radically innovative philosophy of applying design principles to machine technology and mass production.

beam The horizontal stone or timber placed across an architectural space to take the weight of the roof or wall above; also called a *lintel*.

binder The material used in paint that causes *pigment* particles to adhere to one another and to the *support*; for example, linseed oil or acrylic polymer.

biomorphic shape A shape in a work of art that resembles a living organism or an *organic shape*.

bodhisattva A Buddhist holy person who is about to achieve enlightenment but postpones it to remain on earth to teach others. Frequently depicted in the arts of China and Japan, usually bejeweled.

buon fresco See *true fresco*.

burin A tool used in *engraving*.

burr The ridge left by scratching a *drypoint* line in a copper plate. The burr holds ink for printing.

buttress A *support*, usually exterior, for a wall, *arch*, or *vault* that opposes the lateral forces of these structures. A flying buttress consists of a strut or segment of an arch carrying the thrust of a vault to a vertical pier positioned away from the main portion of the building. An important element in *Gothic* cathedrals.

Byzantine art Styles of painting, design, and architecture developed from the fifth century C.E. in the Byzantine Empire of ancient Eastern Europe. Characterized in architecture by round *arches*, large *domes*, and extensive use of *mosaic*; characterized in painting by formal design, *frontal* and *stylized* figures, and rich use of color, especially gold, in generally religious subject matter.

calligraphy The art of beautiful writing. Broadly, a flowing use of line, often varying from thick to thin.

camera obscura A dark room (or box) with a small hole in one side, through which an inverted image of the view outside is projected onto the opposite wall, screen, or mirror. The image is then traced. This forerunner of the modern *camera* was a tool for recording an optically accurate image.

cantilever A beam or slab projecting a substantial distance beyond its supporting post or wall; a projection supported only at one end.

capital In architecture, the top part or head of a column or pillar.

cartoon 1. A humorous or satirical drawing. 2. A drawing created as a full-scale working drawing, used as a model for a *fresco* painting, *mural*, or tapestry.

carving A *subtractive* process in which a sculpture is formed by removing material from a block or mass of wood, stone, or other material, with the use of sharpened tools.

casein Milk protein used as a binder in opaque water-based paint.

casting A substitution process that involves pouring liquid material such as molten metal, clay, wax, or plaster into a mold. When the liquid hardens, the mold is removed, and a form in the shape of the mold is left.

catacombs Underground burial places in ancient Rome. Christians and Jews often decorated the walls and ceilings with paintings.

ceramics; ceramist Clay hardened into a relatively permanent material by firing, and the art form that includes this procedure. A practitioner of the ceramic arts is a ceramist.

charcoal A dry drawing medium made from charred twigs, usually vine or willow.

chiaroscuro Italian word meaning "light dark." The gradations of light and dark *values* in *two-dimensional* imagery. Especially the illusion of rounded, three-dimensional form created through gradations of light and shade rather than line. Highly developed by *Renaissance* painters.

classical 1. The art of ancient Greece and Rome. In particular, the style of Greek art that flourished during the fifth century B.C.E. 2. Any art based on a clear, rational, and regular structure, emphasizing horizontal and vertical directions, and organizing its parts with special emphasis on balance and proportion. The term classic is also used to indicate recognized excellence.

closed form A self-contained or explicitly limited form; having a resolved balance of tensions, a sense of calm completeness implying a totality within itself. A sculptural shape that seems to look inward rather than outward.

coffer In architecture, a decorative sunken panel on the underside of a ceiling.

collage From the French "coller," to glue. A work made by gluing various materials, such as paper scraps, photographs, and cloth, on a flat surface.

colonnade A row of columns usually spanned or connected by *beams* (lintels).

color field painting A movement that grew out of *Abstract Expressionism*, in which large stained or painted areas or "fields" of color evoke aesthetic and emotional responses.

color scheme A set of colors chosen for a work of art in order to produce a specific mood or effect.

complementary colors Two *hues* directly opposite one another on a *color wheel* that, when mixed together in proper proportions, produce a neutral gray.

composition The combining of parts or elements to form a whole; the structure, organization, or total form of a work of art.

Conceptual art An art form in which the originating idea and the process by which it is presented take precedence over a tangible product. Conceptual works are sometimes produced in visible form, but they often exist only as descriptions of mental concepts or ideas. This trend developed in the late 1960s, partially as a way to avoid the commercialization of art.

concrete A liquid building material invented by the Romans. Made of water, sand, gravel, and a binder of gypsum, lime, or volcanic ash.

Constructivism Art movement that originated in Russia at the time of the Soviet Revolution of 1917. Constructivists emphasized abstract art, modern materials (glass, metal, plastic), and useful arts such as set design, furniture, and graphics.

conté crayon A drawing medium developed in the late eighteenth century. Similar to pencil in its graphite content, conté crayon includes clay and small amounts of wax.

content Meaning or message communicated by a work of art, including its emotional, intellectual, symbolic, thematic, and narrative connotations.

contextual theory A method of art criticism that focuses on the cultural systems behind works of art. These may be economic, racial, political, or social.

contrapposto Italian for "counterpose." The counterpositioning of parts of the human figure about a central vertical axis, as when the weight is placed on one foot causing the hip and shoulder lines to counterbalance each other—often in a graceful S-curve.

cool colors Colors whose relative visual temperatures make them seem cool. Cool colors generally include green, blue-green, blue, blue-violet, and violet. Warmness or coolness is relative to adjacent hues. See also *warm colors*.

cross-hatching See *hatching*.

Cubism Art style developed in Paris by Picasso and Braque, beginning in 1907. The early phase of the style, called analytical Cubism, lasted from 1909 through 1911. Cubism is based on the simultaneous presentation of multiple views, disintegration, and geometric reconstruction of subjects in flattened, ambiguous pictorial space; figure and ground merge into one interwoven surface of shifting planes. Color is limited to *neutrals*. By 1912, the more decorative phase called synthetic or collage Cubism began to appear; it was characterized by fewer, more solid forms, conceptual rather than observed subject matter, and richer color and texture.

curtain wall A non-load-bearing wall, typical of the *International Style*. Generally well-endowed with windows.

Dada A movement in art and literature, founded in Switzerland in the early twentieth century, which ridiculed contemporary culture and conventional art. The Dadaists shared an antimilitaristic and anti-aesthetic attitude, generated in part by the horrors of World War I and in part by a rejection of accepted canons of morality and taste. The anarchic spirit of Dada can be seen in the works of Duchamp, Man Ray, Hoch, Hausmann, and others. Many Dadaists later explored *Surrealism*.

daguerreotype An early photographic process developed by Louis Daguerre in the 1830s, which required a treated metal plate. This plate was exposed to light, and the chemical reactions on the plate created the first satisfactory photographs.

design In three-dimensional arts (such as sculpture or architecture), the process of arranging visual elements into a finished work. Also means the product of the process, as in, "The design of that chair is excellent."

De Stijl A Dutch purist art movement begun during World War I by Mondrian and others. It involved painters, sculptors, designers, and architects whose works and ideas were expressed in De Stijl magazine. *De Stijl*, Dutch for "the style," was aimed at creating a universal language of *form* that would be independent of individual emotion. Visual form was pared down to *primary colors* plus black and white, and rectangular shapes.

directional forces Pathways that the artist embeds in a work for the viewer's eye to follow. May be done with actual or implied lines, or lines of sight among the figures depicted in a work.

direct painting Executing a painting in one sitting, applying wet over wet colors.

divisionism See *pointillism*.

dome A generally hemispherical roof or *vault*. Theoretically, an *arch* rotated 180° on its vertical axis.

dressed stone Stone used for building that is cut, trimmed, or ground down to fit into a *masonry* wall.

drypoint An *intaglio* printmaking process in which lines are scratched directly into a metal plate with a steel needle. The scratch raises a ridge that takes the ink. Also, the resulting *print*.

earthenware A type of clay used for ceramics. It fires at 1100°C–1150°C, and is porous after firing.

earthworks Sculptural forms made from earth, rocks, or sometimes plants, often on a vast scale and in remote locations. Some are deliberately impermanent.

edition In printmaking, the total number of *prints* made and approved by the artist, usually numbered consecutively. Also, a limited number of multiple originals of a single design in any medium.

emphasis A method an artist uses to draw attention to an area. May be done with central placement, large size, bright color, or high contrast.

encaustic A type of painting in which *pigment* is suspended in a *binder* of hot wax.

engraving An *intaglio* printmaking process in which grooves are cut into a metal or wood surface with a sharp cutting tool called a burin or graver. Also, the resulting *print*.

entasis In *classical* architecture, the slight swelling or bulge in the center of a column, which corrects the illusion of concave tapering produced by parallel straight lines.

etching An *intaglio* printmaking process in which a metal plate is first coated with acid-resistant wax or varnish, then scratched to expose the metal to the bite of nitric acid where lines are desired. Also, the resulting *print*.

Expressionism The broad term that describes emotional art, most often boldly executed and making free use of distortion and symbolic or invented color. More specifically, Expressionism refers to individual and group styles originating in Europe in the late nineteenth and early twentieth centuries. See also *Abstract Expressionism*.

expressive theory A method of art criticism that attempts to discern personal elements in works of art, as opposed to formal strategies or cultural influences.

eye level In linear *perspective*, the presumed height of the artist's eyes; this becomes the presumed height of the viewer standing in front of the finished work.

Fauvism A style of painting introduced in Paris in the early twentieth century, characterized by areas of bright, contrasting color and simplified shapes. The name *les fauves* is French for "the wild beasts."

feminism In art, a movement among artists, critics, and art historians that began in an organized fashion in the 1970s. Feminists seek to validate and promote art forms that express the unique experience of women, and to redress oppression by men.

figurative art Representational art in which the human form (rather than the natural world) plays a principal role.

figure Separate shape(s) that seem to lie above a background or *ground*.

figure–ground reversal A visual effect in which what was seen as a positive shape becomes a negative shape, and vice versa.

film editing The process by which an editor compiles *shots* into scenes and scenes into a film.

firing Baking clay in a special high-temperature oven to solidify it. Secondary firings may also be done to fix finishing coats on fired pieces.

fixative A light, liquid varnish sprayed over finished charcoal or pastel drawings to prevent smudging.

flamboyant Literally, "flame-like." A style of late Gothic architecture characterized by intricate decorations and sinuous curves.

flying buttress See *buttress*.

focal point The principal area of emphasis in a work of art. The place to which the artist directs the most attention through composition. May or may not be the same as the *vanishing point* in a work.

folk art Art of people who have had no formal, academic training, but whose works are part of an established tradition of style and craftsmanship. Examples include religious carvers, quilt makers, and shop sign painters.

font The name given to a style of type. The text of *Artforms* is printed in the Adobe Garamond font.

foreshortening The representation of *forms* on a *two-dimensional* surface by shortening the length in such a way that the long axis appears to project toward or recede away from the viewer.

form In the broadest sense, the total physical characteristics of an object or event. Usually describes the visual elements of a work of art that create meaning, for example: A huge, looming shape in a painting is a form that may create haunting or foreboding meaning.

formal theory A method of art criticism that values stylistic innovation over personal expression or cultural communication.

format The shape or proportions of a *picture plane*. Format may be large or small, rectangular or oblong.

freestanding Any piece or type of sculpture that is meant to be seen from all sides.

fresco A painting technique in which *pigments* suspended in water are applied to a damp lime-plaster surface. The pigments dry to become part of the plaster wall or surface. Sometimes called *true fresco* or *buon fresco* to distinguish it from painting over dry plaster, or "fresco secco."

Futurism, Futurists A group movement that originated in Italy in 1909. One of several movements to grow out of *Cubism*. Futurists added implied motion to the shifting planes and multiple observation points of the Cubists; they celebrated natural as well as mechanical motion and speed. Their glorification of danger, war, and the machine age was in keeping with the martial spirit developing in Italy at the time.

garba griha Literally, "womb chamber." The sacred room of a Hindu temple, where rituals are performed and the image of the god is kept.

genre painting A type of art work that takes as its subject everyday life, rather than civic leaders, religious figures, or mythological heroes. Flourished in Flanders and Holland between the sixteenth and eighteenth centuries.

geometric shape Any *shape* enclosed by square or straight or perfectly circular lines. Usually contrasted with *organic shapes*.

gesso A mixture of glue and chalk, thinned with water and applied as a *ground* before painting with oil or egg tempera. Most gessos are bright white in color.

glaze 1. In oil painting, a thin transparent or translucent layer brushed over another layer of paint, allowing the first layer to show through but enriching its color slightly. In *ceramics*, a vitreous or glassy coating applied to seal and decorate surfaces. Glaze may be colored, transparent, or opaque. 2. A silica-based paint for clay that fuses with the clay body on

firing. Can be almost any color, or translucent. The silica base makes a glasslike surface on the clay piece.

Gothic Primarily an architectural style that prevailed in Western Europe from the twelfth through the fifteenth centuries, characterized by pointed *arches*, ribbed *vaults*, and flying *buttresses*, which made it possible to create stone buildings that reached great heights.

gouache An opaque, water-soluble paint. *Watercolor* to which opaque white has been added.

ground The background in *two-dimensional* works—the area around and between *figure(s)*. Also, the surface onto which paint is applied, consisting of *sizing* plus *primer*.

happening An event conceived by artists and performed by artists and others, who may include viewers. Usually unrehearsed, with scripted roles but including improvisation.

hatching A technique used in drawing and linear forms of printmaking, in which lines are placed in parallel series to darken the value of an area. Cross-hatching is drawing one set of hatchings over another in a different direction so that the lines cross, suggesting shadows or darker areas. Contour hatching is a set of parallel curved lines that suggest a volume in space.

Hellenistic Style of the later phase of ancient Greek art (300–100 B.C.E.), characterized by emotion, drama, and interaction of sculptural forms with the surrounding space.

hierarchic scale Use of unnatural *proportions* or *scale* to show the relative importance of figures. (Larger relative size = greater importance.) Most commonly practiced in ancient Near Eastern and Egyptian art.

high relief Sculpture in relief in which more than half of a significant portion of the subject emerges from the background. High-relief sculpture thus requires undercutting, in contrast to *low relief*.

horizon line In linear *perspective*, the implied or actual line or edge placed on a *two-dimensional* surface to represent the place in nature where the sky meets the horizontal land or water plane.

hue That property of a color identifying a specific, named wavelength of light such as green, red, violet, and so on. Often used synonymously with *color*.

humanism A cultural and intellectual movement during the *Renaissance*, following the rediscovery of the art and literature of ancient Greece and Rome. A philosophy or attitude concerned with the interests, achievements, and capabilities of human beings rather than

with the abstract concepts and problems of theology or science.

icon An image or symbolic representation, often with sacred significance.

iconoclast Literally, "image-breaker." In Byzantine art, one who opposes the creation of pictures of holy persons, believing that they promote idolatry.

iconography The symbolic meanings of subjects and signs used to convey ideas important to particular cultures or religions, and the conventions governing the use of such forms. For example, in traditional Christian art, a key symbolizes St. Peter, to whom Christ gave the keys to the kingdom of heaven. An hourglass symbolizes the passage of time, etc.

impasto In painting, thick paint applied to a surface in a heavy manner, having the appearance and consistency of buttery paste or of cake frosting.

implied line A line in a composition that is not actually drawn. It may be a sight line of a figure in a composition, or a line along which two *shapes* align with each other.

Impressionism A style of painting that originated in France about 1870. (The first Impressionist exhibit was held in 1874.) Paintings of casual contemporary subjects were executed outdoors using divided brushstrokes to capture the light and mood of a particular moment and the transitory effects of natural light and color.

installation An art medium in which the artist arranges objects or artworks in a room, thinking of the entire space as the medium to be manipulated. Some installations are *site specific*.

intaglio Any printmaking technique in which lines and areas to be inked are recessed below the surface of the printing plate. *Etching, engraving, drypoint*, and *aquatint* are all intaglio processes. See also *print*.

intensity The relative purity or saturation of a *hue* (color), on a scale from bright (pure) to dull. Varying intensities are achieved by mixing a hue with a *neutral* or with another hue.

intermediate color A *hue* between a primary and a secondary on the *color wheel*, such as yellow-green, a mixture of yellow and green.

International Style An architectural style that emerged in several European countries between 1910 and 1920. International Style architects avoided applied decoration, used only modern materials (concrete, glass, steel), and arranged the masses of a building according to its inner uses.

in-the-round See *freestanding*.

iwan A high, vaulted porch frequently used in Islamic architecture to mark an important building or entrance.

joined block construction A method of making large carved pieces from wood. Various parts of a piece are carved separately and then glued together for exterior finishing. The interior is hollowed out to prevent cracking.

kachina One of many deified ancestral spirits honored by Hopi and other Pueblo Indians. These spiritual beings are usually depicted in doll-like forms.

keystone The stone at the central, highest point of a round arch, which holds the rest of the arch in place.

kiln A high-temperature oven in which pottery or *ceramic* ware is *fired*.

kinetic art Art that incorporates actual movement as part of the design.

kore Greek for "maiden." An Archaic Greek statue of a standing clothed young woman.

kouros Greek for "youth." An Archaic Greek statue of a standing nude young male.

krater In classical Greek art, a wide-mouthed vessel with handles, used for mixing wine and water for ceremonial drinking.

line A long, narrow mark. Usually made by drawing with a tool or a brush, but may be created by placing two forms next to each other (see *implied line*).

linear perspective See *perspective*.

linocut, linoleum cut A *relief* process in printmaking, in which an artist cuts away negative spaces from a block of linoleum, leaving raised areas to take ink for printing.

lintel See *beam*.

literati painting In Asian art, paintings produced by cultivated amateurs who are generally wealthy and devoted to the arts, including calligraphy, painting, and poetry. Most commonly used to describe work of painters not attached to the royal courts of the Yuan, Ming, and Qing dynasties (fourteenth to eighteenth centuries) in China.

lithography A planographic printmaking technique based on the antipathy of oil and water. The image is drawn with a grease crayon or painted with *tusche* on a stone or grained aluminum plate. The surface is then chemically treated and dampened so that it will accept ink only where the crayon or tusche has been used.

local color The color of an object as we experience it, without shadows or reflections. (Most leaves show a green local color.)

logo Short for "logotype." Sign, name, or trademark of an institution, a firm, or a publication, consisting of letterforms or pictorial elements.

loom A device for producing cloth or fiber art by interweaving fibers at right angles.

lost wax A *casting* method. First, a model is made from wax and encased in clay or casting plaster. When the clay is fired to make a mold, the wax melts away, leaving a void that can be filled with molten metal or other self-hardening liquid to produce a cast.

low relief Sculpture in relief in which the subjects emerge only slightly from the surface. No undercutting is present.

madrasa In Islamic tradition, a building that combines a school, prayer hall, and lodging for students.

masonry Building technique in which stones or bricks are laid atop one another in a pattern. May be done with mortar or without.

mass Three-dimensional form having physical bulk. Usually a characteristic of a sculpture or a building. Also, the illusion of such a form on a *two-dimensional* surface.

matrix The block of metal, wood, stone, or other material that an artist works to create a *print*.

matte A dull finish or surface, especially in painting, photography, and *ceramics*.

medium (pl. media or mediums) 1. A particular material along with its accompanying technique; a specific type of artistic technique or means of expression determined by the use of particular materials. Examples include oil paint, marble, and video. 2. In paint, the fluid in which *pigment* is suspended, allowing it to spread and adhere to the surface.

metope A square panel, often decorated with relief sculpture, placed at regular intervals above the *colonnade* of a classical Greek building.

mihrab A niche in the end wall of a mosque that points the way to the Muslim holy city of Mecca.

minaret A tower outside a mosque where chanters stand to call the faithful to prayer.

Minimalism A *nonrepresentational* style of sculpture and painting, usually severely restricted in the use of visual elements and often consisting of simple geometric shapes or masses. The style came to prominence in the middle and late 1960s.

mixed media Works of art made with more than one *medium*.

mobile A type of sculpture in which parts move, usually suspended parts activated by air currents. See also *kinetic art*.

modeling 1. Working pliable material such as clay or wax into *three-dimensional* forms. 2. In drawing or painting, the effect of light falling on a three-dimensional object so that the illusion of its *mass* is created and defined by *value* gradations.

mold A cavity created out of plaster, clay, metal, or plastic for use in *casting*.

monochromatic A color scheme limited to variations of one *hue*; a hue with its *tints* and/or *shades*.

montage 1. A composition made up of pictures or parts of pictures previously drawn, painted, or photographed. 2. In motion pictures, the combining of shots into a rapid sequence to portray the character of a single event through multiple views.

mosaic An art medium in which small pieces of colored glass, stone, or ceramic tile called *tesserae* are embedded in a background material such as plaster or mortar. Also, works made using this technique.

motion capture Creation of a three-dimensional representation of a live performance. Done by scanning actions of actors, and using the resulting motion information to create animated characters.

naturalism An art style in which the curves and contours of a subject are accurately portrayed.

nave The tall central space of a church or cathedral, usually flanked by side aisles.

negative shape A background or *ground* shape seen in relation to foreground or *figure* shape(s).

neoclassicism New classicism. A revival of classical Greek and Roman forms in art, music, and literature, particularly during the late eighteenth and early nineteenth centuries in Europe and America. It was part of a reaction against the excesses of *Baroque* and *Rococo* art.

Neolithic art A period of ancient art after the introduction of agriculture but before the invention of bronze. *Neolithic* means "New Stone Age" to distinguish it from *Paleolithic*, or "Old Stone Age."

neutrals Not associated with any single *hue*. Blacks, whites, grays, and dull gray-browns. A neutral can be made by mixing complementary hues.

nonobjective See *nonrepresentational art*.

nonrepresentational Art without reference to anything outside itself—without representation.

Also called "nonobjective"—without recognizable objects.

off-loom A piece of fiber art made without a loom. One of the two major divisions of fiber arts.

offset lithography Lithographic printing by indirect image transfer from photomechanical plates. The plate transfers ink to a rubber-covered cylinder, which "offsets" the ink to the paper. Also called photo-offset and offset lithography.

one-point perspective A *perspective* system in which all parallel lines converge at a single *vanishing point*.

opaque Impenetrable by light; not transparent or translucent.

open form A form whose exterior is irregular or broken, having a sense of growth, change, or unresolved tension; form in a state of becoming or reaching out.

optical color mixture Apparent rather than actual color mixture, produced by interspersing brushstrokes or dots of color instead of physically mixing them. The implied mixing occurs in the eye of the viewer and produces a lively color sensation.

organic shape An irregular, non-geometric shape. A shape that resembles any living matter. Most organic shapes are not drawn with a ruler or a compass. See also *biomorphic shape*.

outsider art Art produced by those with no formal training, outside the established channels of art exhibition. Examples include art by self-directed individuals, prison inmates, and insane persons.

painterly Painting characterized by openness of form, in which shapes are defined by loose brushwork in light and dark color areas rather than by outline or contour.

Paleolithic art A very ancient period of art coincident with the Old Stone Age, before the discovery of agriculture and animal herding.

Pantocrator Literally, "ruler of everything." A title for Christ, especially as he is depicted in Byzantine art.

pastels 1. Sticks of powdered pigment held together with a gum binding agent. 2. Pale colors or *tints*.

pattern Repetitive ordering of design elements.

pediment A shelf above the *colonnade* on the short ends of a classical Greek temple. A triangular space below the gable roof.

pendentive A curving triangle that points downward; a common support for domes in Byzantine architecture.

performance art Dramatic presentation by visual artists (as distinguished from theater artists such as actors and dancers) in front of an audience, usually not in a formal theatrical setting.

persistence of vision An optical illusion that makes cinema possible. The eye and mind tend to hold images in the brain for a fraction of a second after they disappear from view. Quick projection of slightly differing images creates the illusion of movement.

perspective A system for creating an illusion of depth or *three-dimensional* space on a *two-dimensional* surface. Usually used to refer to linear perspective, which is based on the fact that parallel lines or edges appear to converge and objects appear smaller as the distance between them and the viewer increases. Atmospheric perspective (aerial perspective) creates the illusion of distance by reducing color saturation, value contrast, and detail in order to imply the hazy effect of atmosphere between the viewer and distant objects. Parallel lines remain parallel; there is no convergence. A work executed in *one-point perspective* has a single *vanishing point*. A work in two-point perspective has two of them.

petroglyph An image or a symbol carved in shallow relief on a rock surface. Usually ancient.

photomontage The process of combining parts of various photographs in one photograph.

photo screen A variation of *silkscreen* in which the stencil is prepared by transferring a photograph to the stencil.

picture plane The *two-dimensional* picture surface.

pier An upright support for an arch or arcade. Piers fulfill the same function as columns, but piers are more massive and usually not tapered toward the top.

pigment Any coloring agent, made from natural or synthetic substances, used in paints or drawing materials. Usually in powdered form.

plate mark An impression made on a piece of paper by pressing a printing plate onto it. A plate mark is usually a sign of an *original print*.

pointillism A system of painting using tiny dots or "points" of color, developed by French artist Georges Seurat in the 1880s. Seurat systematized the divided brushwork and *optical color mixture* of the *Impressionists* and called his technique "divisionism."

Pop Art A style of painting and sculpture that developed in the late 1950s and early

1960s, in Britain and the United States, and uses mass production techniques (such as silkscreen) or real objects in works that are generally more polished and ironic than *assemblages*.

porcelain A type of clay for *ceramics*. It is white or grayish and fires at 1350°C–1500°C. After firing, it is translucent and rings when struck.

portico A porch attached to a building, supported with columns. Usually surmounted by a triangular *pediment* under a gable roof.

positive shape A *figure* or foreground shape, as opposed to a *negative* ground or background shape.

post-and-beam system (post and lintel) In architecture, a structural system that uses two or more uprights or posts to support a horizontal beam (or lintel) that spans the space between them.

Post-Impressionism A general term applied to various personal styles of painting by French artists (or artists living in France) that developed from about 1885 to 1900 in reaction to what these artists saw as the somewhat formless and aloof quality of *Impressionist* painting. Post-Impressionist painters were concerned with the significance of form, symbols, expressiveness, and psychological intensity. They can be broadly separated into two groups—expressionists, such as Gauguin and van Gogh, and formalists, such as Cezanne and Seurat.

postmodern An attitude or trend of the late 1970s, 1980s, and 1990s. In architecture, the movement away from what had become boring adaptations of the *International Style*, in favor of an imaginative, eclectic approach. In the other visual arts, postmodern art is characterized by influence from all periods and styles, including modernism, and a willingness to combine elements of all. Although modernism makes distinctions between high art and popular taste, postmodernism makes no such value judgments. Postmodern works are not only influened by the past, they make knowing reference to some past style(s).

potter A *ceramist* who specializes in making dishes.

primary colors Those *hues* that cannot be produced by mixing other hues. *Pigment* primaries are red, yellow, and blue; light primaries are red, green, and blue. Theoretically, pigment primaries can be mixed together to form all the other hues in the spectrum.

primer In painting, a primary layer of paint applied to a surface that is to be painted. Primer is used to create a uniform surface.

print (artist's print) A multiple original impression made from a plate, stone, wood block, or screen by an artist or made under the artist's supervision. Prints are usually made in *editions*, with each print numbered and signed by the artist.

proportion The size relationship of parts to a whole and to one another.

qi In Chinese, "life force." The vibrant spirit that animates all things.

readymade A common manufactured object that the artist signs and turns into an artwork. Concept pioneered by Dadaist Marcel Duchamp.

realism 1. A type of *representational art* in which the artist depicts as closely as possible what the eye sees. 2. The mid-nineteenth-century style of Courbet and others, based on the idea that ordinary people and everyday activities are worthy subjects for art.

registration In color printmaking or machine printing, the process of aligning the impressions of blocks or plates on the same sheet of paper.

reinforced concrete Concrete with steel mesh or bars embedded in it to increase its tensile strength.

relief printmaking A printing technique in which the parts of the printing surface that carry ink are left raised, while the remaining areas (negative spaces) are cut away. Woodcuts and linoleum prints (*linocuts*) are relief prints.

relief sculpture Sculpture in which *three-dimensional* forms project from the flat background of which they are a part. The degree of projection can vary and is described by the terms *high relief* and *low relief*.

Renaissance Period in Europe from the late fourteenth through the sixteenth centuries, which was characterized by a renewed interest in human-centered *classical* art, literature, and learning. See also *humanism*.

representational art Art in which it is the artist's intention to present again or represent a particular subject, especially pertaining to realistic portrayal of subject matter.

rhythm The regular or ordered repetition of dominant and subordinate elements or units within a design.

Rococo From the French "rocaille" meaning "rock work." This late *Baroque* (c. 1715–1775) style used in interior decoration and painting was characteristically playful, pretty, romantic, and visually loose or soft; it used small *scale* and ornate decoration, *pastel* colors, and asymmetrical arrangement of curves. Rococo

was popular in France and southern Germany in the eighteenth century.

Romanesque A style of European architecture prevalent from the ninth to the twelfth centuries with round *arches* and barrel *vaults* influenced by Roman architecture and characterized by heavy stone construction.

Romanticism 1. A literary and artistic movement of late-eighteenth- and nineteenth-century Europe, aimed at asserting the validity of subjective experience as a countermovement to the often cold formulas of *neoclassicism*, characterized by intense emotional excitement, and depictions of powerful forces in nature, exotic lifestyles, danger, suffering, and nostalgia. 2. Art of any period based on spontaneity, intuition, and emotion rather than carefully organized rational approaches to form.

Salon An official art exhibition in France, juried by members of the offical French *academy*.

santero Literally, "saint-maker." A person in Hispanic traditions who carves or paints religious figures.

saturation See *intensity*.

scale The size or apparent size of an object seen in relation to other objects, people, or its environment. Also used to refer to the quality or monumentality found in some objects regardless of their size. In architectural drawings, the ratio of the measurements in the drawing to the measurements in the building. A building may be drawn in a scale of 1:300, for example.

screenprinting (serigraphy) A printmaking technique in which stencils are applied to fabric stretched across a frame. Paint or ink is forced with a squeegee through the unblocked portions of the screen onto paper or other surface beneath.

secondary colors Pigment secondaries are the *hues* orange, violet, and green, which may be produced in slightly dulled form by mixing two *primaries*.

serif Short lines that end the upper and lower strokes of a letter in some *fonts*. The capital *I* has two serifs in Adobe Garamond; the small *m* has one.

serigraphy See *screenprinting*.

shade A *hue* with black added.

shape A *two-dimensional* or implied two-dimensional area defined by line or changes in color.

shot Any uninterrupted run of a film camera. Shots are compiled into scenes, then into movies.

silkscreen See *screenprinting*.

site-specific art Any work made for a certain place, which cannot be separated or exhibited apart from its intended environment.

size Any of several substances made from glue, wax, or clay, used as a filler for porous material such as paper, canvas, or other cloth, or wall surfaces. Used to protect the surface from the deteriorating effects of paint, particularly oil paint.

slip Clay that is thinned to the consistency of cream and used as paint on *earthenware* or *stoneware* ceramics.

social realism Representational art that expresses protest at some social condition.

stencil A sheet of paper, cardboard, or metal with a design cut out. Painting or stamping over the sheet prints the design on a surface. See also *screenprinting*.

stoneware A type of clay for ceramics. Stoneware is fired at 1200°C–1300°C and is nonporous when fired.

stupa The earliest form of Buddhist architecture, a domelike structure probably derived from Indian funeral mounds.

subject In representational art, what the artist chooses to depict. It may be a landscape or a mythological scene, or even an invented subject.

subordination Technique by which an artist ranks certain areas of a work as of lesser importance. Areas are generally subordinated through placement, color, or size. See *emphasis*.

substitution The process of making a work of art by *casting*, as opposed to *additive* or *subtractive* processes.

subtractive color mixture Mixture of colored *pigments* in the form of paints, inks, *pastels*, and so on. Called subtractive because reflected light is reduced as pigment colors are combined, generally leading to darker *shades*. See *additive color mixture*.

subtractive sculpture Sculpture made by removing material from a larger block or form.

support The physical material that provides the base for and sustains a *two-dimensional* work of art. Paper is the usual support for drawings and prints; canvas or panels are common supports in painting.

Surrealism A movement in literature and visual arts that developed in the mid-1920s and remained strong until the mid-1940s; grew out of *Dada* and *automatism*. Based upon revealing the unconscious mind in dream images, the irrational, and the fantastic,

Surrealism took two directions: *representational* and *abstract*. Dali's and Magritte's paintings, with their uses of impossible combinations of objects depicted in realistic detail, typify representational Surrealism. Miro's paintings, with his use of abstract and fantastic shapes and vaguely defined creatures, are typical of abstract Surrealism.

Symbolism A movement in late nineteenth-century Europe (c. 1885–1900) concerned with communication of inner emotional states through forms and colors that may not copy nature directly.

symmetry A design (or composition) with identical or nearly identical form on opposite sides of a dividing line or central axis.

Synthetic Cubism See *Cubism*.

taotie mask A mask of abstracted shapes commonly found on ancient Chinese bronze vessels. Represents a composite animal whose symbolism is unknown.

tempera A water-based paint that uses egg yolk as a *binder*. Many commercially made paints identified as tempera are actually *gouache*.

terra cotta A type of *earthenware* that contains enough iron oxide to impart a reddish tone when fired. Frequently used in ancient ceramics and modern building decoration.

tessera Bit of colored glass, ceramic tile, or stone used in a *mosaic*. Plural: *tesserae*.

three-dimensional Having height, width, and depth.

throwing The process of forming clay objects on a potter's wheel.

tint A *hue* with white added.

tooth Degree of roughness present in drawing papers; the presence of tooth gives texture to a drawing.

trompe l'oeil French for "fool the eye." A *two-dimensional* representation that is so naturalistic that it looks actual or real (or *three-dimensional*).

true fresco See *fresco*.

truss In architecture, a structural framework of wood or metal based on a triangular system, used to span, reinforce, or support walls, ceilings, *piers*, or beams.

tusche In *lithography*, a waxy liquid used to draw or paint images on a lithographic stone or plate.

two-dimensional Having the dimensions of height and width only.

typeface See *font*.

typography The art and technique of composing printed materials from type.

unity The appearance of similarity, consistency, or oneness. Interrelational factors that cause various elements to appear as part of a single complete form. See also *variety*.

value The lightness or darkness of tones or colors. White is the lightest value; black is the darkest. The value halfway between these extremes is called middle gray. Sometimes called "tone."

vanishing point In linear *perspective*, the point on the *horizon line* at which lines or edges that are parallel appear to converge.

vantage point The position from which the viewer looks at an object or visual field; also called "observation point" or "viewpoint." Artists who make paintings that use *perspective* create a presumed vantage point for the viewer.

variety The opposite of *unity*. Diverse elements in the composition of a work of art. Most works strive a balance between unity and variety.

vault A curving masonry roof or ceiling constructed on the principle of the *arch*. A *tunnel* or *barrel vault* is a semicircular arch extended in depth; a continuous series of arches, one behind the other. A groin vault is formed when two barrel vaults intersect. A *ribbed vault* is a vault reinforced by masonry ribs.

vehicle Liquid emulsion used as a carrier or spreading agent in paints.

vertical placement A method for suggesting the third dimension of depth in a two-dimensional work by placing an object above another in the composition. The object above seems farther away than the one below.

volume 1. Space enclosed or filled by a three-dimensional object or figure. 2. The implied space filled by a painted or drawn object or figure. Synonym: *mass*.

warm colors Colors whose relative visual temperature makes them seem warm. Warm colors or *hues* include red-violet, red, red-orange, orange, yellow-orange, and yellow. See also *cool colors*.

warp In weaving, the threads that run lengthwise in a fabric, crossed at right angles by the *weft*. Also, the process of arranging yarn or thread on a *loom* so as to form a warp.

wash A thin, transparent layer of paint or ink.

watercolor Paint that uses water-soluble gum as the *binder* and water as the *vehicle*. Characterized by transparency. Also, the resulting painting.

weft In weaving, the horizontal threads interlaced through the *warp*. Also called woof.

woodcut, woodblock A type of *relief print* made from a plank of relatively soft wood. The artist carves away the negative spaces, leaving the image in relief to take ink for printing.

wood engraving A method of relief printing in wood. In comparison to *woodcut*, a wood engraving is made with denser wood, cutting into the end of the grain rather than the side. The density of the wood demands the use of *engraving* tools, rather than woodcarving tools.

work of art What the artist makes or puts in front of us for viewing. The visual object that embodies the idea the artist wanted to communicate.

ziggurat A rectangular or square stepped pyramid, often with a temple at its top.

PRONUNCIATION GUIDE

Ácoma (*ah*-co-mah)
Alhambra (al-*am*-bra)
Tarsila do Amaral (tar-*see*-lah doo ah-mah-*rahl*)
Angkor Wat (*ang*-kohr waht)
Sofonisba Anguissola (so-foh-*nees*-bah ahn-*gwee*-so-la)
Ardabil (ar-*dah*-bil)
Arroyo Hondo (ar-*roy*-yo *ohn*-doh)
Aumakua (ow-mah-*koo*-ah)
avant-garde (ah-vahn *gard*)
Judy Baca (*bah*-kah)
Giacomo Balla (*jah*-koh-moh *bahl*-la)
Jean-Michel Basquait (jawn mee-*shell* bos-kee-*ah*)
Bauhaus (*bow*-house)
Benin (ben-*een*)
Gianlorenzo Bernini (jahn-low-*ren*-tsoh ber-*nee*-nee)
Joseph Beuys (*yo*-sef boyce)
Umberto Boccioni (oom-*bair*-toh boh-*choh*-nee)
Bodhisattva (boh-dee-*saht*-vah)
Germaine Boffrand (zher-*main* bof-*frohn*)
Rosa Bonheur (buhn-*er*)
Borobudur (boh-roh-boo-*duhr*)
Sandro Botticelli (bought-tee-*chel*-lee)
Louise Bourgeois (boorzh-*wah*)
Constantin Brancusi (*kahn*-stuhn-teen brahn-*koo*-see)
Georges Braque (zhorzh brahk)
Pieter Bruegel (*pee*-ter *broy*-guhl)
Michelangelo Buonarroti, see *Michelangelo*
Cai Guo Qiang (tseye gwoh *chyang*)
Callicrates (kah-*lik*-rah-teez)
Michelangelo da Caravaggio (mee-kel-an-jeh-loe da car-ah-*vah*-jyoh)
Rosalba Carriera (roh-*sal*-bah car-*yair*-ah)
Henri Cartier-Bresson (on-*ree* car-tee-ay bruh-*sohn*)
casein (cass-*seen*)
Mary Cassatt (cah-*sat*)
Paul Cézanne (say-*zahn*)

chacmool (chalk-mole)
Marc Chagall (shah-*gahl*)
Chartres (*shahr*-truh)
Chauvet (show-*vay*)
Dale Chihuly (chi-*hoo*-lee)
Chilkat (*chill*-kaht)
chola (*choh*-lah)
Christo (*kree*-stoh)
Constantine (*kahn*-stuhn-teen)
conté (kahn-tay)
contrapposto (kohn-trah-*poh*-stoh)
Gustave Courbet (*goos*-tahv koor-*bay*)
Cycladic (sik-*lad*-ik)
Louis Jacques Mandé Daguerre (loo-*ee* zhahk mahn-*day* dah-*gair*)
Honoré Daumier (awn-ohr-*ay* doh-mee-ay)
Jacques-Louis David (*zhahk* loo-*ee* dah-*veed*)
Edgar Degas (ed-gahr deh-*gah*)
Willem de Kooning (*vill*-em duh *koe*-ning)
Eugène Delacroix (oo-*zhen* duh-lah-*kwah*)
André Derain (on-*dray* duh-*ran*)
de Stijl (duh steel)
Richard Diebenkorn (*dee*-ben-korn)
Donatello (dohn-ah-*tell*-loh)
Marcel Duchamp (mahr-*sell* doo-*shahm*)
Albrecht Dürer (*ahl*-brekht *duh*-ruhr)
Thomas Eakins (*ay*-kins)
Sergei Eisenstein (sair-gay *eye*-zen-schtine)
Olafur Eliasson (o-la-fur ee-*lie*-ah-sun)
M. C. Escher (*esh*-uhr)
Fan Kuan (fahn kwahn)
feng shui (fung shway)
Jean-Honoré Fragonard (zhon oh-no-*ray* fra-go-*nahr*)
Helen Frankenthaler (*frank*-en-thahl-er)
fresco (*fres*-coh)
Ganges (*gan*-jeez)
Paul Gauguin (go-*gan*)
Frank Gehry (*ger*-ree)
genre (*zhan*-ruh)

Artemisia Gentileschi (ahr-tuh-*mee*-zhyuh jen-till-*ess*-kee)
Jean Léon Gérôme (zhon *lay*-on zhay-*roam*)
Lorenzo Ghiberti (low-*rent*-soh ghee-*bair*-tee)
Alberto Giacometti (ahl-*bair*-toh jah-ko-*met*-tee)
Giotto di Bondone (*joht*-toe dee bone-*doe*-nay)
Francisco Goya (fran-*sis*-coe go-yah)
Walter Gropius (*val*-tuhr *grow*-pee-us)
Guo Xi (gwo shr)
Guan Yin (*gwan* yin)
Guernica (ger-nih-kah)
Zaha Hadid (*zah*-hah hah-*deed*)
Hagia Sophia (hah-zhah so-*fee*-ah)
Hangzhou (hung-joe)
Suzuki Harunobu (soo-*zoo*-key hah-roo-*noh*-boo)
Hatshepsut (hah-*shep*-soot)
Heiji Monogatari (hay-jee mo-no-gah-*tah*-ree)
Hannah Höch (*hahn*-nuh *hohk*)
Hokusai (hohk-*sy*)
Pieter de Hooch (*pee*-tuhr duh *hohk*)
Horyuji (hohr-*yoo*-jee)
Ictinus (ick-*tee*-nuhs)
Inca (*eenk*-ah)
Ise (*ee*-say)
kachina (kah-*chee*-nah)
Frida Kahlo (*free*-dah *kah*-loh)
Kandarya Mahadeva (Kan-*dahr*-ya mah-hah-*day*-vuh)
Vasily Kandinsky (vass-see-lee can-*din*-skee)
Anish Kapoor (ah-*neesh* kah-*puhr*)
Katsura (kah-*tsoo*-rah)
Khamererebty (kahm-er-er-*neb*-tee)
Anselm Kiefer (*ahn*-sehlm *kee*-fuhr)
Ernst Ludwig Kirchner (*airnst loot*-vik *keerkh*-ner)
Torii Kiyonobu (tor-ee-ee kee-oh-*noh*-boo)
Torii Kiyotada (tor-ee-ee kee-oh-*tah*-dah)

Paul Klee (clay)
Krishna (*krish*-nuh)
Mitsutani Kunishiro (meet-soo-*tah*-nee
  koo-nee-*shee*-roh)
Laocoön (lay-*oh*-koh-on)
Le Corbusier (luh core-boo-zee-ay)
Fernand Léger (fair-*non* lay-*zhay*)
Li Hua (lee hwa)
Roy Lichtenstein (*lick*-ten-steen)
Maya Lin (*my*-uh *lin*)
Fra Filippo Lippi (frah fill-*leep*-poh
  leep-pee)
Marshall Lomokema (loh-moh-
  keh-mah)
Machu Picchu (*mah*-choo *peek*-choo)
René Magritte (reh-*nay* mah-*greet*)
mandala (*mahn*-dah-lah)
Edouard Manet (ed-*wahr* mah-*nay*)
Maori (*mow*-ree)
Masaccio (mah-*sach*-chyo)
Henri Matisse (on-*ree* mah-*tees*)
Mato Tope (*mah*-toh *toh*-pay)
Chaz Maviyane-Davies (mah-vee-
  yah-neh)
Maya (*my*-uh)
de Medici (deh *meh*-dee-chee)
Ana Mendieta (*ah*-nah men-*dyet*-ah)
metope (*meh*-toe-pee)
Michelangelo Buonarroti (mee-kel-*an*-
  jeh-loe bwoh-nah-*roe*-tee)
Ludwig Mies van der Rohe (*loot*-vig
  mees vahn dair *roh*-eh)
Mihrab (*mee*-rahb)
Moai (*mo*-eye)
Piet Mondrian (*peet mohn*-dree-ahn)
Claude Monet (*klohd* moh-*nay*)
Berthe Morisot (*bairt* moh-ree-*zoh*)
mosque (mahsk)
Mu Qi (moo-chee)
Vera Mukhina (*vir*-ah moo-*kee*-nah)
Edvard Munch (*ed*-vard *moonk*)
Murujuga (mu-ru-*ju*-ga)
Eadweard Muybridge (*ed*-wurd
  moy-brij)
Mycerinus (miss-uh-*ree*-nuhs)
Nadar (Felix Tournachon) (nah-*dar*
  fay-leeks toor-nah-*shohn*)
Emil Nolde (*ay*-meal *nohl*-duh)
Notre Dame de Chartres (*noh*-truh
  dahm duh *shahr*-truh)

Uche Okeke (*oo*-chay oh-*keh*-keh)
Claes Oldenburg (klahs *ol*-den-burg)
Olmec (*ohl*-mek)
José Clemente Orozco (ho-*say* cleh-
  men-tay oh-*rohs*-coh)
Nam June Paik (nahm joon pike)
Andrea Palladio (ahn-*dray*-uh pahl-
  lah-dyo)
Giovanni Paolo Pannini (jyo-*vahn*-nee
  pow-lo pah-*nee*-nee)
Pablo Picasso (pab-lo pee-*cah*-so)
pietá (pee-ay-*tah*)
Jackson Pollock (*pah*-lock)
Polyclitus (pol-ee-*cly*-tus)
Pompeii (pahm-*pay*)
Pont du Gard (pohn duh *gahr*)
Nicholas Poussin (nee-coh-*law*
  poo-*san*)
Praxiteles (prak-*sit*-el-eez)
Qennifer (ken-eh-fer)
qi (chee)
Quetzalcoatl (kets-ahl-*kwah*-til)
Robert Rauschenberg (*row*-shen-buhrg)
Gerrit Reitveld (*gair*-it *ryt*-velt)
Rembrandt van Rijn (*rem*-brant van *ryne*)
Pierre August Renoir (pee-*err* oh-*goost*
  ren-*wahr*)
Gerhard Richter (*gair*-hart *rick*-ter)
Diego Rivera (dee-*ay*-goh ri-*ver*-ah)
Sabatino Rodia (roh-*dee*-uh)
Francois August Rodin (frahn-*swah*
  oh-*goost* roh-*dan*)
Andre Rublev (*ahn*-dray *ru*-blof)
Niki de Saint Phalle (nee-kee duh san *fall*)
Ibrahim Salahi (ee-brah-*heem* sah-
  lah-hee)
Sanchi (*sahn*-chee)
Raphael Sanzio (ra-fay-el *sahn*-
  zee-oh)
Sassetta (suh-*set*-tuh)
scythian (*sith*-ee-ahn)
Sesshû (seh-shoo)
Georges Seurat (zhorzh sur-*ah*)
Bada Shanren (*bah*-dah *shan*-ren)
Yinka Shonibare (sho-ni-*bar*-ee)
Shiva Nataraja (*shih*-vuh nah-tah-
  rah-jah)
Tawaraya Sotatsu (tah-wa-*rah*-ya
  soh-taht-soo)
Alfred Stieglitz (*steeg*-lits)

stupa (*stoo*-pah)
Toshiko Takaezu (tosh-ko tah-kah-
  ay-zoo)
Tang Yin (tahng yin)
taotie (taow tyeh)
Teotihuacan (tay-oh-tee-wah-*cahn*)
Jean Tinguely (zhon tan-*glee*)
Tlingit (*kling*-git)
Félix Gonzáles Torres (*feh*-leeks
  gohn-sa-les *tohr*-res)
Henri de Toulouse-Lautrec (on-*ree* duh
  too-*looz* low-*trek*)
James Turrell (tuh-*rell*)
tusche (too-*shay*)
Tutankhamen (too-tahn-*kahm*-uhn)
Mierle Laderman Ukeles (merl
  lay-duhr-man *yoo*-kuh-lees)
Unkei (*un*-kay)
Ur (er)
Kitagawa Utamaro (kit-ah-*gah*-wah
  ut-ah-*mah*-roh)
Theo van Doesburg (*tay*-oh van
  dohz-*buhrg*)
Jan van Eyck (*yahn* van *ike*)
Vincent van Gogh (*vin*-sent van goe;
  also, van *gawk*)
Diego Velázquez (dee-*ay*-goh behl-
  ahth-kehth; also, veh-*las*-kes)
Robert Venturi (ven-*tuhr*-ee)
Jan Vermeer (*yahn* ver-*mir*)
Versailles (vair-*sy*)
Elizabeth Vigee-Lebrun (vee-*zhay*
  leh-*broon*)
Leonardo da Vinci (lay-oh-*nahr*-doh
  dah *veen*-chi)
Peter Voulkos (*vahl*-kohs)
Wang Xizhi (shee-jr)
Andy Warhol (*wohr*-hohl)
Willendorf (*vill*-en-dohrf)
Xiwangmu (shee-wang-moo)
Xul Solar (shool so-*lar*)
Yaxchilan (yash-chee-*lahn*)
Zhang Daqian (zhang dah-*chyen*)
ziggurat (*zig*-uh-raht)

NOTES

CHAPTER 1

1. "Park's details, sculpture a nod to city's future"; *Arizona Republic*, 20 April 2009, B-6.

2. Georgia O'Keeffe, *Georgia O'Keeffe* (New York: Viking, 1976), opposite plate 13.

3. Charles Glueck, "A Brueghel from Harlem," *New York Times* (February 22, 1970): sec. 2, 29.

4. Quoted in "Romare Bearden," *Current Biography* (1972): 30.

5. Ibid., 72.

6. Félix González-Torres, interview with Tim Rollins, in *Félix González-Torres* (New York: Artpress, 1993), 23.

7. Bergen Evans, *Dictionary of Quotations* (New York: Delacorte Press, 1968), 340.

8. André Derain, *ArtNews* (April 1995): 118.

9. John Holt, *How Children Fail* (New York: Pitman, 1964), 167.

10. *Concise Oxford English Dictionary*. Tenth Edition, Revised ed. Judy Pearsall (London: Oxford University Press, 2002), 75.

CHAPTER 2

1. Gyorgy Kepes, *The Language of Vision* (Chicago: Paul Theobald, 1944), 9.

2. Henri Matisse, "The Nature of Creative Activity," *Education and Art*, edited by Edwin Ziegfeld (New York: UNESCO, 1953), 21.

3. Edward Weston, *The Daybooks of Edward Weston*, edited by Nancy Newhall (Millerton, NY: Aperture, 1973), vol. 2, 181.

4. Maurice Denis, *Theories 1870–1910* (Paris: Hermann, 1964), 13.

5. Quoted in "National Airport: A New Terminal Takes Flight," *Washington Post* (July 16, 1997). http://www.washingtonpost.com/wp-srv/local/longterm/library/airport/architect.htm (accessed May 14, 2000).

6. Faber Birren, *Color Psychology and Color Theory* (New Hyde Park, NY: University Books, 1961), 20.

7. "Notes d'un peintre sur son dessin," *Le Point* IV (1939): 14.

8. Jean Schuster, "Marcel Duchamp, vite," *le surréalisme* (Spring 1957): 143.

9. Georgia O'Keeffe, *Georgia O'Keeffe* (New York: Viking, 1976), opposite plate 23.

CHAPTER 3

1. R. G. Swenson, "What Is Pop Art?" *Art News* (November 1963): 62.

2. Elizabeth McCausland, "Jacob Lawrence," *Magazine of Art* (November 1945): 254.

3. Jack D. Flam, *Matisse on Art* (New York: Dutton, 1978), 36; originally in "Notes d'un peintre," *La Grande Revue* (Paris, 1908).

4. Ibid.

5. Henri Matisse, "Notes of a Painter," translated by Alfred H. Barr, Jr., *Problems of Aesthetics*, edited by Eliseo Vivas and Murray Krieger (New York: Holt, 1953), 259–260; originally in "Notes d'un peintre."

6. Ibid., 260.

CHAPTER 4

1. Quoted in David Bayles, *Art and Fear* (Santa Barbara, 2001), 79.

2. Frederick Franck, *The Zen of Seeing: Seeing/Drawing as Meditation* (New York: Vintage, 1973), 6.

3. Vincent to Theo van Gogh, April 1884, Letter 184. *Vincent van Gogh: The Complete Letters*. http://www.vangoghgallery.com (accessed October 21, 2004). Edited by Robert Harrison.

4. Robert Wallace. *The World of Van Gogh* (New York: Time-Life, 1969), 90.

5. Anthony Blunt, *Picasso's Guernica* (New York: Oxford University Press, 1969), 28.

6. Marjane Satrapi, "On Writing *Persepolis*"; http://www.randomhouse.com/pantheon/graphicnovels/satrapi2.html (accessed July 26, 2007).

CHAPTER 5

1. Quoted in Erika Doss, *Spirit Poles and Flying Pigs: Public Art and Cultural Democracy in American Communities* (Washington, DC: Smithsonian Institution Press, 1995), 179.

CHAPTER 6

1. Quoted in Barbara Isenberg, "Prices of Prints." *Los Angeles Times,* 14 May 2006, E27.

CHAPTER 7

1. "Edwin Land," *Time* (June 26, 1972): 84.

2. Henri Cartier-Bresson, *The Decisive Moment* (New York: Simon & Schuster, 1952), 14.

3. All quotes in this essay from Margaret Bourke-White, *Portrait of Myself* (New York: Simon & Schuster, 1963).

CHAPTER 9

1. "Do You Know Your ABCs?" *Advertising Age*, June 19, 2000.

2. All quotes from this article from "Chaz Maviyane-Davies, Artist and Designer," *The Idea: Indian Documentary of Electronic Arts* No. 5, July 2002.

CHAPTER 10

1. Henry Hopkins, *Fifty West Coast Artists* (San Francisco: Chronicle Books, 1981), 25.

2. Ruth Butler, *Western Sculpture: Definitions of Man* (New York: HarperCollins, 1975), 249; from an unpublished manuscript in the possession of Roberta Gonzáles, translated and included in the appendices of a Ph.D. dissertation by Josephine Whithers, "The Sculpture of Julio González: 1926–1942" (New York: Columbia University, 1971).

3. Brassaï, *Conversations with Picasso* (Paris: Gallimard, 1964), 67.

CHAPTER 11

1. John Coyne, "Handcrafts," *Today's Education* (November–December 1976): 75.

2. Grace Glueck, "In Glass, and Kissed by Light," *New York Times*, August 29, 1997: Bl.

3. All quotes in this essay from Faith Ringgold, *We Flew Over the Bridge: The Memoirs of Faith Ringgold* (Boston: Little, Brown, 1995).

CHAPTER 12

1. Louis Sullivan, "The Tall Office Building Artistically Considered," Lippincott Monthly Magazine, March 1986: 408.

2. Zaha Hadid: *Complete Buildings and Projects* (New York: Rizzoli, 1998), 43.

3. Frank Lloyd Wright, *The Future of Architecture* (New York: Horizon Press, 1953), 227.

CHAPTER 14

1. "Picasso Speaks," *The Arts* (May 1923): 319.

CHAPTER 15

1. Titus Burckhardt, *Chartres and the Birth of the Cathedral* (Bloomington, IN: World Wisdom Books, 1996), 47.

CHAPTER 16

1. *The World of Michelangelo* (New York: Time-Life Books, 1966), 192.

2. Saint Teresa of Jesus, *The Life of Saint Teresa of Jesus*, translated by David Lewis, edited by Benedict Zimmerman (Westminster, MD: Newman, 1947), 266.

CHAPTER 17

1. Wen C. Fong, "The Literati Artists of the Ming Dynasty," Wen C. Fong and James C. Y. Wyatt, *Possessing the Past: Treasures from the National Palace Museum, Taipei* (New York: Metropolitan Museum of Art, 1996), 387.

CHAPTER 20

1. Katherine Solender, *Dreadful Fire! The Burning of the Houses of Parliament* (Cleveland: Cleveland Museum of Art, 1984), 42–56.

2. Beaumont Newhall, "Delacroix and Photography," *Magazine of Art* (November 1952): 300.

3. Margaretta Salinger, *Gustave Courbet, 1819–1877, Miniature Album XH* (New York: Metropolitan Museum of Art, 1955), 24.

4. From *Reminiscences of Rosa Bonheur*, published in 1910 and quoted in Wendy Slatkin, ed., *The Voices of Women Artists* (Englewood Cliffs, NJ: Prentice Hall, 1993), 132.

5. Ibid.

6. William Seitz, *Claude Monet* (New York: Abrams, 1982), 13.

7. Albert E. Elsen, *Rodin* (New York: Museum of Modern Art, 1963), 53; from a letter to critic Marcel Adam, published in an article in *Gil Blas* (Paris: July 7, 1904).

8. John Rewald, *Cézanne: A Biography* (New York: Abrams, 1986), 208.

9. Vincent van Gogh, *Further Letters of Vincent van Gogh to His Brother, 1886–1889* (London: Constable, 1929), 139, 166.

10. Ronald Alley, *Gauguin* (Middlesex, England: Hamlyn, 1968), 8.

11. Paul Gauguin, *Lettres de Paul Gauguin à Georges-Daniel de Monfried* (Paris: Georges Cres, 1918), 89.

12. John Russell, *The Meanings of Modern Art* (New York: HarperCollins, 1974), 35.

13. Jean Leymarie, "Paul Gauguin," *Encyclopedia of World Art* (London: McGraw-Hill, 1971), vol. 6, 42.

14. Yann Le Pichon, *Gauguin: Life, Art, Inspiration* (New York: Abrams, 1987), 240.

CHAPTER 21

1. Wassily Kandinsky, "Reminiscences," *Modern Artists on Art*, ed. Robert L. Herbert (Englewood Cliffs, NJ: Prentice Hall, 1964), 27.

2. William Fleming, *Art, Music and Ideas* (New York: Holt, 1970), 342.

3. Alfred H. Barr, Jr., ed., *Masters of Modern Art* (New York: Museum of Modern Art, 1955), 124.

4. H. H. Arnason, *History of Modern Art*, rev. ed. (New York: Abrams, 1977), 146.

5. Nathan Lyons, ed., *Photographers on Photography* (Englewood Cliffs, NJ: Prentice Hall, 1966), 133.

6. Beaumont Newhall, *The History of Photography* (New York: Museum of Modern Art, 1964), 111.

7. Joshua C. Taylor, *Futurism* (New York: Museum of Modern Art, 1961), 124.

CHAPTER 22

1. Hans Richter, *Dada 1916–1966* (Munich: Goethe Institut, 1966), 22.

2. Paride Accetti, Raffaele De Grada, and Arturo Schwarz, *Cinquant'annia Dada—Dada in Italia 1916–1966* (Milan: Galleria Schwarz, 1966), 39.

3. André Breton, *Manifestos of Surrealism*, translated by Richard Seaver and Helen R. Lane (Ann Arbor: University of Michigan Press, 1972), 14.

4. Sam Hunter and John Jacobus, *Modern Art* (New York: Harry N. Abrams, 1985), 148.

5. Herbert Read, *A Concise History of Modern Painting* (New York: Praeger, 1959), 160.

6. *San Francisco Chronicle*, October 6, 1935; quoted in Evangeline Montgomery, "Sargent Claude Johnson," *Ijele: Art Journal of the African World* (2002), 1–2.

7. Romare Bearden and Harry Henderson, *A History of African American Artists from 1792 to the Present* (New York, 1993), 152.

CHAPTER 23

1. Edward Lucie-Smith, *Sculpture Since 1945* (London: Phaidon, 1987), 77.

2. Calvin Tomkins, *The World of Marcel Duchamp* (New York: Time-Life Books, 1966), 162.

3. Richard Hamilton, *Catalogue of an Exhibition at the Tate Gallery*, March 12–April 19, 1970 (London: Tate Gallery, 1970), 31.

4. R. G. Swenson, "What Is Pop Art?" *Art News* (November 1963): 25.

5. Claes Oldenburg, "I am for an art . . ." from *Store Days*, Documents from the Store (1961) and Ray Gun Theater (1962), selected by Claes Oldenburg and Emmett Williams (New York: Something Else Press, 1967).

6. Donald Judd, "Specific Objects," *Arts Yearbook* 8 (1965): 78.

7. Patricia Failing, "James Turrell's New Light on the Universe," *Art News* (April 1985): 71.

8. Andy Goldsworthy, "Artist's Statement," http://www.thinker.org/deyoung/about/subpage.asp?subpagekey=847 (accessed July 20, 2007).

9. Lucy R. Lippard, *From the Center: Feminist Essays on Women's Art* (New York: Dutton, 1976), 48.

CHAPTER 24

1. Quoted in Vivian Sundaram, "Amrita Sher-Gil: Life and Work"; *Sikh Art*, http://www.sikh-heritage.co.uk/arts/amritashergil/amshergil.htm (accessed June 21, 2004).

2. Daniel Herwitz, *Husain* (Bombay, 1988), 17.

3. Uche Okeke, "Natural Synthesis," Art Society, Zaire, Nigeria, October 1960. Found in Okui Enwezor, *The Short Century: Independence and Liberation Movements in Africa, 1945–1994* (Munich: Prestel, 2001), 453.

CHAPTER 25

1. Joel L. Swerdlow, "To Heal a Nation," *National Geographic* (May 1985): 557.

INDEX